Marketi
In 4 We

The Complete Guide to Success

Eric Davies,
Nick Smith and
Brian Salter

The Teach Yourself series has been trusted around the world
for over 75 years. This series of 'In 4 Weeks' business books is
designed to help people at all levels and around the world to
further their careers. Learn, in 4 weeks, what the experts learn
in a lifetime.

Eric Davies BA (Hons), MPhil, DipM has a broad-based business experience, including board-level positions in industry and marketing services agencies and setting up a number of new business ventures. He has consulted widely in both the private and public sectors and provided a range of management programmes for the British Institute of Management (now CMI), the British Council and the Institution of Chemical Engineers and contributed to postgraduate programmes at the University of Glamorgan and post-experience programmes at University College Lampeter. In addition, he has contributed articles to a number of journals including *Accountancy, European Journal of Marketing, The Pakistan Management Review, Management Consultancy* and *The Municipal Journal.*

Nick Smith runs a successful online marketing consultancy advising companies how to increase sales and profits using the power of the Internet and by leveraging forgotten assets hidden in their business. Companies hire Nick and his team to devise effective traffic strategies using a combination of paid marketing sources, search engine optimization and social media marketing. In addition, Nick is considered to be one of the leading direct response marketing consultants in the UK after logging more than 33,000 hours implementing successful online marketing strategies during the past 12 years. In his spare time, Nick writes for his blog (NickTheGeek.com) and also maintains CamStudio (CamStudio.org), the world's most popular free desktop recording software downloaded 100,000 times every week.

Brian Salter began his career in the BBC where he produced and presented features, business and current affairs programmes before leaving to join Heathrow Airport as Media Relations Manager immediately following the bombing of Pan Am 103 over Lockerbie. Following a variety of communication roles, he started his own consultancy in the 1990s advising companies and giving training in PR, marketing and presentation techniques, as well as Internet technology for business use when it was still in its infancy. He now works in Beijing for a major media company.

Teach Yourself®

Marketing In 4 Weeks

The Complete Guide to Success

Eric Davies,
Nick Smith and
Brian Salter

First published in Great Britain in 2015 by Hodder & Stoughton. An Hachette UK company.

First published in US in 2015 by The McGraw-Hill Companies, Inc.

This edition published 2015 by Hodder & Stoughton.

British Library Cataloguing in Publication Data: a catalogue record for this title is available from the British Library.

Library of Congress Catalog Card Number: on file.

Paperback ISBN 978 1 473 605 299

eBook eISBN 978 1 473 605 305

1

Typeset by Cenveo® Publisher Services.

Printed and bound in Great Britain by CPI Group (UK) Ltd., Croydon, CRO 4YY.

Hodder & Stoughton policy is to use papers that are natural, renewable and recyclable products and made from wood grown in sustainable forests. The logging and manufacturing processes are expected to conform to the environmental regulations of the country of origin.

Hodder & Stoughton Ltd
338 Euston Road
London NW1 3BH
www.hodder.co.uk

Contents

Week 1: Marketing In A Week

Introduction   7

Sunday   10
What is marketing?

Monday   24
Marketing and the customer

Tuesday   40
Marketing information and marketing research

Wednesday   64
Strategic marketing

Thursday   82
The marketing mix – product and price

Friday   102
The marketing mix – place

Saturday   114
The marketing mix – promotion

Week 2: Digital Marketing In A Week

Introduction   129

Sunday   130
Building the ultimate sales website

Monday   142
SEO: The backbone of any digital marketing
strategy

Tuesday   158
Social media marketing madness

Wednesday   176
Pay per click (PPC) simplified and explained

Thursday   196
Mobile optimization and getting mobile users

Friday   212
Email marketing – why you should do it no
matter what

Saturday   226
Other marketing tricks and tips in the
modern world

Week 3: Social Media Marketing In A Week

Introduction   243
Sunday   246
Introduction to social media

Monday   262
Successful case studies

Tuesday   272
Getting started with social media marketing

Wednesday   294
Phase one of your social media takeover

Thursday   312
Phase two of your social media takeover

Friday   326
   Phase three: quality content creation

Saturday   336
   Managing, metrics and scaling up

Week 4: Public Relations In A Week

Introduction   351
Sunday   354
   Who needs PR?

Monday   366
   External audiences

Tuesday   380
   Dealing with the media

Wednesday   394
   Social media

Thursday   412
   Practical pointers for powerful press releases

Friday   430
   Marketing communications

Saturday   444
   Internal PR

Surviving in tough times   461
Answers   465
Notes   466

WEEK 1

Marketing In A Week

Introduction

Marketing is about the relationship between an organization and its marketplace, and in particular its customers and potential customers. Customers are the lifeblood of a business; without customers a business has no future. In order to succeed and make a profit, a business must therefore aim to identify and satisfy the needs of its customers. The purpose of marketing is to help the business achieve these aims. This week you will learn about the nature and techniques of successful marketing and how it can improve business performance.

On Sunday we will consider the definition of marketing, what it is and what it is not, and the relationship between marketing and business performance. On Monday we will study the customer, their motives, values and attitudes and buyer behaviour (in customer and business-to-business markets). On Tuesday we focus on marketing information and marketing research and look at the techniques and processes used to obtain information to reduce risk in marketing decision making. Wednesday's chapter describes marketing as a strategic activity and looks at the marketing decision process, as well as some of the most famous strategic techniques including the Boston Box, the Ansoff Box and Michael Porter's Three Generic Strategies.

We spend the rest of the week looking in detail at the marketing mix – product, price, place and promotion, also known as the 4 Ps. On Thursday we consider first the product element, which covers tangible and intangible benefits, brands, the product life cycle, new product development and product strategy decisions. We also look at price, which includes customers' perceptions of value, our cost structure and competitors' prices and value offerings. On Friday we focus on place – specifically the channels of distribution that are used to make the product or service available to the customer. Finally, on Saturday we review promotion, the fourth P of the marketing mix, which includes the communications process and the seven key decision areas of the promotional strategy.

Today's business world is highly competitive and changing fast, and marketing, as a body of knowledge and best practice, must respond to these changes. However, there is one fundamental fact about marketing that remains constant: it is that, to become successful and remain successful, an organization must be better at meeting customers' needs than the competition.

SUNDAY

What is marketing?

Today we will set out to define marketing and to dispel some of the common misunderstandings regarding the meaning and nature of marketing. We will look at established UK and American definitions of marketing and some current European thinking about the definition of marketing for the 21st century. We will also summarize the history of marketing and how this business philosophy developed in response to increased competition.

We will consider the relationship between marketing and business performance and some of the key evidence to support the view that a 'customer/marketing orientation' can have a positive effect on profitability and performance.

We will also touch on the issue of competition and the need to consider the relationship between our customers/potential customers and our competitors in any discussion of our approach to marketing our business. We will return to this theme in more detail later in the week.

Finally today we will look at marketing and the business as a whole, and identify some of the key behaviours of businesses that have effectively (and profitably) made the customer/marketing orientation the basis of their operations.

SUNDAY

MONDAY

TUESDAY

WEDNESDAY

THURSDAY

FRIDAY

SATURDAY

Defining marketing

In essence, marketing is a relatively simple concept but at its root lies a fundamental approach to directing a business. Its simplicity can lead to the real meaning of marketing being misunderstood or misconstrued – and this can lull us into a false sense of security. And, if we don't understand what marketing is, we had better hope that our competitors don't know either – because, if they do, they will have a competitive advantage over us.

A good way to explain marketing is to start by dispelling two common misunderstandings regarding its meaning and nature.

- **Marketing is just a posh name for selling.** WRONG! A sale is often the ultimate objective of a marketing strategy, but marketing covers a much broader range of activities than just the sale event. Selling is the exchange of a product or service for, most commonly, a monetary value. Selling can be viewed as the last step in the marketing process. If marketing has been effective, it should make selling 'easier' (although selling is never easy!) because promotional and sales effort will have been directed at those customer groups who have a perceived need for the company's offering.
- **Marketing just means advertising.** WRONG! Promotion (including advertising) is a strategic activity that focuses on transmitting informative and/or persuasive messages via a medium or range of media to defined target audiences. In simple terms promotion is, again, *part* of the

marketing strategy (as we will see later). This potential misunderstanding is further compounded when news media talk about a 'marketing gimmick' when they mean a 'promotional gimmick'.

Some definitions of marketing

The UK Chartered Institute of Marketing (CIM) says that

'Marketing is the management process responsible for identifying, anticipating and satisfying consumers' requirements profitably.'

The American Marketing Association (AMA) defines marketing as

'the process of planning and executing the conception, pricing, promotion, and distribution of ideas, goods, and services to create exchanges that satisfy individual and organizational objectives.'

Both of these definitions are manifestations of the prevailing view of what constitutes marketing. However, a number of commentators are now suggesting that it is time to redefine marketing for the 21st century. For instance, one suggested definition, from C. Grönroos of the Swedish School of Economics, Helsinki, is:

'Marketing is to establish, develop and commercialize long-term customer relationships, so that the objectives of the parties involved are met. This is done by mutual exchange and keeping of promises.'

It is worth noting that both the AMA and Grönroos definitions refer to 'exchange'. At the heart of marketing is the process of enabling individuals and organizations to obtain what they need and want through exchanges with others.

For the purposes of this book a simple, usable definition might be:

'Marketing is the identification and anticipation of customers' needs and the profitable satisfaction of those needs.'

SUNDAY
MONDAY
TUESDAY
WEDNESDAY
THURSDAY
FRIDAY
SATURDAY

In essence, marketing is a business philosophy that says *it is easier to achieve your business objectives if you understand and meet customers' needs*. Customers should be the *raison d'être* of the business.

There are **four key issues** encompassed in our simple definition:

'Marketing is the identification and anticipation of customers' needs and the profitable satisfaction of those needs.'

1 **Identification** To be truly marketing oriented, a business must **identify** customer **needs**. Marketing research linked to marketing decision making is the hallmark of a marketing-oriented company.

2 **Satisfaction** Customers must feel that the **benefits** offered by the company's products or services **meet** their **needs**. If this does not happen, there is little opportunity for repeat sales.

3 **Profitable** Profit is an obvious business objective, and part of the 'consideration' (to use a term from contract law) for satisfying customer needs is to make a profit. In addition, for a business to survive and satisfy customer needs in the future, profit is essential.

4 **Anticipation** Part of what marketing needs to do is study customers' behaviour and attitudes to make it possible to **predict** how changes will affect future demand for products and services.

It is also important to stress that, when establishing and maintaining customer relationships, the seller gives a set of **promises** based on the performance of a product or service offered, i.e. the benefits inherent in the offering that the seller believes are matched to the needs of the customer. In return the buyer promises to meet his/her commitment in the exchange, generally some form of payment. Promise is a key component of marketing, not only during the first purchase but also as central to the ongoing relationship between buyers and sellers.

One way to get a better understanding is to take a brief look at the history of marketing.

A history of marketing

Some argue that marketing has been in existence whenever and wherever there have been buyers and sellers, i.e. a market. However, it is generally considered that marketing, as we understand it, developed when competition for customers intensified.

Before and during the Industrial Revolution (roughly 1750–1850 in the UK), goods were relatively scarce and producers could sell all that they could produce. The focus was therefore on production and distribution at the lowest cost. This approach to organizing a business is often referred to as a **'production orientation'**.

From the late 19th and early 20th centuries, competition grew and the focus turned to selling what could be produced, by persuading buyers to choose the seller's product, regardless of whether it was the best match to the customer's needs. A clear problem with this approach is that, if the product does not meet the customer's needs, they will not purchase it again. Consequently, there will be no repeat sales and this will impact on the survival of the business. This approach to organizing a business is often referred to as a **'sales orientation'**.

From the 1950s onwards, most markets displayed intense competition for customers, and this competition drove the need to understand and satisfy customers' needs if the business was to succeed. In essence, this approach puts the customer at the centre of a firm's thinking and strategy, an approach to organizing a business that we often refer to as a **'customer or marketing orientation'**.

Marketing was once seen as the preserve of fast-moving consumer goods (FMCG) companies; now marketing and its techniques can be found in most industries. Even the public sector and charities are embracing the marketing orientation. In not-for-profit environments the main differences are that the objectives of the organization may not be expressed in terms of profitability or market share, and there is generally no real 'competitive' element.

In addition, marketing became an important academic subject – there is a reference to 'marketing' in a course syllabus at Ohio State University from 1921 – and is a central

SUNDAY

MONDAY

TUESDAY

WEDNESDAY

THURSDAY

FRIDAY

SATURDAY

plank of management education, both undergraduate and postgraduate, across the world. I recently 'Googled' the term 'marketing MBA' and got 87.8 million results!

It is important to point out that, even now, 'production-oriented' and 'sales-oriented' organizations can still be identified in some business sectors. This situation seems to be related to:

- the nature of the particular market environments of these sectors, e.g. large purchase values, very small number of customers, complex contractual arrangements
- the attitudes/perceptions of senior management in these sectors.

Perhaps such management has been sceptical about whether marketing helps improve business performance and has therefore been reluctant to adopt the customer/marketing orientation.

Marketing and business performance

Both managers and academics have long been exercised by the 'value' of marketing to a business. In other words, if your business is marketing orientated, will you be more profitable than businesses that are not?

From a manager's perspective, the issue is straightforward: why should you invest any scarce resource (including time and money) in marketing unless there is evidence that it will make you more profitable?

Academics have also focused on this issue, not only to support managers (by seeking to distil best practice) but also to understand the fundamental relationships between independent variables (such as what we do) and dependent variables (the results of what we do).

Academic research in this area began seriously in the 1970s. Probably one of the most important studies was the Profit Impact of Market Strategies (PIMS) study from Harvard University. The basis of the study was a huge survey and a large multiple regression model. It started with hundreds of independent variables that were considered to affect the key dependent variables (i.e. profit and return on investment (ROI), often referred to as return on capital employed (ROCE) in the UK) and finished up with 37 variables that explained most (80 per cent) of the causal effect. The study identified that profit margins and ROI are strongly, and positively, related to four key variables:

1 **business share of the target market**, relative to the share held by the top three competitors (relative market share)
2 **customer rating of product/service performance**, relative to competitors (customer perceived relative quality)
3 **asset productivity**, measured in terms of value added/capital employed
4 **employee productivity**, measured in terms of real value added per person.

As might be expected, a range of variables influences profitability, including those associated with the relationship between the business and its marketplace (including customers and competitors) and others within the firm (such as asset productivity and employee productivity, both related to the effective management of the business).

What seems to be clear from the PIMS study is that high market share is an important predictor of business performance. This is achieved by providing customers with the products/services that deliver benefits that they perceive match their needs best and this, fundamentally, is what marketing is all about. The second variable, customer perceived relative quality, confirms this: to be a leader in any market you must have a better offering than that of your competitors. So marketing, as a business philosophy and as a way of organizing a business, is one important independent variable affecting the key dependent variables of profit margin and ROI.

Researchers turned their attention to the relationship between 'customer/marketing orientation' (i.e. the implementation of the marketing concept encapsulated in our definition set out above) and business performance. During the 1990s, a number of key studies were published and most indicate a positive, if sometimes weak, relationship between customer/marketing orientation and business performance.

What we can say is that the evidence shows that a customer/marketing orientation is associated with improved business performance.

 Customer/marketing orientation cannot deliver improved business performance on its own; all other elements of the business, including operational management, financial management and human resources management, must be managed in an effective way to contribute to the overall performance of the business.

The four 'big ideas' in marketing

1 Exchange At the heart of marketing is the process of enabling individuals and organizations to obtain what they need and want through exchanges with others.

2 Promise In establishing and maintaining customer relationships, the seller gives a set of promises based on the performance of a product or service offered. In return the buyer promises to meet his/her commitment in the exchange, generally some form of payment.

3 Matching Marketing matches the benefits in the organization's offerings with the customer's needs.

4 'Customer' or 'marketing' orientation A business that is customer (or marketing) oriented puts customer needs at the centre of their thinking and strategy.

Customers and the competition

One important aspect of the real-world situation we have not addressed yet is competition. So far, the customer/marketing orientation has placed the customer as the focus of the business. This seems intuitively acceptable – if we understand and meet customers' needs, we should win their business – but while we are focusing on customers, so are our competitors. Consequently, any effective marketing strategy must take into account our competition and the relationship between them and our customers/potential customers.

The first issue to consider is the nature of the customers' perceived needs – the customer/marketing orientation. Customers will seek to identify the best match of benefits to their perceived needs and in doing so will make judgements about the various offerings available to them.

In addition, customers will consider the price of each competitor's offering along with the benefits they perceive in each offering. In essence, customers will make a value judgement – which offering provides the most benefits at the lowest price.

We will return to these issues in more detail later in the week.

Marketing and the business

A reasonable question to ask at this stage is this: if a customer/marketing orientation is linked to profitability, what is it we have to do to make it operational (and therefore effective) in our business?

A wide range of studies has distilled **five key behaviours** that characterize businesses which have effectively (and profitably) made customer/marketing orientation the operational basis of their businesses.

1 Market sensing

This is the foundation of an effective customer/marketing orientation. We must know what our customers' needs are and, to do this, we need to use a range of sources including direct contact with our customers and tools like marketing research (which we will look at later in the week). In addition, we know that we do not live in a static environment so therefore we need to track changes in customers' needs.

2 Quality focus

The PIMS research highlighted the relationship between product/service quality and business performance, and the message is that the business must seek to improve product/service quality to maintain a competitive differential. Clearly, this must include monitoring competitive actions.

3 Internal 'marketing'

It was once said that 'Marketing is too important to be left to the marketing department' and, like many humorous quotes, this has a strong basis in reality. While specialist marketing-related functions still exist, in many modern businesses large marketing departments have been replaced by a business-wide focus on satisfying customer needs. Quite simply, all employees must know what they have to do to satisfy customers' needs, must be able to do it and must be motivated to do it.

4 Adaptive response

We all know that we live in a time of rapid change and it is therefore critical that businesses are flexible and able to adapt to changing market conditions and customer needs. This includes understanding how broader political, economic, social and technological factors impact on our customers and competitors.

5 External relationships

It is all too easy for business managers to feel they must focus all their attention on matters within the business but, as we have seen, the success of the business depends on how we interact with the outside world. Constructing effective means of two-way communication with customers is therefore paramount. This can be as simple as ensuring that customers are encouraged to tell the business about problems or any gaps in meeting their needs to using sophisticated barcode/customer loyalty card data analysis and customer satisfaction research. Managers need to identify and focus on key account relationships (KAR), i.e. those accounts that are responsible for the majority of the business. Such KARs could be with your main customers or perhaps your major distributors/retailers.

TIP

Customer relationship management (CRM) programmes are designed to formalize the process of customer/ business relationships, with customer retention often a key objective. A number of software companies provide bespoke software to support the CRM function.

Summary

Developed as a strategic response to intensified competition for customers, marketing is a relatively simple concept but a fundamental approach to directing a business.

In essence, marketing is a business philosophy that says it is easier to achieve your business objectives if you understand and meet customers' needs, and research indicates that marketing improves business performance. Customers should be the *raison d'être* of the business.

Four 'big ideas' are central to marketing: exchange, promise, matching, and customer or marketing orientation. Another key aspect of strategic marketing is our competitors, who are also interacting with our customers/ potential customers.

Finally, there are five key behaviours that characterize businesses which have effectively (and profitably) made customer/marketing orientation the operational basis of their businesses: market sensing, quality focus, internal marketing, adaptive response and external relationships.

SUNDAY

MONDAY

TUESDAY

WEDNESDAY

THURSDAY

FRIDAY

SATURDAY

Questions (answers at the back)

1. Why can the meaning of marketing be misunderstood?
   a) Because it is a relatively simple concept but a fundamental approach to directing a business ❏
   b) It is not related to the real world of business ❏
   c) It is a complex academic subject ❏
   d) It is only relevant to the US market ❏

2. How can marketing be defined?
   a) As a posh word for selling ❏
   b) It is the same as advertising and promotion ❏
   c) As the identification and anticipation of customers' needs and the profitable satisfaction of those needs ❏
   d) None of the above ❏

3. What is the business philosophy of marketing?
   a) Spending the most on advertising guarantees you a profit ❏
   b) It is easier to achieve your business objectives if you understand and meet customer needs ❏
   c) Customers will buy whatever you can produce ❏
   d) You only have to convince the customer once to be successful ❏

4. Persuading buyers to choose the seller's product regardless of whether it is the best match to the customer's needs is known as what?
   a) Production orientation ❏
   b) Sales orientation ❏
   c) Customer or marketing orientation ❏
   d) Retail orientation ❏

5. Why did companies start to embrace marketing from the 1950s onwards?
   a) There were more advertising media, such as TV, available ❏
   b) Advertising agencies had been invented ❏
   c) Most markets displayed intense competition for customers ❏
   d) Mail order was a new sales method ❏

6. What does the Profit Impact of Market Strategies (PIMS) study?
   a) The relationship between strategy and profit ❏
   b) The characteristics of the best managers ❏
   c) The size of the US export market ❏
   d) The differences between capitalist and communist systems ❏

7. What are the two marketing outcomes that PIMS identified as strongly and positively related to profitability?
a) Brand logo and colour ❏
b) Relative market share and customer perceived relative value ❏
c) Size and frequency of advertisements ❏
d) Range and content of sponsorship deals ❏

8. Why must a marketing strategy take the competition into account?
a) The rate of change in society is so fast ❏
b) They too are focusing on our customers/potential customers ❏
c) International trade is important ❏
d) The Internet is important ❏

9. What are market sensing, quality focus, internal 'marketing', adaptive response and external relationships?
a) Terms used in new product testing ❏
b) Sales management techniques ❏
c) Key behaviours of businesses that have effectively made customer/marketing orientation an operational basis of their businesses ❏
d) None of the above ❏

10. What is a key concept of the customer/marketing orientation?
a) Exchange ❏
b) Promise ❏
c) Matching process ❏
d) All of the above ❏

MONDAY

Marketing and the customer

We learned yesterday that the customer is at the heart of the customer/marketing orientation and that it is easier to achieve our business objectives if we understand and meet customers' needs. Clearly, customers are very important to a business and to the development of marketing thought, and today we will focus on customers as individuals and as organizations.

We will begin by considering customers' motives, values and attitudes and how these influence the way they perceive their needs, and look at customer behaviour as a problem-solving process and the stages involved in that. We shall also review the differences between individual customers and organizational customers and look at the importance of decision-making units (DMUs) in the latter. We will review the importance of market segmentation and look at the ways in which markets can be segmented.

Finally, we will consider the impact of political, economic, social and technological (PEST) drivers that shape the world in which customers exist and therefore have a major influence on customers' behaviour.

Who are our customers?

A good place to start is with the question, 'Who are our customers?' At first sight this might seem a simple question. Our customers are the people who buy our products or services. Customers can be individuals, families, small and medium-sized businesses, public limited companies (PLCs), government departments, and so on. It is possible, therefore, to divide customers into two broad markets:

- **consumer markets** – e.g. individuals and families
- **organizational or business-to-business (B2B) markets** – e.g. businesses, not-for-profit/charitable organizations and government departments.

Customers in consumer markets

We can all relate to customers in consumer markets – a subject that is often referred to as consumer behaviour – since we are all customers: we all buy products and services as individuals.

Our definition of marketing focuses on 'customers' needs'. Some writers distinguish between a 'need' and a 'want': they say a need is something fundamental to life, such as water, food, shelter, etc., whereas a want is a desire to possess something that is less important to life. The *Concise Oxford English Dictionary* defines a 'need' as 'a want or requirement' and a 'want' as 'a desire, wish for possession, need'. For the purposes of understanding customers' needs, we can assume that a need and a want are one and the same.

When considering how customers perceive their needs, we have to embrace some concepts and knowledge developed in disciplines such as psychology and sociology. We are going to look at customers' motives, values and attitudes, and customer behaviour as a problem-solving process.

Motives

At the heart of a perceived need is a **driver**, a motive. Abraham Maslow produced a hierarchical structure of needs based on five core levels.

	Need	Motive
Lower level ↓	Physiological	Water, sleep, food
	Safety	Security, shelter, protection
	Belongingness	Love, friendship, acceptance by others
	Ego	Prestige, status, accomplishment
Upper level	Self-actualization	Self-fulfilment, personal enrichment

At each level, different priorities exist in terms of the benefits a customer is seeking. The implication is that one must first satisfy basic needs before ascending to higher needs. Of course, one product or service may satisfy a number of different needs simultaneously. For example, a meal at a fashionable and expensive restaurant can meet a range of needs from physiological to ego and self-actualization.

Sex, in particular, transcends the levels of Maslow's hierarchy. A basic biological drive, sex is also a more complex motive that can involve belongingness, ego and self-actualization.

Many of the products and services we purchase in modern economic markets have a significant element of the upper-level motives at the root of our perceived needs. Examples include clothing (designer clothes and shoes) and cars (luxury saloon cars, performance cars, 'super cars').

Some commentators (e.g. J. K. Galbraith in his 1967 book *The New Industrial State*) have seen this as businesses exercising control over consumers through advertising and related salesmanship activities – in effect, creating artificial needs and wants among consumers.

Values

Our motives are filtered through our values. Values can be defined as our broad preferences concerning appropriate courses of action or outcomes and reflect our sense of 'good' and 'bad'. Our values develop in a number of ways but the family (socialization of children) is a major factor, along with school, religion and peer group influence.

For example, motives such as prestige and status (ego needs) would be manifested as different perceived needs in individuals with different values. We can take this example further if we consider the purchase of a prestige car: a customer whose values include a heightened sense of environmental issues is likely to have a different set of perceived needs from a customer who does not share that value. A hybrid vehicle would therefore not to be equally attractive to both customers.

Attitudes

Over time, we all develop a set of attitudes. Attitudes are a predisposition or a tendency to respond positively or negatively towards a certain stimulus – an idea, a person, a situation, a product, etc. Our attitudes incorporate both our motives and our values but are also influenced by our experiences.

For instance, following the tragedy at Hillsborough football stadium in Sheffield, England, in 1989, *The Sun* newspaper published an article accusing Liverpool fans of appalling behaviour on the day. There was no truth in these claims, and the people of Liverpool responded with justifiable anger. Sales of the newspaper on Merseyside plunged from 200,000 copies a day to just a couple of thousand. *The Sun's* customers in Liverpool changed their attitude to the newspaper in a matter of days.

Behaviour

Customer behaviour has traditionally been seen as a problem-solving process. Implicit in this is that customers act in a logical manner when selecting solutions to their needs. The steps in the process are set out below.

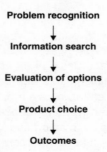

The problem-solving process

For some purchases (particularly more expensive ones) customers do actually follow such a process. However, for lower-cost (and therefore lower-risk) purchases evidence suggests that the decision process is significantly less rigorous. In addition, different customers go through more or less rigorous decision processes depending on their socio-economic and cultural situation.

Let's look at the different stages of the process in detail.

1 Problem recognition

Problem recognition is the point at which a customer articulates their 'perceived need' (see our definition of marketing from Sunday). In reality customers usually have a number of perceived needs that are important to them in meeting their overall needs. Such needs tend to have different levels of importance to them – the customer's 'hierarchy of needs' – a ranked list of those needs that must be satisfied to convince the customer to buy.

For major purchases (like a home or a car) customers may have a long list of perceived needs, sometimes running into double figures. Marketers have spent considerable effort to both identify and rank customers' needs in such situations. One important finding is that, even when there is a relatively long list of perceived needs, the actual purchase decision is often based on the three or four most important perceived needs.

2 Information search

The next stage can involve a wide range of activities, including looking at manufacturers' brochures and advertisements, reviews in magazines and reports from specialist consumer advisory groups (such as *Which?*) and making online searches for user blogs. Personal contacts, such as family, friends and colleagues, and word-of-mouth are also important sources of information and help with forming opinions.

3 Evaluation of options

To evaluate the options, the customer compares the benefits of a number of solutions (our offering and our competitors') against their perceived needs. The customer will decide which offering has the best match of benefits to their needs, and this will normally produce a ranking of best match to least good match. One element will be price.

The customer now has to decide which offering is the best **value**, i.e. represents the most benefits at the lowest price. This can be difficult for the customer when both the number of benefits and the price vary between offerings.

Second best?

During the 1970s a leading domestic durables manufacturer (we'll call them 'the client') commissioned a research study that asked customers to rank their product and competitive products in terms of the best match to the respondents' needs. In all the studies, the client's product topped the list. However, they achieved poor market share figures. Further research identified that the reason for this apparent contradiction (i.e. we have the best match of benefits to the customers' needs but they don't buy our product) was that the price differential between the client's product and the next best-ranked product was large enough to persuade customers to buy the second-ranked rather than the first-ranked offering.

4 Product choice

The penultimate stage in the problem-solving process, product choice, leads to the act of purchase. At this stage, buyers may experience pre-purchase anxiety, a worry about the ramifications of the act they are about to commit. Is it the right product for me? Can I afford it? Will my friends like it? In some cases this leads to the customer postponing a purchase decision. Marketers are obviously keen to minimize the effect of pre-purchase anxiety.

5 Outcomes

The final outcomes stage can be described as the 'consumption' stage, when the customer actually gets to consume the benefits carried by the offering. What we can see is that there are two stages when the customer is evaluating the product:

- the pre-purchase stage up to and including the purchase
- the post-purchase stage.

In the post-purchase stage the product must fulfil the promises made at the pre-purchase stage. Failure to do so will mean there is little likelihood of repeat purchase. This is an important business imperative: it is costly to 'create' a customer and, if we fail to satisfy them, we will provide an opportunity for our competitors.

Customers may also experience post-purchase anxiety – again experiencing the same worries that they may have had before the purchase. Marketers need to help customers deal with post-purchase anxiety by reinforcing the positive messages used at the pre-purchase stage. We will return to this on Saturday.

The customer decision is further complicated when the person who buys (i.e. pays for) the product or service is different from the person who consumes the product or service. For instance, when someone buys a present for another person, the buyer is not the consumer. In this situation the buyer is assessing whether the benefits they perceive in the offering will match the needs of the third party.

Other factors in decision making

Some of the current thinking about human decision making comes from the Nobel Prize winner Daniel Kahneman. In his book *Thinking, Fast and Slow* (2011) he presents evidence that humans are far from being 'rational agents' and are often inconsistent, emotional and biased in their decision making. Kahneman refers to two 'systems' of thinking. *System Two* is the conscious, thinking mind that considers, evaluates and reasons. *System One*, on the other hand, is responsible for the automatic and effortless mental response. *System One* works on as little or as much information as it has and is responsible for snap decisions regarding major courses of action including buying decisions. So *System One* thinking may lead a customer to select a product that they would reject if they adopted *System Two* thinking.

Neuromarketing is a further, parallel approach to looking at the brain from a marketing perspective. The term 'neuromarketing' is thought to have been coined by Ale Smidts of Erasmus University in the early 2000s and is the application of brain-scan technology, especially functional magnetic

resonance imaging (fMRI), to marketing problems. One of the findings indicates that brain activity for an action begins about half a second before a person consciously decides to take an action. This suggests that we are not so much consciously 'making' a decision as becoming aware that a decision has been made. These are early days for neuromarketing and we can expect more developments soon.

Customers in organizational or B2B markets

It is generally considered that organizational markets differ from consumer markets in four key ways.

1 B2B markets have a relatively small number of customers – e.g. there are relatively few car manufacturers in Europe.
2 Demand for products and services is 'derived demand', i.e. derived from the need to meet organizational objectives rather than to be consumed for their own sake, as is the case in consumer markets – e.g. car manufacturers buy steel sheet not for its own sake but as a part of the process of producing cars for consumption by consumers.
3 Decision making concerned with specifying and procuring products and services is normally a complex interaction of individuals within and sometimes from outside the organization (including consultants) – e.g. technical staff will specify and buying professionals will procure.

4 The perceived needs of the organization will involve a complex interaction of the stated corporate needs and the personal needs of the individuals involved in the decision. The company will specify what is required but this will be interpreted by individuals and will therefore be filtered through their own motives, values and attitudes.

Like consumer buyer behaviour, organizational buyer behaviour is a problem-solving process. However, in the latter case the stages of the process are normally more rigorous. There are eight steps.

Step 1   Need recognition
Step 2   Definition of the characteristics and quantity needed
Step 3   Development of the specifications to guide procurement
Step 4   Search for and qualification of potential sources
Step 5   Acquisition and analysis of proposals
Step 6   Evaluation of proposals and selection of supplier(s)
Step 7   Selection of an order routine
Step 8   Performance feedback and evaluation

It is worth comparing this with the model of individual customer behaviour as a problem-solving process, set out above. The similarities are quite clear and, again, the real difference is in the rigour required by organizations (which is not to say that some individuals do not also adopt very rigorous processes).

The eight steps set out above are associated with a **new-task** purchase situation in which an organization is buying a product or service for the first time. It involves greater potential risk and the involvement of the largest number of decision participants.

Some organizations use decision theory models to support the buying process. The steps in the process are as follows.

1 A list of selection criteria is assembled.
2 Each criterion is given a weight in terms of its importance.
3 Each identified potential supplier is scored on each criterion.
4 Suppliers are then ranked in terms of these weighted scores.

Once a selection has been made, purchases can become more routine, even automated, and this is known as **straight rebuy**.

Between the two extremes of new-task and straight rebuy is **modified rebuy**. In this case the organization needs to modify the specification, terms, price, etc., and this requires more decision participants than straight rebuy but not as many as new-task.

When the decision participants act together, they are known as a buying centre or a **decision-making unit (DMU)**. Research has identified five key roles in the DMU.

- **Users** – those who use the purchased item such as the production department
- **Influencers** – members of the organization who influence the purchasing decision even though they may not be centrally involved, e.g. members of the marketing department
- **Buyers** – those members of the organization who have authority to select suppliers and arrange terms of purchase
- **Deciders** – those members of the organization with formal or informal power to determine the final choice of supplier
- **Gatekeepers** – Those individuals who control the flow of information into the organization and therefore indirectly influence the purchasing decision, e.g. members of the finance department through their control of budgets.

It has also shown that the DMU usually has one member (known as the 'salient member') who has the major influence on the selection decision. This person is not always the most senior member of the group, however. The DMU can contain a number of 'champions' who favour particular solutions.

Market segmentation

Customers are different – in their values and attitudes, their incomes, age, gender, location and so on – and these differences are the reason why marketing managers seek to **segment** markets. Segmentation refers to dividing customers into segments where customers within one segment have similar characteristics and as a segment are different from customers in other segments.

Examples of market segments

Geographical – countries, regions within countries, etc.

Demographic – based on age, gender, family size, income, occupation, education, race, religion, etc.

Behavioural – consumer knowledge, perceptions, attitudes, uses of and responses to a product or service.

Fundamentally, segmentation of a market must be based on differences in customers' perceived needs. However, in practical terms, it is sometimes difficult to identify (and therefore to direct marketing effort at) potential customers on this basis.

While it is relatively easy to identify customers/potential customers by age or gender or where they live, such variables do not always correspond to customers' buying preferences. This has led marketers to seek to record customers' preferences through mechanisms such as loyalty programmes (store cards, air miles). An alternative approach combines a range of data sources to profile customers and create segments based on customers' buying behaviour. For example, CACI Ltd ACORN is a geodemographic tool used to identify and understand the UK population and the demand for products and services.

Other characteristics of effective segmentation

Measurable We need to be able to measure the market – usually in terms of market worth (i.e. monetary spend) or number of customers. If we can't, it is difficult to develop strategies to exploit these segments.

Accessible We need to be able to access customers in terms of the media they are exposed to and where they shop. If we lack information about these factors, it is again difficult to develop strategies to exploit these segments.

Critical mass The segment must be big enough to make it cost-effective for the company to target it.

Recent research in *McKinsey Quarterly* (January 2011) suggests that businesses should consider more rather than fewer segments ('think in terms of 30–50 segments, not 5 or so').

> **'Defining and understanding these segments correctly is one of the most practical things a company can do to improve its strategy.'**
> 'Have you tested your strategy lately?' *McKinsey Quarterly*, January 2011

Effective segmentation is critical to successful strategic marketing and we shall return to this topic on Wednesday.

The 'PEST' environment

Finally, we need to remember that all customers are subject to the influences and pressures of the broader 'environment'. In this context we are using the term 'environment' to include the political, economic, social and technological (PEST) drivers that shape the world in which customers exist and that therefore have a major influence on customers' behaviour. We can expand each element.

- **Political** includes aspects such as law making and tax policy.
- **Economic** includes the general economic climate, rate of inflation and interest rates.
- **Social** includes the prevailing attitudes in society, e.g. attitudes to smoking, recycling and energy conservation.
- **Technological** includes the increasing use of mobile communications technology and alternative (non-fossil fuel) power sources.

Some analysts have added legal and rearranged the mnemonic to SLEPT; others have inserted environmental (the physical environment) factors and expanded it to PESTEL or PESTLE. The model has recently been further extended to STEEPLE and STEEPLED, adding ethics and demographic factors.

PEST factors have an influence not only on customers but also on all participants in the marketplace, including our organization, competitors, suppliers and distributors, and we shall return to this later.

Summary

Customers can be individuals or organizations. Behind every perceived consumer need is a driver or *motive*. Motives are filtered through our *values*, our broad preferences concerning appropriate and good actions or outcomes. Family, school, religion and peer group are major influences on these.

The *attitudes* we develop are our tendency to respond positively or negatively towards certain stimuli. Our attitudes incorporate our motives and values but are also affected by our experiences. Customer behaviour has traditionally been seen as a *problem-solving process*. PEST drivers in the wider environment influence this behaviour.

Organizational markets differ from consumer markets in four key ways: they are smaller, demand is derived from organizational objectives, decisions are made by groups of participants, and perceived needs contain corporate and personal elements.

Effective *market segmentation* divides customers into measurable and accessible segments of appropriate critical mass according to differences in perceived needs.

SUNDAY
MONDAY
TUESDAY
WEDNESDAY
THURSDAY
FRIDAY
SATURDAY

Questions (answers at the back)

1. What is at the heart of a perceived need?
   a) An advertisement ❑
   b) A motive ❑
   c) A film ❑
   d) A book ❑

2. What, according to Maslow, is the lowest level need?
   a) Physiological level ❑
   b) Wants level ❑
   c) Ego level ❑
   d) Self-actualization level ❑

3. What does Maslow consider motives such as self-fulfilment and personal enrichment to be?
   a) Spending to the limit on your credit cards ❑
   b) Self-actualization needs ❑
   c) Basic needs ❑
   d) Being wealthy ❑

4. What are values?
   a) Our broad preferences concerning appropriate courses of action or outcomes ❑
   b) Our ability to detect falsehoods ❑
   c) Our ability to solve puzzles ❑
   d) Our ability to recall dreams ❑

5. What are attitudes?
   a) Our ability to play sports ❑
   b) Our ability to learn a musical instrument ❑
   c) Our ability to tell jokes ❑
   d) A predisposition to respond positively or negatively towards a certain stimulus ❑

6. What has customer behaviour traditionally been seen as?
   a) A problem-solving process ❑
   b) Linked to advertising ❑
   c) Totally linked to the weather ❑
   d) Unexplainable ❑

7. Why are organizational markets different from consumer markets?
   a) There are relatively few customers in organizational markets ❑
   b) Demand is derived from the needs of the organization ❑
   c) Decision making is complex and involves both organizational needs and the personal needs of the individuals involved ❑
   d) All of the above ❑

8. In the decision-making unit (DMU), what does the 'gatekeeper' role involve?
   a) Making sure the doors are closed ❑
   b) Controlling the flow of information ❑
   c) Preventing non-DMU members from entering the room ❑
   d) Keeping the minutes to the meeting ❑

9. In addition to differences in customers' perceived needs, for market segmentation to be effective what do the segments need to be?
a) Measurable ❏
b) Accessible ❏
c) An appropriate critical mass ❏
d) All of the above ❏

10. What are the elements of the PEST 'environment'?
a) Painting, English, sociology and training ❏
b) Power, engineering, selling and transport ❏
c) Processes, experiences, solutions and testing ❏
d) Political, economic, social and technological ❏

SUNDAY
MONDAY
TUESDAY
WEDNESDAY
THURSDAY
FRIDAY
SATURDAY

TUESDAY

Marketing information and marketing research

Marketers n...
decision maki...
of the way they ...

We will consider ...
Association's (AMA) ...
the elements of this de...
of research application...

Today we will cover:

- research within the organi...
  information generated by the...
  the more formal marketing in...   ...ystem
  (MkIS) used by some companies...
- marketing intelligence – its nature and some
  examples of sources of marketing intelligence
- secondary research – its nature and some
  examples of the four main sources of secondary
  research
- primary research – we will set out a model for
  the primary research process and look in some
  detail at each element including sampling frame
  and sampling, research instruments (particularly
  the questionnaire), question content and type,
  data collection methods, analysis and reporting.

What is marketing

On Sunday we said that ...
marketing decision mak...
oriented company ...
element of th...
underst...
co...

...keting research (MR), linked to ...aking, is the hallmark of a marketing- ... Identifying customers' needs is an essential ...arketing and, as we then saw on Monday, ...nding customers' motives and buying behaviour is ...plex and MR is central to how we do this.

A definition of marketing research

The American Marketing Association (AMA) defines MR as follows.

Marketing research is the function that links the consumer, customer, and public to the marketer through information – information used to identify and define marketing opportunities and problems; generate, refine, and evaluate marketing actions; monitor marketing performance; and improve understanding of marketing as a process. Marketing research specifies the information required to address these issues, designs the method for collecting information, manages and implements the data collection process, analyses the results, and communicates the findings and their implications.

There are three key issues encompassed in the comprehensive definition shown in the box above.

1 **MR acts as a link** between the customer and the organization and allows a two-way flow of information; the organization can use research to understand the customer and can present the customer with ideas and offerings and gauge the customers' likes and dislikes.
2 **MR captures information** about marketing opportunities and problems; the purpose of research therefore is to reduce risk in decision making and help managers make better and more successful decisions.

3 MR is a process involving research design, data collection, analysis and communication of the findings.

Marketing research is an investment for organizations: they are investing resources (normally money) to reduce the risk of wrongly allocating a scarce resource or failing to maximize an opportunity. Consequently, there is a trade-off between the cost of MR and the benefit the organization will obtain in reducing risk in decision making. Clearly, the higher the perceived risk, the more managers are likely to be prepared to invest in MR.

To understand the scope of MR, consider some examples of applications:

- market/segment size and trends – focusing on establishing the size (monetary value, unit value) of a market and/or segments of the market
- customer need analysis and attitudes to competitive offerings – to establish the perceived needs that a customer group (or segment) holds regarding a defined product/service, the ranking of these needs in their minds, and their perceptions of the benefits inherent in the various offerings (the client's and their competitors') available to them
- customer care research – to monitor customers' levels of satisfaction, etc.
- corporate identity research – to support the development or updating of a company's corporate identity
- message research – to test the effectiveness of different promotional messages
- new product development (NPD) research – assessing the appeal of a new product to a market segment.

This chapter will look at research within the organization, marketing intelligence, secondary research and primary research.

Research within the organization

It is important to place MR within the overall organizational information process. Modern information technology (IT) enables organizations to produce a wide range of information including financial and accounting, production and process. From a marketing perspective, businesses also generate a wide range of information concerning the relationship between the organization and its customers. For instance:

- sales volumes – by product range, etc.
- sales trends – tracked over time, seasonality, etc.
- sales by segment – type of customer, geographical location, etc.
- requests for product information – responses to advertisements, website 'hits', etc.
- complaints – obviously it is important that complaints are dealt with effectively, but complaints also provide a useful source of information: customers who complain may be articulating the view of a larger, silent group of customers
- reports from salespeople – particularly in B2B markets, sales reports are very important in managing the marketing/ sales effort.

Many organizations have an established formal process known as a **marketing information system (MkIS)**.

A definition of a marketing information system

An MkIS is a system in which marketing data are formally gathered, stored, analysed and distributed to managers in accordance with their informational needs on a regular basis.

The MkIS process involves four stages.

1 **Information requirements** An MkIS starts with a definition of the information requirements, i.e. the information required by managers to help them reduce risk in decision making.
2 **Data sources** The MkIS will draw on a wide range of information both from within the business (as suggested above) and from other sources outside the business. External sources include:

- marketing intelligence
- secondary research
- primary research (qualitative and quantitative).

3 **Data processing (to generate information)** There is a difference between data and information. Data are the raw facts, which may not necessarily be related to helping management reduce risk in decision making. Modern IT systems can generate significant volumes of data that can threaten to engulf managers. Information, on the other hand, is knowledge relevant to a specific requirement. The critical focus for the MkIS is that it must produce information appropriate to the decision needs of the users.

4 **Dissemination of information** For the information to be of value it must be disseminated to those who can obtain value from it. It is therefore important that the output of the MkIS is designed to meet the needs of the users, i.e. it is relevant, easily understood, clear and concise.

Marketing intelligence

There is a fairly strong link between marketing intelligence and secondary research. Marketing intelligence sources include customers, intermediaries, competitors, suppliers, new employees and the PEST environment.

A definition of marketing intelligence

Marketing intelligence is the process of gathering and analysing information relevant to reducing risk in decision making from sources that are not formal marketing research sources.

Customers

Particularly in B2B markets, companies can learn a great deal from maintaining a close dialogue with their customers, in addition to formal client relationship management (CRM) or marketing research studies.

Intermediaries

Many businesses use intermediaries such as retailers, wholesalers and distributors to take their products to market. Intermediaries are closer to the customer and often purchase from our competitors as well as from us. Intermediaries offer an excellent marketing intelligence source.

Competitors

Competitors are an excellent source of marketing intelligence. Their annual reports provide performance information, commentary on their strategy (Chairman's and CEO's statements) and information about future initiatives. Reports for all UK limited companies are available from Companies House www.companieshouse.gov.uk.

Also, competitors place information in the public domain to inform and persuade customers and potential customers: on their websites, in press releases (published in the business and general press), in publicity material, at exhibitions and on social networking sites, for instance. Some companies take studying their competitors to quite exhaustive lengths including monitoring their recruitment advertising to see what type and number of employees they are seeking to hire.

Suppliers

In a similar way to intermediaries, suppliers offer a good source of marketing intelligence. They are 'upstream' from our customers but are also likely to be focusing on our customers as part of their strategic activity. In addition, they are likely to supply our competitors as well as us and so have an understanding of our competitors' strategies.

New employees

Industries and sectors can be quite 'incestuous'. Companies are often trying to attract the same type of employee, and experienced new employees are likely to have worked with one or more of our competitors. Some businesses have formal 'debriefing' sessions for new employees to obtain information from them regarding customers and competitors.

PEST

We have seen that the broader 'environment' has a marked effect on our customers and, as we will see later, on both our business and our competitors. Consequently, it is important that our marketing intelligence monitors trends and changes in our PEST environment. Businesses engage with specialist associations and trade bodies, and maintain strong links with appropriate public bodies, to help them obtain 'early warning' of opportunities or threats that may be approaching.

Secondary research

Secondary research can be described as research conducted by others, not necessarily focusing on our particular information needs. It offers the advantages of relatively low cost (compared with primary research) and is often instantly available. Moreover, some research, such as a national census, would be impossible for one organization to undertake.

However, there are drawbacks. Because secondary research does not necessarily focus on our particular information needs, care must be taken not to 'fit' the needs of the research to the information available. Also, as the research is already available, it may be too old to meet the researcher's requirements. Fundamentally, the researcher must assess the degree of accuracy of the secondary research in terms of both how and when it was gathered, analysed and interpreted.

A huge range of information can be accessed through Internet search engines but, when assessing any particular source, take care to consider both the advantages and drawbacks set out above.

There are four main sources of secondary research: government, non-departmental public bodies, trade and professional bodies, and commercial research.

Government

Governments are the main source of secondary research. They conduct research as part of the process of government and the scope of the research therefore covers virtually all aspects of life. By way of illustration, we can look at three sources.

- **UK Office for National Statistics (ONS)** (www.ons.gov. uk) collects data and conducts research on a wide range of themes including the economy, business and energy, agriculture and environment, education, health and social care, the labour market and population (including the census data). Most reports are available as free downloads and some data are available as data sets that the user can construct into tables to meet their particular needs.
- **European Commission Eurostat** (www.epp.eurostat.ec.europa. eu) provides a very similar service for the 27 European Union (EU) countries as ONS does for the UK. Over a number of years the EU has harmonized the data collection activities of member states to allow for like-for-like comparisons.
- **US Dept of Commerce, Bureau of Economic Analysis** (www. bea.gov) follows a similar format both in terms of content and flexibility to ONS and Eurostat.

Non-departmental public bodies

Non-departmental public bodies (NDPBs) are set up to provide regulation to specific sectors. Examples in the UK include Ofwat (the Water Services Regulation Authority) and Ofcom (the independent regulator and competition authority for the communications industries). More general agencies include the following:

- **the Competition Commission** (www.competition-commission. org.uk) publishes reports on investigations into particular businesses in the UK

- **the Office of Fair Trading** (www.oft.gov.uk) publishes reports on investigations into particular UK industries.

Trade and professional bodies

These organizations representing particular industries or professions collect data and conduct research to inform their members and to provide evidence for public relations and lobbying. For example:

- **the Society of Motor Manufacturers and Traders** (www.smmt.co.uk) publishes a wide range of reports, e.g. *Motor Industry Facts*, a profile of the UK motor industry
- **the Law Society** (www.lawsociety.org.uk) represents solicitors in the UK and their research department publishes reports such as *Trends in the solicitors' profession*, an annual statistical report that presents a profile of the profession.

Commercial research

A number of organizations sell research studies they have already conducted (known as multi-client research). Some organizations cover a wide range of products and services while others specialize in specific sectors. Here are three good examples.

- **Mintel** (www.mintel.com) focuses particularly on consumer markets, e.g. mobile phones and network providers in the UK.
- **Keynote** (www.keynote.co.uk) has a mainly UK focus and includes non-consumer markets, e.g. arts and media sponsorship.
- **Euromonitor** (www.euromonitor.com) carries out international research covering a wide range of products and services, e.g. Apparel in the USA.

Primary research

Primary research refers to research designed and conducted to meet specific research needs. Often it builds on secondary research, but primary research will engage directly with the defined marketplace.

1 Quantitative

This uses some form of random sampling and structured data collection (such as a questionnaire). The findings from quantitative research are representative of the population from which the sample is drawn within defined levels of representativeness, and they can be presented in quantitative form, e.g. '65 per cent of respondents think our product is very good.' Many people will be familiar with quantitative research from being asked to participate in a survey or from seeing survey findings (such as opinion poll results) referred to in the media.

2 Qualitative

Qualitative research focuses more on understanding the underlying motives and drivers for people's actions. Typically, judgement rather than random sampling is used, and sample sizes are much smaller. Consequently, the findings cannot be said to be representative in quantitative terms (as in quantitative research). Qualitative research uses tools such as depth interviews and focus groups.

3 Observation

This involves gathering data by observing relevant people, actions and situations and is selected when researchers cannot obtain the required information through direct questioning. Observation can include using trained observers (e.g. observing customers' behaviour in a supermarket) and machine-based observation (e.g. electronic counting of foot fall into a shopping mall).

4 Experimental

Control samples (two samples drawn from different populations, for instance) are used to obtain causal information about links between independent variables (e.g. socio-economic group, age, gender) and dependent variables (e.g. product preferences).

The primary research process

Primary research is a process that can be illustrated as follows.

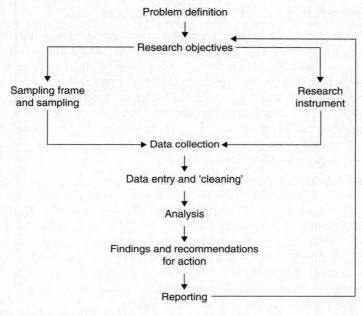

The primary research process

We can look at each part of the process in turn.

Problem definition

It is essential that the problem is clearly defined. One major issue is that the actual problem can be confused with the symptoms of the problem, and this confusion can lead to misdirected research effort. There is an old adage in consulting that says, 'A problem well defined is half solved.'

Research objectives

This stage establishes the foundation of the research study; all other stages will be based on the research objectives. Some researchers draw up a 'need-to-know' (N2K) list with the research user to ensure that all information requirements are covered by the study.

SUNDAY MONDAY TUESDAY WEDNESDAY THURSDAY FRIDAY SATURDAY

Sampling frame and sampling

The sampling frame is the 'population' of units under study, also known as the 'target population'. Units can be any group that the researcher is focusing on (e.g. individuals, households, businesses). Sampling refers to taking a representative portion of the target population. Clearly, a census (i.e. taking all units in the target population) provides the highest level of representativeness, but in most cases the cost and the time required to execute the research are prohibitive. There are two broad approaches to sampling.

- **Probability (or random) sampling** Simple random sampling means that each unit in the target population has the same chance (probability) of being sampled. There are other forms of probability sampling and one used quite extensively is stratified random sampling. In this the sample is drawn in line with the profile of the target population under study; so if 60 per cent of a target population is over the age of 50, then the sample would reflect this by ensuring that 60 per cent of the sample was also over that age.
- **Non-probability sampling** As the name suggests, this form of sampling is not based on units having the same chance (probability) of being sampled. Non-probability sampling can be selected for a number of reasons: for instance, a B2B company may wish to discover the attitudes and perceptions of their major customers and would therefore want specific individuals to be included in the target population. Qualitative research often uses a form of non-probability sampling.

There are two other aspects of sampling we need to consider.

- **Representativeness** Researchers and users of research need to know how representative a sample is of the target population from which it is drawn. There are two elements, allowable error and level of confidence. **Allowable error** is defined as the difference between the value achieved from the sample and the true value for the population. This is normally expressed as a ±%. **Level of confidence** is defined as the probability that the true value (for the population) will fall within the interval created by adding and subtracting the allowable error.

- **Sample size** is a function of the degree of variability in the population under study and the level of accuracy of representativeness required. If all the units in a population are identical, we will need to sample only one unit, regardless of the size of the population. Where researchers do not know the degree of variability in the population (which is often the case), they take the worst-case scenario and assume that the population is equally split on any measure.

The following table shows the relationship between three examples of sample size and the associated degrees of allowable error and levels of confidence.

Sample size	Level of confidence 95%	Level of confidence 90%
500	±4.4%	±3.7%
1,000	±3.1%	±2.6%
1,500	±2.5%	±2.1%

Allowable error (±) at 95 and 90 per cent levels of confidence associated with various sample sizes

You will note that as the sample size increases, so the allowable error decreases. The higher the level of confidence, the greater the allowable error is for the same sample size.

Research instrument

The research instrument is the means by which primary data are gathered. Some research designs use electronic or mechanical devices to gather data. Examples include website counts of 'hits', meters attached to viewers' televisions to monitor the programmes they watch, and eye cameras to study viewers' eye movements when watching advertisements. The main method of gathering primary data, however, is the **questionnaire**.

Questionnaires are a systematic way of gathering data and can broadly be divided into structured and semi-structured. A structured questionnaire is one where questions and potential answers are set up in advance (often using 'closed' questions); a semi-structured questionnaire uses a list of topics and allows the respondent to answer in their own words. Generally, structured questionnaires are used in quantitative research and semi-structured questionnaires are used in qualitative research, although there are times when formats are mixed.

Question content It is important that questions are drafted in a way that ensures that the respondents' views are recorded as accurately as possible. Questions (or statements) should aim to avoid:

- leading the respondent – e.g. 'Shopping centres are better than high streets.'
- embarrassing or pressurizing the respondent – e.g. questions about income/wealth or sexuality must be worded sensitively to ensure accurate and complete responses
- creating a status bias – e.g. 'Most intelligent shoppers compare prices. Do you?'
- ambiguous questions – questions must be unambiguous to prevent respondents interpreting the words differently, which would introduce a bias to the study.

Question types As mentioned above, there are two broad question types.

- **Open questions** allow the respondent to answer in his/ her own words. This type captures the respondents' actual words but open questions are much more difficult to analyse than closed questions.
- **Closed questions** are those where the answers are set up in advance and are therefore much easier to analyse. However, closed questions 'force' the respondent to choose an answer and care must be taken to ensure that his/her opinion is represented in the predetermined list. One approach to dealing with this problem is to include an 'open' element in a closed question, e.g. 'Other, please state'.

The following are some of the most commonly used closed question types.

- **Dichotomous questions** require a simple Yes/No answer, e.g. 'Is this your first visit?'
- **Multiple-choice questions** offer the respondent several options: the respondent may be instructed to select only one option or, alternatively, all that are appropriate to them.

● **Projective questions** use a more indirect approach and techniques like sentence completion, word association, pictorial (e.g. adding words to a picture) and storytelling.
● **Attitudinal scales** Measuring attitudes is important and researchers use a range of scales. Some of the most widely used scales are:
  – itemized – various responses are itemized to help the respondent make his/her selection, as follows:

Buy every day	Buy once a week	Buy monthly	Buy rarely	Don't buy at all
1	2	3	4	5

  – constant sum – the respondent is asked to divide up or allocate a number of points (normally 100) to indicate the relative importance of two or more attributes, e.g. 'Please divide up 100 points to reflect how important any of the following features are to you.'
  – Likert – this scale is a symmetrical agree–disagree scale where each point in the scale has a constant value relationship with the other points. In some cases the middle point is removed to create a 'forced' response, i.e. the respondent has to agree or disagree. Likert scales are complex to develop and most researchers use currently tested versions.

Strongly agree	Agree	Neither agree nor disagree	Disagree	Strongly disagree
+2	+1	0	-1	-2

  – semantic differential – this scale uses bipolar adjectives (hot–cold, reliable–unreliable, old–new, etc.) and is often constructed with seven categories between the two poles allowing the respondent to select the position that best matches their opinion.

Hot						Cold
*	*	*	*	*	*	*

Data collection

Data collection is a form of communication: the researcher poses a question and the respondent answers. There are four broad data collection approaches, two of which involve an interviewer and two of which are based on self-completion.

● **Face-to-face (f2f) interviewing** includes the 'street intercept' interviews that many of us have experienced while shopping. This is the most versatile and productive method but it is also the most expensive. The method allows for in-home interviewing, which is particularly valuable when sampling is based on the demographic distribution of a population. Trained interviewers conduct the interview, often using CAPI (computer-assisted personal interviewing) systems to aid the process.

● **Telephone interviewing** again uses a trained interviewer and can also involve computer-based systems to aid the process (CATI or computer-aided telephone interviewing). This method is the fastest and is not as expensive as f2f but it lacks the more personal contact between the interviewer and respondent provided by f2f and is therefore not so versatile.

● **Self-completion postal questionnaires** are posted to respondents who are asked to complete the questionnaire and return it in a pre-paid envelope. This is a less expensive method than both f2f and telephone. However, non-response rates are much higher with postal surveys and a major issue is the problem of non-response error – i.e. if those who do respond are different from those who do not, this may skew the results. In practice, researchers use a range of techniques to maximize response rates (e.g. primer letters, reminder letters, incentives) and also test for the likely direction of non-response error.

● **Self-completion web surveys** are a new method made available to researchers by the rapid growth of the Internet. Also based on self-completion, they are less expensive. Web-based surveys can use questionnaires on a website or send them out by email. The Internet can be valuable for researching groups that are difficult to reach through other methods (e.g. heavy web users such as teenagers). The main drawback is again the problem of non-response error.

Focus groups

Focus groups are a standard qualitative data collection technique used to capture respondents' views and attitudes about a subject. A focus group is generally made up of a group of respondents drawn from a defined 'population'. The group meets under the guidance of a 'moderator' who introduces topics to the group for discussion.

Data entry and 'cleaning'

Data collected are generally entered into an electronic database, either directly in the case of computer-aided data collection (such as CATI and CAPI) or manually where completed questionnaires are returned as 'hard copy'. In the latter case the process of transferring the data from the questionnaire to the database can be a source of error and it is therefore important to control for such error. The researcher must be sure that what is contained in the questionnaire is identical to that entered to the database for analysis. Researchers take a random sample of entered questionnaires and compare them with the original completed questionnaires to ensure accuracy.

An alternative to manual data entry is questionnaire scanning involving a scanner and dedicated software. In addition, the researcher will be concerned that the questionnaire has been completed correctly. For instance, a particular response to a question may ask the respondent to go to another section of the questionnaire (known as 'gate' questions). Sometimes, particularly in self-completion, a respondent may complete the wrong section and this type of error needs to be 'cleaned' before analysis.

Analysis

Analysis of data has been supported by specialist software since the 1970s and became available on PCs in the 1980s. Today there is a wide range of providers of data analysis software available, e.g. SPSS and SNAP.

Primary research data in a database has two elements: the **cases** (the respondents) and the **variables** (the information captured by the questions). A question in a questionnaire can have more than one variable, such as in the case of multiple-choice questions.

The starting point in analysing the data is to run a simple count of the numbers of responses in each category for each variable, known as **frequency analysis** or one-way tabulation. Here's an example.

1 Value label	2 Value	3 Frequency	4 Percentage	5 Valid percentage	6 Cumulative percentage
Yes	1	90	32.14	32.14	32.14
No	2	180	64.29	64.29	96.43
Don't know	3	10	3.57	3.57	100.0
Total		280	100.0	100.0	

1 The value labels: the predetermined answers to the question. In this example the question would have been a dichotomous question (Yes/No answer) with a Don't know option.

2 The 'value' or coding (1 = Yes, etc.) assigned to the value label and entered in the database.

3 The number of respondents by each category (Yes, No, Don't know) for this variable = the frequency of that answer. The total sample size in this example was 280.

4 The simple percentage values for each value label: here the majority of respondents (64 per cent) had answered No to this question.

5 If some respondents do not answer all the questions the software recalculates the percentage value based on the actual total number of respondents to that question. Here all respondents have responded, so the values in columns 5 and 4 are the same.

6 The cumulative percentage count based on column 4.

The next most common level of analysis counts two variables simultaneously. This is known as **cross-tabulation**. Cross-tabulation allows a researcher to investigate relationships between dependent variables (such as respondents' attitudes and behaviour) and independent variables (such as their age, gender, socio-economic position). As we saw on Monday, these relationships are important to the marketer. Below is an example of a cross-tabulation of gender and agreement/disagreement with a cited statement.

Value label	Value		Strongly agree	Agree	Disagree	Strongly disagree	Total
Male	1	Frequency	6	25	45	21	**97**
		Percentage	6.2	25.8	46.4	21.6	**100.0**
Female	2	Frequency	18	36	76	23	**153**
		Percentage	11.8	23.5	49.7	15.0	**100.0**
Total		**Frequency**	**24**	**61**	**121**	**44**	**250**
		Percentage	**9.6**	**24.4**	**48.4**	**17.6**	**100.0**

This cross-tabulation shows that there is little difference in agreement/disagreement with the cited statement between male and female respondents.

To further the researcher's understanding of the data, a wide range of statistical tests can be used.

Findings and recommendations for action

We have seen that the primary research process is a complex project management of a number of interrelated elements. This stage of the process must bring meaning and value to the research user. The starting point is to link the findings to the research objectives, assembling them in line with each element of the objectives.

Reporting

The way the findings are presented to users must be appropriate to their needs. Often this means using:

- **graphical representations** – e,g, pie charts, histograms
- **data 'reduction'** – i.e. simplifying numbers such as rounding them to make them easier to digest, e.g. 45.67 per cent 'reduced' to 46 per cent
- **summaries** – using 'executive' summaries, abstracts, etc.
- **presentations** – e.g. PowerPoint presentations.

Omnibus surveys and agencies

Omnibus surveys are multi-client surveys, so called because clients can join and leave the 'omnibus' according to their needs. The advantages to the research client include cost savings (because the sampling and screening costs are shared across multiple clients) and timeliness (because omnibus samples are large and interviewing is ongoing). For further information go to www.ipsos-mori.com/omnibusservices.aspx

While it is feasible for organizations to conduct their own research studies, managers often choose to use **marketing research agencies** because of their experience and expertise. In addition, agencies bring emotional detachment to the problem and by providing extra resources enable client staff to concentrate on their core objectives. For more information about selecting and commissioning MR agencies, visit www.mrs.org.uk

Summary

Marketing research (MR) acts as a link between customer and organization. It is an investment for organizations, and there is a trade-off between the cost and the benefit obtained in capturing information that reduces risk in decision making.

MR can be applied to many marketing problems including establishing segment size, and defining customers' needs or attitudes to the benefits perceived in different products. Modern IT enables organizations to produce information valuable for marketing decision making.

Secondary research is research that has been conducted by others, not necessarily focusing on our needs. The major sources are government, public bodies, trade/professional bodies and commercial research providers.

The primary research process involves defining the problem, research objectives, sampling frame and method, and research instrument and questions. When the data have been collected using an appropriate method, the findings are analysed and can be reported.

SUNDAY
MONDAY
TUESDAY
WEDNESDAY
THURSDAY
FRIDAY
SATURDAY

Questions (answers at the back)

1. What is a key issue of the AMA definition of marketing research (MR)?
   a) It's a link between customer and organization ❏
   b) It's another name for the R&D department ❏
   c) It's specific to pharmaceutical businesses ❏
   d) It's mainly an American activity ❏

2. What is a system that formally gathers, analyses and distributes information to managers known as?
   a) A talking shop ❏
   b) A marketing information system ❏
   c) An in-house website ❏
   d) A company newsletter ❏

3. What is information gathered about the general marketing environment including customers, intermediaries, competitors, suppliers and the general PEST environment known as?
   a) Office gossip ❏
   b) Marketing intelligence ❏
   c) Making contacts ❏
   d) Networking ❏

4. What is secondary research?
   a) Research conducted by others, not necessarily focusing on our particular needs ❏
   b) Research conducted after the main research ❏
   c) Research that is of less value ❏
   d) Research conducted by our customers ❏

5. Why is quantitative research different from qualitative research?
   a) There is much more of it ❏
   b) The results from quantitative research can be presented in quantitative form, e.g. 65% like our product ❏
   c) It can only be done by academics ❏
   d) It is free ❏

6. What is sampling, where each unit has the same chance of being sampled, known as?
   a) Probability or random sampling ❏
   b) Unknown sampling ❏
   c) Researcher's sampling ❏
   d) Explainable sampling ❏

7. What are the two broad question types?

a) Right and wrong ❏
b) Open and closed ❏
c) Short and long ❏
d) Difficult and easy ❏

8. What is one of the problems with self-completion data collection (including web-based)?

a) Analysing them ❏
b) Non-response bias ❏
c) Preventing fraud ❏
d) Handling complaints ❏

9. A primary research database has which two elements?

a) Time and cost ❏
b) Completed and aborted ❏
c) Right and wrong ❏
d) Cases and variables ❏

10. What is cross-tabulation?

a) An error report ❏
b) Corrupted data ❏
c) Analysis of two variables simultaneously ❏
d) Processing of incorrect cases only ❏

WEDNESDAY

Strategic marketing

Today we shall consider marketing as a strategic activity – how marketers decide what they must do to meet the organization's objectives. Marketing strategy can be seen as a marketing decision process involving a series of steps to analyse, plan, implement and control a range of activities designed to achieve the organization's objectives.

We will start by considering how marketers must review the strengths and weaknesses of their own organization (business audit) and assess the opportunities and threats in the marketplace (market audit) before conducting a 'targeting' exercise that matches the strengths of the organization to opportunities presented by different market segments. We will then see how marketers develop an integrated marketing strategy (marketing mix), and implement and control the execution of the strategy to meet the organization's objectives.

Finally today we will look at three famous approaches to developing strategy: the Boston Box, the Ansoff Box and Porter's Three Generic Strategies.

Marketing planning

Marketing planning is a strategic activity; marketers have to make a range of decisions that translate into actions in the future to achieve their objectives. Marketers have to **plan** and they have to develop a **strategy**.

> ## Two definitions
>
> **Plan** – a formulated and especially detailed method by which a thing is to be done; a design or scheme
>
> **Strategy** in game theory, business theory, etc. – a plan for successful action based on the rationality and interdependence of the moves of opposing or competing participants

Planning in marketing seeks to apply a logical and objective approach to deciding how a company's capabilities will be matched to opportunities in the marketplace so that the corporate objectives can be met. Strategy takes into consideration the 'moves' of others. For marketers, the key group of 'others' is competitors, i.e. 'opposing or competing participants'. However, for marketers, a key additional participant group is customers, whom we are neither 'opposing' nor 'competing' with. On first sight, these militaristic terms may seem to contradict the basic ethos of the marketing orientation we described on Sunday. The reason they are used in this context is that they reflect the nature of the process of deploying the organization's resources to achieve a defined objective.

Developing a strategic marketing plan involves a series of interrelated stages of analysis, planning, implementation and control. One might say that there are two broad elements to strategic marketing planning – thinking and doing. The ancient Greek proverb 'Think slowly, act quickly' extols the virtue of taking time to weigh up the options before acting, but it stresses the need to carry out the selected strategy without delay. Thinking helps us to reduce the risk in deciding what we should do and therefore significantly improves the probability of success. This simple proverb encapsulates the value of strategic marketing planning for the marketer.

The marketing planning process

We can translate the four stages of strategic marketing planning into a marketing planning process, as shown below.

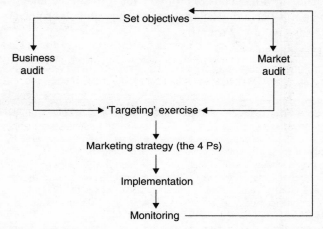

The marketing planning process

We shall consider each part of the process in turn.

Objectives

The organization will need to establish a set of objectives for the planning period (probably 12 months). It is likely that setting objectives will start with a description of a series of qualitative objectives (such as a mission statement). These will need to be 'operationalized' (made quantitative) so that performance against these objectives can be measured. Ultimately, objectives are defined in terms of, for example, percentage turnover growth on last year, improving operating profit from $y\%$ to $z\%$, achieving market leadership in a defined market/segment, and so on. There are two important points to note.

1 These objectives will be the basis for developing the strategic direction of the organization and will involve the commitment of corporate resources.

2 We must consider the objectives in the context of the market audit (i.e. the audit of the market environment within which the business operates, which we shall look at later in this chapter). Basically, we must assess how realistic the objectives are in terms of what is possible, given the market conditions. For example, it would be unrealistic for a small business with access to limited capital to set an objective to be the world market leader in building nuclear power stations within 12 months.

Business audit

The business audit is a review of the strengths and weaknesses of the business.

Examples of business strengths	Examples of business weaknesses
• Market leadership	• Low market share
• Some uniqueness as perceived by the customers (a differential advantage in terms of quality and/or price)	• No uniqueness perceived by the customers
• Control of a scarce resource related to differentiating our offering from that of the competition, e.g. access to a scarce resource (such as aggregates in construction), control of patents	• Poor brand appeal
	• Poor business performance (lack of capital for reinvestment)
	• Poor employee morale
• A market-beating 'business process model' (i.e. how we organize our business), e.g. McDonald's, Lidl	
• Profitability	
• Brand loyalty	

While in no way meant to be exhaustive, the following demonstrates the types of analysis undertaken during a business audit.

Business performance (last three years)

1 Sales and contribution by type of product/service
2 Sales and contribution by type of customer
3 Sales and contribution by geographical area
4 Top ten customer segments (profile)

Marketing mix

1 Product (width and depth of product range, features and benefits, product portfolio analysis)

2 **Price** (cost versus price, basis for pricing decisions)
3 **Channels** (channel selection and positioning)
4 **Promotion** (including current activities and budgets/spend levels, advertising, press relations, mail, outlets, personal selling, Internet)

Management knowledge

1 Perceptions of the company's strengths and weaknesses
2 Perceptions of customers' perceived needs (e.g. of value, price benefits)
3 Perceptions of the competition (market/segment shares, high profile accounts, capabilities in terms of strengths and weaknesses, geographical coverage, business objectives, policies, strategies, etc.)
4 Perceptions of the PEST environment in which the business operates

Market audit

This is a review of the **opportunities** and **threats** existing in the organization's business/market environment. There are two levels: the 'immediate' level and the 'general' level.

Immediate level

● **Customers** We have noted that customers/potential customers need to be segmented, i.e. placed into groups whose members share attitudes to product/service selection and differ from other segments within the same market.
● **Competitors** Perhaps surprisingly, companies embarking on a strategic marketing planning exercise often show a poor understanding of this group. We need to understand such issues as:
  – our competitors' recent 'track record' (business performance)
  – their declared corporate objectives/strategies
  – within segments, customers' perceptions of their offerings.
● **Intermediaries**
● **Suppliers**

General level
This level covers the PEST environment we have discussed previously.

- **Political** – e.g. prevailing political policies towards climate change
- **Economic** – e.g. level of growth in GNP, unemployment
- **Social** (or cultural) – e.g. society's attitudes to sustainability, energy conservation
- **Technological** – e.g. 'smartphone' technology

By combining the findings from the business audit and market audit, the marketer can assemble a **SWOT analysis** of strengths, weaknesses, opportunities and threats. This can be a powerful and very useful tool for developing the plan. One way to think about SWOT analysis is to consider it as a planning 'balance sheet': within the organization there will be strengths (+) and weaknesses (–), and in the marketplace there will be opportunities (+) and threats (–).

Within the organization	In the marketplace
Strengths +	Opportunities +
Weaknesses –	Threats –

The 'targeting' exercise
Targeting refers to deciding which segments the organization will select to focus on. It is the heart of the marketing planning

process and decisions made at this stage have a significant effect on the overall success of the plan. The task is to match the organization's strengths to opportunities in the marketplace so that the firm can obtain the best return on effort. There are two distinct tasks:

● to rank the market segments in terms of their attractiveness to the organization
● to rank the organization against the competition in terms of attractiveness to the market segments.

These two tasks can be represented in the following matrix.

Market/segment
attractiveness to the organization

The targeting matrix

● *Cell 1* This cell is the segment or segments that are highly attractive to the organization and to whose buyers the organization is highly attractive. This is the most effective matching of the organization to the segments.
● *Cell 2* Here the organization is still highly attractive to the segments but these segments are less attractive to the organization (they may be too small or offer poor creditworthiness). In this case the marketer may choose to 'sub-segment' the segments to isolate the most attractive parts that may be worth targeting.
● *Cell 3* While the segments are attractive to the organization, the segments do not perceive the organization to be attractive to them. In this case the marketer needs to assess

the basis of this perception. If our offering is objectively poorer than our competition, we must do something to address this disadvantage (e.g. improve product quality). However, if we can find no objective difference between our offering and that of our competitors, the problem is one of communication.

- *Cell 4* In this case the segments are unattractive to the organization and the organization is unattractive to the segments. Marketers 'de-target' (redirect resources *away* from these segments) in such circumstances.

Marketing strategy

Establishing a successful marketing strategy involves deciding what to produce, how much to charge, where the customer will buy the product, and how to inform and persuade the customer to buy the product. Marketers have described this as the 'marketing mix' – product, price, place and promotion (i.e. the 4 Ps). We will look at the 4 Ps in more detail later in the week, but we can summarize each element here.

- **Product** This term encapsulates both tangible and intangible benefits carried by products and services. The product strategy must ensure that the firm's offering carries benefits that can be matched to customer needs.
- **Price** Prices must be set to reflect the benefits customers perceive in our offering compared to offerings from our competitors; i.e. which offers the best value.
- **Place** This term generally refers to channels of distribution, i.e. where the products are sold, including direct marketing channels such as the Internet.
- **Promotion** This is how we inform and communicate the benefits in our offering to the target market segments.

It involves developing messages and selecting the most cost-effective media to carry the messages to the target market segments. People will usually think of advertising (TV, radio, press, posters, etc.) and direct mail, but promotion also encompasses e-marketing (on the web) and public relations.

The marketer should draft separate marketing mixes (or marketing strategies) for each targeted segment, blending all the mix elements together to deliver satisfied customers and to meet the organization's stated marketing objectives.

Implementation

As we have already seen, the purpose of planning is to make our actions more effective. Planning without action is an arid academic exercise and of no real value to the organization. How the plan is implemented is therefore critical. Organizations often produce **tactical action plans** that:

1 set operational variables
2 establish time limits and deadlines
3 communicate and assign tasks
4 develop sales forecasts
5 determine action plans for individuals
6 prepare budgets.

 Action plans need to be 'SMART' – specific, measurable, attainable, relevant and time bound.

Monitoring

Monitoring is a critical part of the planning process; only by using monitoring for control can we ensure that the strategy will achieve our objectives.

Not surprisingly, the first issue is monitoring the implementation of the plan in terms of achieving the stated objectives. In effect we are considering a loop that can be couched in a simple question: we have set measurable objectives but are we delivering to these objectives? We need to set appropriate timescales for monitoring and establish mechanisms to compare 'actual' to 'budget'. The purpose of this type of monitoring review is to ensure that the plan is 'on track' and, if not, to identify and make changes to ensure that we get it back on track. For some organizations, it is necessary to define the organization's objectives as 'milestones': what do we need to have achieved by the end of period 1 (to be defined by the organization) to be confident that we shall achieve our ultimate objective(s)?

In addition, the marketer needs to monitor the environment. Customers and competitors must be the main focus but general trends in the PEST environment must also be noted. We have seen that marketing research and the MkIS have an important role to play here. Where changes impact on the plan, action will be needed to respond to the changes so that they do not undermine its successful execution.

Effective marketing planning and the organization

At the beginning of the week we looked at the relationship between marketing and organizational performance and the body of evidence that suggests marketing is associated with improved profitability. However, there is also evidence that marketing planning does not always deliver improved performance, and research has been able to identify the following key requirements for the effective (and commercially successful) execution of marketing planning.

- **Ownership** It is important that those who have to implement the plan are given the opportunity to contribute to its development.
- **Rigour** The audit process (business and market) requires a significant amount of information, both from within the firm and from the marketplace. Lack of rigour in gathering, analysing and interpreting data can seriously undermine the effectiveness of the planning process. Marketers need to obtain thorough and objective information to reduce risk in decision making.

● **Environmental sensitivity** Marketers must guard against trying to 'fit' the world outside to the plan. Change is endemic to all market situations, and planning processes must be reviewed in the light of the changing environment. Organizations must be environmentally sensitive and have the flexibility to be able to respond to changes, both opportunities and threats.

● **Company-wide appreciation** All employees need to appreciate the broad issues involved in the plan so that they can contribute to its success (i.e. share the same agendas as other staff).

● **Management belief** Senior management must believe that the process of planning will reduce risk in decision making and contribute to the success of the business. Without this belief, the process can easily lose staff enthusiasm and rigour and ultimately become a pointless bureaucratic exercise marginalized in the business.

Alternative approaches

The marketing decision process described above is used, in different formats, by a wide range of organizations, both large and small, manufacturing and services and for profit and not-for-profit. In addition, marketing consultants often use this approach when supporting clients in improving the benefits they can derive from marketing planning.

However, there are a number of other approaches to managing the strategic direction of a business. Among them are the Boston Box, the Ansoff Box and Porter's Three Generic Strategies.

The Boston Box

Larger organizations often face the problem of managing their portfolio of products (all the products they offer to the marketplace). It is important that the organization's resources support those products that offer the best return on investment. One famous approach to analysing this problem is known as the Boston Box.

Relative market share

	High	Low
High	Star	Problem child
Low	Cash cow	Dog

(Market growth rate — vertical axis)

The Boston Box

Source: Boston Consulting Group

The Boston Box classifies products in terms of two variables: relative market share and market growth rate.

Star These products are in high growth markets and the organization has a high relative (to the competition) market share. These products often need high investment to maintain their market position but may become 'cash cows'.

Cash cow These are low-growth, high market share products. They are established and successful, have low investment needs and produce a positive cash flow.

Problem child These products are in high growth markets but have low relative market share. They require investment to maintain (let alone increase) market share and marketers have to decide whether these products will succeed or fail.

Dog These products are low growth, low market share. They may generate enough cash to maintain themselves but do not offer any medium/long-term potential for the organization.

Balancing the portfolio

Organizations must balance their product portfolios: too many of any one type can create major problems. Even too many 'cash cows', which would seem like the best situation for an organization, cause a problem – markets are dynamic and the current demand for cash cows will eventually decline. The organization needs 'stars' to replace the current 'cash cows' in the future.

The Ansoff Box

An alternative way to look at the organization's relationship with its customers is to study the relationship between products and customers. Igor Ansoff created another famous tool, often referred to as the Ansoff Box, which looked at an organization's product mix in terms of the relationship between existing and new products and existing and new customers. The Ansoff Box ranks the best return on effort in the short term based on four product/customer relationships.

	Customer	
	Existing	New
Product Existing	1	3
Product New	2	4

The Ansoff Box

Source: H. Igor Ansoff, *Corporate Strategy* (Harmondsworth: Penguin, 1965)

The numbers in the cells represent the ranking of each product/customer relationship and identify that selling existing products to existing customers offers the best return on effort in the short term. However, selling 'new' (i.e. new to the customers) products to existing customers offers the second-best return on effort in the short term.

Porter's Three Generic Strategies

In his book *Competitive Strategy*, Michael Porter developed the concept of the Three Generic Strategies for outperforming other businesses in an industry.

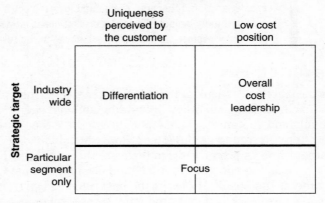

Three Generic Strategies

Source: Michael E. Porter, *Competitive Strategy* (Free Press, 1998)

Overall cost leadership Here emphasis is on cost minimization and control, so the business can still earn returns after its competitors have competed away their profits through rivalry.

Differentiation Here management seeks to differentiate the product or service by creating something that is perceived industry wide to be unique: perhaps through brand, technological advantages, patents or control of scarce resources.

Focus The management focus here is on a particular buyer group and seeks to serve that target particularly well, through either uniqueness perceived by the customer or low cost.

Porter's Three Generic Strategies are viable approaches for dealing with competitive forces. However, a business failing to develop its strategy in at least one of the three directions – a 'stuck in the middle' firm – is in an extremely poor strategic situation and is almost guaranteed low profitability.

Summary

Marketing planning is a strategic activity – marketers have to make a range of decisions that translate into actions in the future to achieve their objectives. It is a decision process that focuses on matching the strengths of the organization to market opportunities and creating detailed action plans designed to deliver the organization's objectives.

The steps involved in market planning are:

1 setting objectives

2 reviewing the strengths and weaknesses of the organization (through a business audit)

3 assessing the opportunities and threats in the marketplace (through a market audit)

4 conducting a 'targeting' exercise that matches the strengths of the organization to opportunities presented by different market segments

5 developing an integrated marketing strategy (marketing mix)

6 implementing and controlling the execution of the strategy to meet the organization's objectives.

Marketing planning is a key strategic link between the organization and its marketplace and plays a vital part in the successful management of a business.

SUNDAY
MONDAY
TUESDAY
WEDNESDAY
THURSDAY
FRIDAY
SATURDAY

Questions (answers at the back)

1. What is marketing planning?
a) A strategic activity ❏
b) A gift some businesspeople are born with ❏
c) A skill you can only learn from a business school ❏
d) A technique only management consultants use ❏

2. What does the marketing planning process start with?
a) Advertising ❏
b) Selling ❏
c) Setting objectives ❏
d) Retailing ❏

3. What does the business audit review?
a) Economic climate ❏
b) Strengths and weaknesses of the organization ❏
c) Trends in social attitudes ❏
d) Competition ❏

4. What does the market audit review?
a) Opportunities and threats in the business/market environment ❏
b) Skills in our organization ❏
c) Our sales growth over the last three financial years ❏
d) Our operating profit over the last three financial years ❏

5. What does the 'targeting' exercise help marketers do?
a) Decide which segments the organization will focus on ❏
b) Check if the plan is going to be effective ❏
c) Win prizes in business competitions ❏
d) Respond positively to journalists' requests for information ❏

6. The marketing mix involves decisions regarding what?
a) Rebates, rates, revisions and returns ❏
b) Product, price, place and promotion ❏
c) Scales, summaries, shifts and scenarios ❏
d) Training, timetables, tokens and tolls ❏

7. What is the purpose of monitoring?
a) To ensure that the plan achieves the stated objectives ❏
b) To check that employees are doing their jobs ❏
c) To decide who will receive bonuses ❏
d) None of the above ❏

8. What is the Boston Box based on?

a) Making sure that the product's packaging meets customers' needs ❏

b) Improving the in-house flow of information ❏

c) Preventing competitors discovering our strategy ❏

d) Relative market share and market growth rate ❏

9. What is the Ansoff Box based on?

a) The relationship between existing and new customers and existing and new products ❏

b) Relative market share and market growth rate ❏

c) The critical mass of markets and segments ❏

d) None of the above ❏

10. What are Porter's Three Generic Strategies?

a) Processes, solutions and testing ❏

b) Leadership, motivation and remuneration ❏

c) Production, selling and marketing ❏

d) Overall cost leadership, differentiation and focus ❏

THURSDAY

The marketing mix – product and price

Yesterday we looked at marketing planning and introduced the idea of developing an integrated marketing strategy, the marketing mix. We saw that a successful marketing strategy involves deciding what to produce, how much to charge, where the customer will buy the product, and how to inform and persuade the customer to buy the product using the 4 Ps: product, price, place and promotion.

In this and the following chapters we are going to look at each of these four elements of the marketing mix in more detail.

Today we are going to look at *product* and *price*. We will consider tangible and intangible product benefits, explore the differences between products and services, and review the relationship between product features and benefits. We will then go on to discuss brands, the product life cycle, new product development and product strategy decisions.

Three forces act on pricing – the target audience's perception of value in our and competitors' offerings, our cost structure and the competition's price levels. We will look at these before considering some key issues of pricing strategy decisions.

Product

'Product' is the fundamental basis of the marketing mix. Our 'product' carries benefits that satisfy customers' needs and, while it can be a tangible, physical entity, 'product' can also be something quite intangible such as a service, an experience or an idea. In the context of the marketing mix, we can define 'product' as follows.

> **'A product is anything that is offered to the marketplace that can satisfy a customer's perceived need.'**

Our **product strategy** is the method by which we **satisfy** customers' needs. Here we are going to look at the factors affecting our product strategy: tangible and intangible benefits; the differences between products and services; features and benefits; brands; the product life cycle; new product development; and product strategy decisions.

Tangible and intangible benefits

A product can be tangible or intangible. Some writers have tried to establish a tangible–intangible continuum, with highly tangible products at one extreme (e.g. salt) and highly intangible products at the other extreme (e.g. insurance).

Tangible	**Intangible**
Salt	Insurance

The tangible–intangible continuum

It's probably accurate to say that most offerings have some element of tangible and intangible benefits as part of their appeal. Let's look at some examples.

- **Cars** The physical nature of the product has a high element of tangibility, but there are intangible benefits such as the brand and dealer service.

- **Personal computers** Again, these have a high element of physical product, but aspects such as brand and pre- and post-service support add intangible benefits.
- **Restaurants** The food is tangible but the overall benefit is made up of intangibles like the decor, the ambience, the service and the restaurant's reputation.
- **Perfumes** The core offering is intangible in terms of the benefits customers derive from the purchase but the offering is 'delivered' as a tangible product.

Differences between products and services

Given that most offerings have some element of tangible and intangible benefits as part of their appeal, it is still possible to distinguish **products** (i.e. with a high degree of tangibility) from **services** (i.e. with a high degree of intangibility). There are five key differences between products and services:

- **Heterogeneity** Services can usually be designed around a specific requirement: a consultancy assignment can be designed to meet one client's unique needs. Products tend to be more homogeneous: for volume car producers one can only select from the specifications on offer.
- **Intangibility** As we've seen, products with a high tangible element can be touched, tasted and taken apart to examine how they work; there is a 'trial' element. Services do not have this trial element.
- **Inseparability** The production of a service and its consumption occur at the same time: there is a direct link between provider and customer. The production and consumption of highly tangible products, on the other hand, are separate.
- **Perishableness** Unlike products, services cannot be stocked or held over. A hotel bedroom that is not occupied on a particular night is a revenue opportunity lost.
- **Lack of ownership** Access to or use of a service facility does not mean the customer obtains ownership. The purchase is often time related, e.g. a hotel room reservation for three nights.

Features and benefits

Whether predominately tangible or intangible, a product must carry benefits that satisfy customers' needs. **Benefits** are those elements of the product that meet customers' needs (as discussed on Monday). **Features** carry benefits.

It is important to differentiate between a benefit and a feature. Telling a customer about a feature may not enable him/her to understand how the product meets his/her perceived needs. Features are the product's capabilities; benefits are the outcomes customers 'consume' by way of meeting their perceived needs.

Features carry benefits

Let's consider an example. Many cars today have antilock braking systems (ABS) as standard. ABS is not a benefit per se but a feature that carries a benefit that fulfils a need.

- Feature: ABS
- Benefit: safer braking
- Need: safety

Customers don't care about features unless they're experienced in buying the specific type of product we are offering. For example, when personal computers (PCs) were first marketed to individuals and Small Office Home Office (SoHo) users, the promotional emphasis was on technical performance features, such as RAM, hard disc size and CPU speed. Many potential customers were put off by the 'jargon' because they could not see what benefits these features would offer to them. In essence, they asked, 'What's in it for me?' Most people now understand these terms and can judge the benefits in an offering from a list of features. In effect, the features list can become a type of shorthand between the experienced customer and the producer.

SUNDAY
MONDAY
TUESDAY
WEDNESDAY
THURSDAY
FRIDAY
SATURDAY

TIP When presenting a customer with a benefit, the marketer can use a feature as evidence that the benefit exists. Our ABS example demonstrates this point well.

Brands

An important form of intangible benefit is the **brand**. A brand is a name, term, sign, symbol, association, trademark or design which is intended to identify the products or services of one provider or group of providers, and to differentiate them from those of competitors.

Customers develop loyalty to a brand, based on previous experience if they have purchased the product before and found that it has met their perceived needs. Alternatively, a brand can be associated with a lifestyle or particular condition that is important to the customer and that they aspire to.

In addition, brands can add value to a product: for instance, many customers would perceive a bottle of Chanel perfume as a high-quality, exclusive and expensive product. But the same fragrance in an unmarked bottle would probably be viewed as lower quality even if the two fragrances were identical. Some commentators have cited this as an example of marketers taking advantage of customers, but the intangible benefits the customer obtains from the brand meet important needs such as self-actualization and the esteem of others.

Brand extension

Although the Chanel brand started as a French fashion house, the product range now includes fragrances, fine jewellery and watches, leather goods and shoes, and even eyewear and sporting goods. This is known as brand extension – the application of a brand beyond its initial range of products or outside its category. This becomes possible when the brand image has contributed to a perception with the consumer/user, where brand and not product is the decision driver.

From the marketer's perspective, brand management seeks to make the product or services relevant to the target segments. Brands should be seen as more than the difference between the actual cost of a product and its selling price: brands represent the sum of all valuable qualities of a product to the customer. It follows that marketers must be careful not to allow anything to damage the brand's reputation. For example, when the presence of the chemical benzene was found in a small sample of bottles of Perrier water in the USA in 1990, Perrier voluntarily recalled its entire inventory of Perrier from store shelves throughout the United States. This action demonstrated to the market the importance Perrier placed on the quality of their product and their commitment to deal with any problem quickly and thoroughly – to do whatever was necessary to protect the integrity of the brand.

The product life cycle

Most products display similar characteristics to living organisms – they are 'born', grow to maturity, decline and 'die'. They have a product life cycle (PLC). For example, the stand-alone facsimile (fax) machine was launched in the 1970s and was adopted by a wide range of organizations and individuals during the 1980s. However, the spread of Internet access, email and scanning had a major impact on the sales of fax machines.

While the life expectancy of products varies greatly, most products go through four stages: introduction, growth, maturity and decline, as shown graphically below.

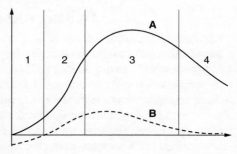

The product life cycle

The horizontal axis of the graph represents time and the vertical axis represents sales (depicted by graph line A) and profit (depicted by graph line B). We can consider some of the properties of the four stages.

1 Introduction

At this stage the product has been introduced to the market, sales growth is slow and profits are negative due to the costs of launch. A particular group of buyers is adopting the new product. These are known as 'innovators' and are characterized by their desire for new experiences and a relatively high degree of risk taking. As a marketing rule of thumb, this group accounts for around 10 per cent of the market.

2 Growth

If the product is perceived to have benefits matched to customers' needs, it will become more widely adopted. Sales will grow quickly and profits will follow suit. The growth stage is driven by a group of buyers known as 'early adopters' who have an appetite for new (and better) solutions to their needs but who lack the risk taking of the innovators. This group generally accounts for around 20 per cent of the market.

3 Maturity

At some point the product's sales growth will slow and it will enter its mature stage. Commonly the longest period, sales and profits peak during the maturity stage. This stage is characterized by the adoption of the product by the majority of the market, known as the 'late adopters'. This group accounts for around 60 per cent of the market.

4 Decline

Eventually, the product's sales are likely to decline. This can be due to new products being seen as a better match to customers' needs, changing customers' attitudes or increased competition. Even during this stage, new customers are adopting the product. These 'laggards' can be characterized by a generally conservative outlook and a low threshold to risk. This group accounts for around 10 per cent of the market.

The marketer will obviously face different strategic issues for each stage of the PLC and may have a portfolio of products at different stages. It is worth noting the relationship between the PLC concept and the Boston Box we looked at on Wednesday. In simple terms we can align the two as shown below.

PLC	Boston Box
Introduction	Problem child
Growth	Star
Maturity	Cash cow
Decline	Dog

New product development

Customers change and the PEST factors change and exert an influence on customers. Consequently, the marketer must be alert to the need for new solutions to customers' needs. **New product development (NPD)** is therefore an important element of the organization's product strategy. New products cost an organization until they reach growth stage and some products do not achieve this stage and fail, with the resultant impact on the organization's profitability. The marketer needs to maximize the chances of a new product becoming established (i.e. reaching maturity in PLC terms or becoming a 'cash cow' in Boston Box terms). NPD success is linked to the **diffusion of innovation**, i.e. the way new ideas or products are communicated through certain channels over time to a marketplace. Several factors determine whether and how quickly an innovation will be adopted.

- **Relative advantage** Potential adopters must perceive that the innovation is an improvement over the previous solution to their needs. In some NPD situations, the customer has a poorly defined need because there had been no solution to their needs up to that point. This is the 'anticipation' element of our definition of marketing.
- **Compatibility** Potential adopters must perceive the innovation as being consistent with their existing values, past experiences and needs. An idea that is incompatible with their values and norms will either not be adopted at all or not be adopted as rapidly as an innovation that is compatible.

- **Relative complexity/simplicity** If the innovation is too difficult to understand or use, it is less likely to be adopted.
- **Trialability** If the potential adopter may try or experiment with the innovation, this will increase the chances of it being adopted.
- **Observability** The more easily an innovation is visible to others, the more this will drive communication among peers and personal networks. In turn this will create more positive or negative reactions (i.e. the effect of 'innovators' on 'early adopters').

Product strategy decisions

Marketers have to make a series of decisions regarding the product offering. We can summarize these decisions under four headings.

1 **Core benefit** As we have seen, the product must carry benefits to meet the customers' perceived needs. In general terms the marketer needs to understand the hierarchy of needs (the relative importance of customers' perceived needs) and ensure that the product carries benefits (tangible and intangible) matched to these needs.

2 **Actual product** Decisions in this area include product design, styling, quality, colours, branding and packaging. In effect this is the manifestation of the core benefits.

3 **Augmented product** Decisions in this area involve anything that can add value to the customer (and differentiate our offering from that of the competition) and could include installation, warranty, credit facilities and after-sales service.

4 **Product range (depth and width)** Decisions in this area involve the 'width' of the product range (e.g. small family hatchback, family saloon car, executive saloon car) and the 'depth' (e.g. range of engines on offer, trim levels, equipment levels).

For companies to ensure continued evolution, they must define their industries broadly to take advantage of growth opportunities. They must ascertain and act on their customers' needs and desires, not bank on the presumed longevity of their products. An organization must learn to think of itself not as producing goods or services but as doing the things that will make people want to do business with it.

Price

This is the second part of the marketing mix and, while all parts of the mix are inextricably linked, there is a particularly strong link between the product and price parts of it. At its basic level, price is the amount a customer must pay to obtain the benefit(s) from a product or service – the **exchange** we referred to on Sunday.

In considering price strategy, we are going to look at the three interrelated forces acting on any organization's decisions regarding pricing (the **'pricing triangle'**) and pricing strategy decisions:

- the target audience's perception of value in our and the competition's offerings
- our cost structure
- the competition's price levels.

We can represent this interrelationship as the pricing triangle.

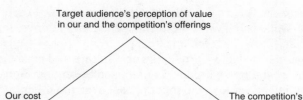

The pricing triangle

The target audience's perception of value

Value is the customer's perception of the match of benefits in an offering to their needs and is measured by the customer's willingness to pay for it. We can illustrate this with a simple example: a customer sees three products (A, B and C) as having *exactly the same* benefits matched to his/her needs. However, the products have different prices.

Product	Price
A	225.00
B	264.00
C	210.00

In this situation the product with the lowest price (i.e. product C) offers the best value, i.e. the most benefits at the lowest cost. We can present this as a simple equation:

$$Value = \frac{Benefits}{Price}$$

Many of us will be familiar with the process of deciding on a particular make and model of a product and searching for the lowest price supplier.

However, if the three products are perceived to have *different* bundles of benefits, the job of assessing the value in each product is made more difficult for the customer. Customers adopt a range of strategies to deal with this situation. Some do a thorough analysis of the benefits offered by the competing products and calculate the best value on this basis. Others will focus on just one or two of their most important perceived needs and decide on that basis. Others will rely on their experiences of particular brands, while some will always choose the lowest price option, regardless of the benefits on offer.

Consumer durables (products such as cars and washing machines) and many products purchased by organizations have an added value component of **cost over time**. For instance, an airline company will be interested not only in the purchase price of an aeroplane but the running cost over time. It may include issues such as taxes on carbon emissions.

Price can also be inextricably linked to the customers' perception of quality and hence value. With a luxury brand such as Chanel, if the product were 'too cheap' it would be difficult for the customer to accept that the benefits they perceive in the product can be obtained for such a 'low' price. This phenomenon is known as '**customer dissonance**' and further illustrates the link between product and pricing strategies.

Quality and price

The Belgian brewer Stella Artois ran a promotional campaign in the UK between 1982 and 2007 using the slogan 'Reassuringly expensive'. The intention was to make the relatively high price of the product a benefit rather than a barrier and take advantage of the consumer linking quality with price.

Our cost structure

Price and cost are not the same. Price is ultimately controlled by customers' value perceptions; cost is the monetary value of producing and delivering the product, including profit. We need to define costs, which fall into two broad groups.

- **Variable costs** are so called because they vary directly with the level of production – the more we produce, the more variable costs we incur. Examples are raw materials, labour and operating expenses directly related to production.
- **Fixed costs,** also known as overheads, do not vary with the level of production. Whether we make anything or not, we will still incur these costs. Examples are office/factory rent, business rates and salaries of sales staff and management.

At a certain level of units of production (and hence revenue), the total cost (fixed and variable) matches the revenue value. This is known as the **breakeven point**: as production increases from this point, the organization will make profits.

From the marketer's perspective, cost sets the limit to the low end of pricing. The following table considers six scenarios (A–F) of differing relationships of the key variables of units of production, which are number of units, unit price, revenue (units of production x unit price), variable cost (VC) per unit, VC per unit x units of production, fixed cost (FC) and profit/loss.

	Scenario					
	A	B	C	D	E	F
Units number	5,000	5,000	5,000	15,000	5,000	20,000
Unit price £	10	20	10	10	10	10
Revenue (units × unit price) £	50,000	100,000	50,000	150,000	50,000	200,000
VC per unit £	4	4	8	8	10.5	10.5
VC per unit × units £	20,000	20,000	40,000	120,000	52,500	210,000
FC £	30,000	30,000	30,000	30,000	30,000	30,000
Profit/loss £	0	50,000	–20,000	0	–32,500	–40,000

A This is an example of the simple breakeven position. In this scenario 5,000 units at a selling price of £10.00, a variable cost (VC) per unit of £4.00 and fixed costs (FC) of £30,000 will yield breakeven.

B In this scenario the price is double that of scenario A while all other factors remain the same. In this case the organization would deliver a profit of £50,000. This example demonstrates the effect on the 'bottom line' of increasing price levels.

C This scenario is the same as A apart from increased variable costs (up from £4.00 per unit to £8.00) and this yields a loss of £20,000.

D This is the breakeven position based on the costs in scenario C. The units of output need to triple (from 5,000 to 15,000). This demonstrates that, when the difference (known as the 'contribution') between the selling price and the variable cost is relatively low (£2.00 in this case), units of output have to increase significantly to achieve breakeven.

E This scenario is the same as A but with increased variable costs (up from £4.00 per unit to £10.50), £0.50 *more* than selling price. This scenario yields a loss of £32,500.

F In this scenario units of output have quadrupled but losses have increased (from £32,500 to £40,000). This demonstrates that increasing output will only worsen the organization's losses when variable costs are *above* selling price.

The competition's price levels

This is the third point of our pricing triangle. We can do everything we can to understand our customers' needs, match benefits to needs and try to give the customer the best value proposition, but we mustn't forget that our competitors will be doing the same.

Some products are difficult to differentiate from one another – such as nails and screws (fixings) and petrol – and with these the lowest price strategy will win.

Different approaches

Organizations adopt different approaches to pricing. For instance, the US retailer Walmart (Asda in the UK) bases its strategic positioning on being the lowest price provider in a broad industry sector. BMW, on the other hand, seeks to differentiate its offer across a range of market segments and it bases its product pricing on customers' perceptions of the value they see in the BMW brand. Chanel adopts the focus approach, targeting particular market segments and differentiating its offering through its exclusivity.

In many organizations pricing offers the marketer the most immediate and flexible tool in the marketing mix because it is relatively easy to change prices. Consequently, many organizations rely on price cuts to generate sales or to meet a competitive threat. But this may be a 'double-edged sword': although a price cut may generate sales in the short term, it may undermine the customers' perceptions of the value of the product. Price-cut sales promotions seem to promise two important benefits:

- they generate increased sales volume
- they induce non-buyers to trial and then perhaps become regular customers.

We can consider each in turn.

- It is true that temporary price promotions do generate a sales 'spike'. However, research by Ehrenberg, Hammond & Goodhardt (1994) suggests that around 80 per cent of the people who buy a brand on a price promotion deal already use the brand anyway and the company has a reduced margin on these sales. Sales volume is one thing but profitability is quite another.
- Ehrenberg *et al.* demonstrated that there is no long-term effect on loyalty/repeat buying rates from price-related sales promotions. Where customers 'brand switch' in line with the promotion, they return to their original brand when the price promotion is lifted.

TIP *To be effective, the marketer must remain vigilant and aware of not only what the competitors are doing but, equally importantly, what customers are thinking and doing with regard to their offering and that of their competitors. This underlines the importance of marketing information and research.*

Pricing strategy decisions

Pricing decisions must take into account the three forces described in the pricing triangle above. However, price is also part of the overall marketing mix and interrelated with the other parts of the mix. If we choose to operate in an undifferentiated market (e.g. petrol retailing), our pricing strategy will reflect the fact that it is difficult to differentiate our offering from that of the competition in terms of additional benefits matched to customers' needs. On the other hand, if we operate in the luxury goods market (e.g. fragrances, fine jewellery, watches), we can expect to be able to use our benefits (including intangibles such as brand) to differentiate our offering from that of the competition. Products and services must therefore be '**price positioned**' so that:

- the customer perceives the value in the offering
- the customer perceives our offering to be better value than that of the competition
- we are able to make a profit (defined here as the surplus after subtracting total costs from total revenue) in the medium term.

Time and pricing

Time is an additional variable to consider. The product life cycle demonstrates the link between units purchased (revenue) and time. When a new product is launched, some organizations choose to set a high price. This is called **market-skimming pricing**. As the product moves into the mature stage, prices can be reduced to stimulate increased adoption. This is known as **market-penetration pricing**.

Summary

Today we focused on two parts of the marketing mix: product and price.

Product is anything that satisfies a customer's perceived needs, and involves both tangible and intangible elements. Services tend to be more intangible than products. Features are a product's capabilities and carry benefits, which may be tangible (such as safer braking) or intangible (such as brand).

The product life cycle is introduction–growth–maturity–decline. Although new product development is expensive, finding new solutions to changing customer needs is vital.

Three forces influence pricing: audience perception of value, cost structure and competitors' prices. A key concept is value – benefits against price. When all offerings carry the same benefits, the lowest price offering represents the best value.

Cost is not the same as price but is the monetary value of profitable production/delivery and includes fixed and variable elements.

SUNDAY

MONDAY

TUESDAY

WEDNESDAY

THURSDAY

FRIDAY

SATURDAY

Questions (answers at the back)

1. What is a product ?
   a) The outcome of customers' spending ❏
   b) The motive driving customers' needs ❏
   c) The end result of a purchase ❏
   d) The fundamental basis of the marketing mix ❏

2. Do products have either intangible or tangible benefits, but not both?
   a) Yes, that's correct ❏
   b) Only for services ❏
   c) No, products can have both intangible and tangible benefits ❏
   d) Only for luxury food products ❏

3. What is a product feature?
   a) The basis for an advertising campaign ❏
   b) The product's capabilities that carry benefits to customers' needs ❏
   c) The best aspect of a product ❏
   d) An article in a magazine about a new product ❏

4. What is a brand?
   a) The packaging ❏
   b) The theme for an advertising campaign ❏
   c) A new product idea ❏
   d) An important form of intangible benefit ❏

5. What is the growth and subsequent decline in a product's revenue over time known as?
   a) Product life cycle ❏
   b) Product trajectory ❏
   c) Product roller coaster ❏
   d) Product big dipper ❏

6. What is new product development (NPD) success linked to?
   a) The diffusion of innovation ❏
   b) The advertising budget ❏
   c) The product's time in development ❏
   d) The time of year it is launched ❏

7. What does Levitt's concept of 'marketing myopia' say?
   a) Customers do not see all the products available to them ❏
   b) Customers do not see all advertisements ❏
   c) Marketers cannot see all the potential customers in the market ❏
   d) Organizations must be customer oriented rather than product oriented ❏

8. What is price?
a) What it costs to make a product ❏
b) The printed price before you start haggling ❏
c) The amount a customer must pay to obtain the benefits from a product or service ❏
d) Always set to be 10% lower than the competition ❏

9. What is the value equation?
a) Needs/benefits ❏
b) Tangible benefits/intangible benefits ❏
c) Price/cost ❏
d) Benefits/price ❏

10. What are total costs made up of?
a) Prices and costs ❏
b) Variable and fixed costs ❏
c) New and existing costs ❏
d) None of the above ❏

FRIDAY

The marketing mix – place

Yesterday we focused on the first two parts of the marketing mix – product and price. Today we are going to focus on the *place* part of the mix, the third of the 4 Ps.

In its simplest terms and probably original sense, place is where the 'exchange' (of product or service for the price) takes place. The term marketplace can conjure up images of stalls in open market squares, bazaars and souqs and, as we said at the beginning of the week, marketing began with this fundamental relationship between buyers and sellers. In the modern context, however, place focuses on how products and services are distributed to customers.

Today we will look at channels of distribution, types of channels, channel characteristics and some of the key issues in decisions related to distribution channel strategy.

Place and distribution

In the modern context the 'place' part of the marketing mix focuses on how products and services are distributed to customers. This **distribution** may refer to the physical distribution of products or the channels of distribution.

● **Physical distribution** is the *planning, monitoring and control of the distribution and delivery of manufactured goods* and forms an important part of ensuring that the product is available to customers in the quantities required at the time they want to buy.

● **Channels of distribution** are the third parties that make the product or service available for use or consumption by the customer.

We can imagine a simple channel of distribution as follows:

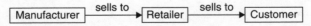

In our example, if a manufacturer uses a retailer, then the retailer must add a cost to the manufacturer's price. For this to make business sense, the retailer must **add value** to the marketing process. Retailers, or intermediaries in general, can add value in a number of ways.

● Dealing with a small number of retailers is more **economical** for the manufacturer than dealing directly with a large number of end customers.

- Retailers will take much **larger volumes** of products than end customers and this offers cost savings to the manufacturer in terms of physical delivery.
- The **location** of retail premises meets customers' buying behaviour, e.g. in out-of-town shopping centres.
- For some goods, the **reputation** of the retailer can enhance the product's perceived value, e.g. Harrods.

It is probably easier to think of channels of distribution in the context of products than of services because, as we have seen, 'inseparability' is a characteristic of services (its production and consumption occur at the same time). However, services can be delivered through intermediaries too. Examples are travel agents and mortgage brokers.

The channel relationship should provide a mutual benefit to the manufacturer/service provider and the intermediary.

Channel types

There are two broad types of distribution channel available to the marketer: intermediaries and direct.

Intermediaries

Intermediaries are independent organizations that carry out a number of activities associated with adding value to the marketing process. The two main groups are retailers and wholesalers.

Retailers include organizations such as:

- supermarkets (Tesco, Sainsburys)
- department stores (House of Fraser, John Lewis Partnership)
- high street chains (Topshop, Next)
- convenience store groups (Martin McColl, Spar)
- independent retailers, including speciality stores
- franchises (McDonald's, IKEA, Subway).

Wholesalers primarily sell goods and services to those buying for resale and/or business use. They include:

- wholesale merchants – sell primarily to retailers and can be general (i.e. sell a range of products, e.g. Booker Wholesale) or specialist (i.e. fish wholesalers, e.g. M&J Seafood, part of the Brakes Group)
- cash-and-carry wholesalers – sell from fixed premises and do not normally deliver; buyers come to them for their requirements (e.g. Selco Builders' Warehouse)
- industrial distributors – sell to manufacturers rather than retailers and can carry a range of stock to meet customers' needs (e.g. Nationwide Fuels who supply a range of industrial lubricants to industry in the UK)
- producers' co-operatives – are prevalent in the agricultural market; members assemble groups of products to be sold to customers and share the profits.

Direct channels

Organizations often choose to trade directly with customers because of cost issues but also because of the potential for building customer relations. Direct channels can be broadly divided into two groups: traditional and new media.

Traditional channels

These are 'traditional' in the sense that they have been used for some time. The following are some of the best-known examples.

- Direct mail – involves posting promotional material direct to the potential customers' home or office and encouraging customers to buy direct (e.g. Readers' Digest).
- Catalogue-based home shopping – is a variant of direct mail, where a catalogue is forwarded to the customer and they are encouraged to purchase products represented in the catalogue (e.g. Littlewoods catalogue).
- Inserts – are promotional material placed in selected magazines with instructions for buying direct.
- Telemarketing – uses the telephone to sell directly to customers in both consumer and B2B markets.
- Direct selling – includes door-to-door selling and party plan (e.g. Party Plan UK) in consumer markets.
- Personal selling – can include own salaried staff and/or sales agents. Sales forces are common in B2B markets where there is a strong benefit from personal relationships between the salesperson and the buyer.
- TV shopping – is more accurately known as direct response television marketing (DRTV). DRTV is common in the US and now more widespread in other markets such as the UK following the proliferation of satellite and free-to-air channels. DRTV involves the direct promotion of a product to the audience and typically a freephone number for them to make their purchase.

New media
The explosion of digital-based technology has opened up a wide range of new channels for marketers. Of major use in promotion (which we will discuss tomorrow), new media also offer additional channels of distribution.

- Websites – are widely used by all sorts of organizations and individuals and have been described as 'online shop windows'. Clearly, with the addition of e-commerce (the transactional element), organizations can trade directly with their customers, opening a new channel. Many organizations have traditional retail channels but also trade direct from their websites.
- Specialist sites – e.g. eBay have a seller development team committed to helping sellers grow their business within the eBay channel.

- E-direct mail – is used in the same way as traditional direct mail but using email to communicate a particular message or to direct the recipient to a website.
- Mobile phone marketing – has been made possible by the growth in ownership of smartphones and 3G/4G networks and associated software so customers can purchase through their mobile phone.
- Podcasts and vodcasts – are audio and video (respectively) files that can be downloaded to a mobile device. Marketers are experimenting with different approaches to using these technologies as effective channels.

Changing channels

One important component of distribution channels is **change**. As with the influence of change on the marketing process, decisions related to distribution channels are no different. Channels are subject to similar PEST and market forces as products, and over time different channels grow and then decline in a way that resembles the product life cycle.

Traditional channels are making way for new media channels, and one major change has been the Internet share of retailing. The chart below shows the Internet share in percentage terms of the average weekly value of all retailing in the UK in the period 2006–11.

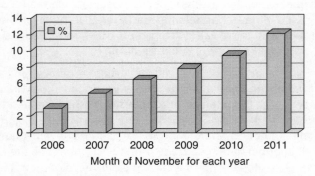

Internet share (%) of average weekly value for all retailing in UK

Source: Retail sales – November 2011: Office for National Statistics, UK

These data show the significant growth (up from 3 per cent in 2006 to 12.2 per cent in 2011) in market share obtained by Internet-based retailing out of all UK retailing. Perhaps one of the best-known Internet retailers is Amazon.com. The business was incorporated in 1994 and trades in the USA and a number of other countries in Europe and Asia. Net sales in the year to 31 December 2010 were $34.2 billion, up 319 per cent on 2006 (sales in 2006 being $10.7 billion).

Channel characteristics

The type and nature of channel relationships are based on an agreement between the parties involved and can be quite diverse. To take a simple manufacturer/retailer example, this could be a medium-term contractual relationship or a more informal, flexible relationship.

Some producers establish exclusive channels; car manufacturers, for example, have 'dealer networks'. In this case there is a much stronger 'partnering' theme to the relationship than there would be in a less formal manufacturer/retailer relationship. Dealers agree to invest in their business in support of the investment of their manufacturer partner, and manufacturers commit to supporting their dealers through promotions and so on.

The relative 'power' of the players in a distribution channel can vary quite significantly. For instance, in our example of the car manufacturer and dealer, one might say there is a 'symbiotic' (mutually advantageous) relationship. However, in different markets different members of the channel can have significantly more 'power' than the other members. Two extreme examples of this **'channel captaincy'** are:

- **UK supermarkets** Keynote estimates that Tesco, ASDA, Sainsbury's and Morrisons, followed by Waitrose, Aldi, Lidl and Marks & Spencer, accounted for around 93 per cent of retail food sales in the UK in 2009. This places the large supermarkets in an extremely strong bargaining position with their suppliers.
- **luxury goods** With luxury goods the manufacturer selects the retailer and gives that retailer an exclusive territory,

agreeing not to sell to any other retailer in a designated area. Rolex, the luxury watch manufacturer, operates in this way. Its 'dealer locator' page on their website enables customers to identify where they can buy Rolex watches in a particular area. The strength of the brand gives the manufacturer the power to select retailers and negotiate terms.

While channel members depend on one another, they often act alone in their own short-term best interests. Maintaining a mutually beneficial relationship can therefore be difficult. Clearly, the greater the investment and the longer the contractual relationship, the more likely it is that channel members can operate in a mutually beneficial way.

Distribution channel strategy decisions

As with all aspects of marketing, the starting point must be the organization's target customer segments. They must ask two key questions.

● Does the channel put the product in the right place: where the target customer wants to buy it?
● Does the channel add value?

Marketers often consider the channels their competition utilizes and may choose to be in the same channel so that customers see their product at the same time as they see their competitors'. For example, a proprietary food brand might want to be in the same supermarkets as their direct competitors. Alternatively, marketers may wish (or be forced) to adopt different channels from their competitors. A good example is smaller specialist food producers using online and other channels (such as farmers' markets) to 'bypass' the supermarkets to reach their target customers.

The marketer must be alert to channels changing over time. The growth in online channels is part of the reason for the recent decline in revenue experienced by UK high street retailers.

Summary

Today you learned that 'place' in the marketing mix is largely about channels of distribution – how a product/service is made available to the customer. Marketers can use intermediaries – retailers, wholesalers – if they add value to the marketing process, or they can trade directly with customers to reduce costs and increase the potential for building customer relations.

Direct channels can be broadly divided into traditional and new media. The recent significant growth of the Internet in terms of percentage share of the value of all UK retailing is one example of how different channels grow and decline over time.

Channels can have different characteristics. Some are exclusive relationships, like the dealer networks in the automotive market. Sometimes the intermediary can be the most powerful member of the distribution channel, as is the case with leading UK supermarkets.

Some organizations choose to be in the same channels as their competitors; others select channels offering a different route to their customers, such as direct marketing rather than retailers.

SUNDAY

MONDAY

TUESDAY

WEDNESDAY

THURSDAY

FRIDAY

SATURDAY

Questions (answers at the back)

1. What is a channel of distribution?
   a) Selling to Europe ❏
   b) Those third parties that make the product or service available for use or consumption by the customer ❏
   c) The spread of sales in different markets ❏
   d) None of the above ❏

2. Why must an intermediary like a retailer add value?
   a) Because of the common law of contract ❏
   b) They are only a service provider ❏
   c) They add cost so if they do not add value, there is no reason for a producer to use them ❏
   d) They are overrated ❏

3. Why are wholesalers different from retailers?
   a) They do not advertise ❏
   b) They sell to those buying for resale or business use ❏
   c) They have the highest sales volumes ❏
   d) All of the above ❏

4. What are two aspects of direct marketing?
   a) Traditional and new media ❏
   b) Profitable and non-profitable ❏
   c) Bulk based and individual units ❏
   d) Products and services ❏

5. Why is change over time important when considering channels?
   a) Because of seasonality ❏
   b) Because of the increasing cost of travelling ❏
   c) Over time different channels grow and then decline ❏
   d) Because of the lack of opportunities for out-of-town developments ❏

6. What does channel captaincy refer to?
   a) Taking the lead in developing a marketing campaign ❏
   b) Having control of shipping lines to Europe ❏
   c) The best retailers to use for products targeted at the leisure sailing market ❏
   d) Those members of the channel that have the most power ❏

7. Although channel members depend on one another, what do they often do?
   a) Act alone in their own short-term best interests ❏
   b) Misunderstand their roles ❏
   c) Fail to communicate with each other ❏
   d) Have different views about marketing ❏

8. What is the starting point for deciding a distribution strategy?
a) Who is available ❏
b) The production department ❏
c) Whether the channel puts the product where the customer wants to buy it ❏
d) Falling sales volumes ❏

9. Why do organizations often want to be in the same channel as their competitors?
a) They may be missing something ❏
b) Customers see their product at the same time they see their competitors' product ❏
c) They don't want to be left out ❏
d) It is what they have always done ❏

10. What dramatic increase in sales illustrates the growth of the Internet as a channel?
a) The BBC ❏
b) The Charities Commission ❏
c) Amazon.com ❏
d) Marmite ❏

SATURDAY

The marketing mix – promotion

Today we will look at the last of the 4 Ps of the marketing mix – *promotion*. This is the part of the mix that involves the organization in advancing and furthering its product or service in the minds of customers.

Promotion is also the most visible part of the marketing mix and can be seen alongside general entertainment on TV, radio and in the cinema and now increasingly on the Internet. It is understandable, therefore, that a large proportion of the general public perceives promotion to be synonymous with marketing. However, we know that promotion is only a *part* of marketing.

We will consider promotion in terms of marketing communications, the communication process, and the seven key decision areas of the promotional strategy. We will also discuss briefly ethics and regulation in this area.

Promotion and marketing communications

Promotion is the fourth part of the marketing mix and it can be thought of as the advancement or furtherance of a product or service in the mind of the customer. It is really about marketing communications and is concerned with **informing** and **persuading** customers.

Marketing communications involves developing and delivering co-ordinated messages designed to create a desired effect in a target audience. Ideally, marketing communications should manage the customer relationship over time, from the pre-purchase and purchase stages through to post-purchase and the brand's ongoing relationship with customers.

Communication is a process as depicted in the following model.

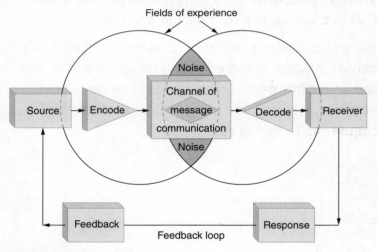

The communication process

The communication process involves ten elements.

1 **Source** – the organization sending the message to another party
2 **Encode** – the process of putting the intended message or thought into symbolic form, i.e. words and images

3 **Message** – the set of words, pictures or symbols that the source transmits
4 **Channel of communication** – the medium or media used by the source to carry the message to the receiver
5 **Decode** – the process by which the receiver assigns meaning to the message sent by the source
6 **Receiver** – the party receiving the message, normally the customer or potential customer but also including groups that may influence their opinions and behaviour
7 **Response** – the reactions of the receiver exposed to the message; this may be either a move from a state of unawareness of an offering to awareness or a move to a more committed position that will lead to a purchase
8 **Feedback** – the part of the receiver's response that is communicated back to the source, e.g. marketing research results
9 **Noise** – the unplanned 'static' or distortion during the communication process, which results in the receiver getting a different message from the one sent by the source. 'Static' could include competitors' messages, articles in magazines, blogs, etc.
10 **Fields of experience** – the more the source's and the receiver's fields of experience overlap, the more effective the message is likely to be.

Promotional strategy decisions

There are seven key decision areas involved in developing a promotional strategy.

1 Defining the target audience

On Wednesday we discussed the strategic process of defining which market segments the organization will target (the 'targeting' exercise). This exercise will have enabled us to define and profile the target customers in terms of both their perceived needs and their exposure to media. The organization may have multiple target segments and many of the following decision areas will be affected by their characteristics.

For example, younger target audiences can be difficult to reach using traditional media and the marketer would need to use new media (Internet and mobile-based).

2 Setting promotional objectives

While the ultimate objective is likely to be a purchase, promotional objectives will need to be drafted in terms of 'moving' the target audience towards this ultimate aim. Customers may move through a series of attitudinal stages – starting with **unawareness**, moving to **awareness**, developing an **understanding** of the benefits in the offering, and then becoming **convinced** that the offering meets their needs before taking **action** (purchasing). For instance, if the target audience is unaware of the organization's offering, the promotional objective is likely to be creating awareness. The marketer could therefore set an objective of 40 per cent of the target audience to be aware of the offering following the first stage of the campaign.

3 Creating the message(s)

The starting point for creating a message is an understanding of the task in hand. What are our promotional objectives? The message can be informative or persuasive, or both. A simple informative message may be 'Our new store opens on Monday at 8 a.m.' Persuasive messages form much of the media we all see and hear every day, in print, on television and radio, and on the Internet and mobile phones. These messages are developed by matching benefits to customers' perceived needs. Often marketers will seek to focus on the most important needs (from the hierarchy of needs discussed on Monday) as the basis for their messages.

To communicate this we need to 'encode' our message so that the customer will 'decode' it with maximum fidelity. It follows that the more we know about our target audience, the more effective our messages will be – marketing research at pre-campaign stage offers a valuable resource in this context. Message design can also be influenced by the nature of the medium. For instance, an advertisement in a magazine that could be re-read would be able to carry a more detailed message than a TV advertisement, but a TV advert would be able to use a range of moving images and sounds including music and dialogue.

4 Selecting the media

Media carry the message(s) to the target audiences and there are many media available to marketers.

- Advertising in print – includes national and regional newspapers, free press, special interest magazines (e.g. music, gardening), age-group targeted (e.g. *Saga Magazine*), lifestyle (e.g. *Tatler*)
- TV (terrestrial, cable and satellite) – carries sophisticated multimedia promotional messages
- Cinema – can run longer versions of TV adverts and can be targeted at audiences based on the nature of the film being shown
- Commercial radio – audio advertisements which, like cinema, can be targeted at particular groups based on the content of the programmes on air
- Personal selling – a very effective promotional medium because trained and experienced salespeople can interact with the customer; often a key part of B2B promotion and high-cost domestic durables, e.g. cars
- Direct marketing – postal, leaflet drop, telephone (including auto-dialling)
- Outdoor poster – includes large fixed billboards, bus stop, motorway, airport, underground, mobile (vehicle-based), inflatables
- Public relations – is the discipline which looks after reputation, with the aim of earning understanding and support and influencing opinion and behaviour. It is the planned and sustained effort to establish and maintain goodwill and mutual understanding between an organization and its public. Key to its success is the ability of the PR practitioner to place press releases in appropriate media
- Sponsorship – cash or in-kind support of anything from small regional events to major international events such as the Olympics and football's World Cup

- Online – from the proliferation of websites to sponsored links on search engines to specially designed adverts running on host sites including social networking sites such as Twitter and Facebook
- Mobile – the growth in ownership of smartphones and 3G/4G networks has given advertisers a new medium to deliver promotional messages to people's phones based on platforms including mobile browsers, apps (software applications) and SMS (short message service).

The marketer must select carefully. The first thing to consider is which media best 'reach' the target audience. By this we mean the number of people who will be exposed to the message carried by the medium. Clearly, the more of our target audience covered by the medium the better.

Secondly, the marketer must assess the relative cost of reaching an audience. Different media have different costs and reach, and marketers seek to create a reasonable comparison by dividing the cost of an advertisement in a particular medium by the reach (or coverage) of that medium, often expressed as a cost per 1,000 audience.

Thirdly, he/she will be interested in what the medium can 'do' for the message. Some media, such as exclusive magazines, can enhance the message by adding credibility to a product's advertisement.

5 Creating the promotional programme

The promotional programme has two components, the mix of media to be used and the schedule of activities over the time of the campaign. The following is an example of a simple programme.

Medium	Activity	Month 1	Month 2	Month 3	Month 4
TV	4 × 60 seconds	×		×	
Radio	6 × 20 seconds		×		×
Press	4 × 1/4 page	×		×	
Twitter	Weekly feed	×	×	×	×
Public relations	News releases	×		×	

The key thing for the marketer is to ensure an **integrated** programme of promotional activity that enables messages to build on earlier work and for themes to be **reinforced** as the campaign progresses. All too often, messages emanate from different parts of the organization with the result that the customer receives a mixed set, at worst contradictory, that can seriously reduce the effectiveness of the campaign.

6 Setting the budget

Setting the budget is often difficult. Some organizations base their decision on what they can afford. However, this method fails to link what needs to be done (the promotional objectives) with the resources to do it. Others use a percentage of sales approach, perhaps 10 per cent of last year's total sales made available for this year's promotional budget. Again, this method fails to link resources to objectives. Probably the best approach is the objective-and-task method – assessing what has to be achieved, the tasks involved and the estimated cost of performing these tasks.

7 Evaluating the results

Promotional spend is a business investment and therefore must be measured to assess its effectiveness. Unfortunately, it is difficult to measure the return on promotional spend (in sales and profit) because so many factors influence such measures. Effectiveness must therefore be measured in terms of meeting the promotional objectives through post-campaign research.

Ethics and regulation

In promoting a product or service it is particularly important that marketers maintain an ethical approach – that they do not use the promotional process to mislead customers. It may be tempting to make unsubstantiated claims to attract attention but, in addition to the fact that such action is immoral, it is bad for business and also illegal.

1 **Making unsubstantiated claims is bad for business**
   Although an organization might obtain a short-term advantage by misleading a customer, if the product or service does not satisfy customers' needs, they will not buy the product again. In addition, customers who feel badly treated by a supplier will tell their relations, friends and colleagues and this form of word-of-mouth communication is very powerful.

2 **Making unsubstantiated claims is illegal**
   Most developed economies legislate against bad promotional practice. In the UK the **Trade Descriptions Act 1968** prevents manufacturers, retailers and the service sector from misleading customers about what they are spending their money on. The Act empowers the courts to punish companies or individuals who make false claims.

   Each product sold must be '**as described**', of '**satisfactory quality**' and '**fit for purpose**'. 'As described' refers to any advertisement or verbal description made by the trader. 'Satisfactory quality' covers minor and cosmetic defects as well as substantial deficiencies and means that products must last a reasonable time. 'Fit for purpose' covers not only the obvious purpose of an item but also any purpose determined at the point of sale by the trader.

Independent regulators

The **Advertising Standards Authority (ASA)** is the UK's independent regulator of advertising, working to ensure that advertisements are **legal, decent, honest and truthful**. The US equivalent is the **Federal Trade Commission**. Their mission is to uphold standards in all media on behalf of consumers, business and society at large.

Summary

Today you learned that promotion is about marketing communications and is concerned with informing and persuading your target market. It is the most visible part of the marketing mix, appearing alongside entertainment on TV and radio, in the cinema and on the Internet.

Ideally, marketing communications should manage the customer relationship with the brand. At its root, communication involves encoding a message to be decoded by the receiver.

The seven key decision areas involved in developing a promotional strategy are: defining the audience; setting objectives; creating the message(s); selecting the media; creating the programme; setting the budget; and evaluating the results.

When promoting a product/service, marketers must not use the promotional process to mislead customers. Legislation and regulation exist to protect customers, but it is the responsibility of professional marketers to act ethically and not to make unsubstantiated claims.

SUNDAY

MONDAY

TUESDAY

WEDNESDAY

THURSDAY

FRIDAY

SATURDAY

Questions (answers at the back)

1. What is the promotion part of the marketing mix?
   a) Marketing communications ❏
   b) The 'glossy' part ❏
   c) All about TV ❏
   d) Not important to the success of the business ❏

2. Why does a large proportion of the general public perceive promotion to be synonymous with marketing?
   a) Advertising *is* marketing ❏
   b) Promotion is the most visible part of the marketing mix ❏
   c) It's part of the entertainment business ❏
   d) All of the above ❏

3. What does the heart of the communication process involve?
   a) Closing the sale ❏
   b) Getting the best price for printed materials ❏
   c) The source encoding a message to be decoded by the receiver ❏
   d) Subliminal messages ❏

4. How must promotional objectives be set?
   a) In terms of moving the audience through a series of attitudinal stages to the purchase stage ❏
   b) In terms of sales ❏
   c) According to the time of the year ❏
   d) According to the number of specialist sales staff available ❏

5. What can messages be?
   a) Read or heard ❏
   b) Seen or viewed ❏
   c) Informative and/or persuasive ❏
   d) None of the above ❏

6. What is media reach?
   a) The number of people in an audience that will be exposed to the message carried by the medium ❏
   b) The reputation of a newspaper or TV channel ❏
   c) The amount a customer must pay to access a medium ❏
   d) Always much higher than the medium claims ❏

7. What are the two components of creating a promotional programme?
   a) The mix of media to be used and the schedule of activities over the time of the campaign ❏
   b) Sales staff and marketing staff ❏
   c) Time of year and product type ❏
   d) Retailer and competitor activity ❏

8. Why is it difficult to measure the financial return, such as sales or profit, on promotional spend?
   a) Because of the way costs are accounted for ❏
   b) Seasonal factors need to be taken into account ❏
   c) So many factors additional to the promotional activities influence such measures ❏
   d) Because of differences in retailers' sales systems ❏

9. Why may it be tempting to make an unsubstantiated claim?
a) To attract attention ❑
b) To mislead the competition ❑
c) To get the campaign under way quickly ❑
d) To make the shareholders happy ❑

10. In addition to regulation, for what reason must the professional marketer guard against making unsubstantiated claims?
a) It's bad for business ❑
b) Because of competitors' reactions ❑
c) Because of retailers' reactions ❑
d) None of the above ❑

WEEK 2

Digital Marketing
In A Week

Introduction

Hello my fellow Marketing Warriors ...

What, that isn't what you want to be? Sorry, but whether or not you like it very much it is war out there. That makes you a warrior and that means you need this book.

This week is what I consider essential basic training for every small business owner or department manager before they hope to trek deeper into the marketing woods.

This week trains you in the basics of what you need to know to survive and thrive with marketing in this digital age:

- social marketing
- search engine optimization
- 'paid' advertising on Google/Facebook, and so on
- creating the perfect website that makes sales
- and more ... (lots of tips and tricks on everything from Yahoo Answers to press releases).

SUNDAY

Building the ultimate sales website

Welcome to the starting line of your 'digital marketing' race.

This is more of a marathon then a sprint but as the saying goes 'The journey of a thousand miles begins with one step'.

So take what you learn in this week and *apply it* as this can change you and your business for the better.

And so to begin, before we get into the 'sexy' stuff, like social media marketing and search engine optimization, we need to talk about some far more important things.

First, we need to talk about your website, because all the traffic in the world will not make you money if you have a crappy website that can't convert all those visitors into buyers.

This is where you really start to make money.

At the same time you don't want to spend too much time trying to fine-tune every detail on the site but not enough time on generating traffic.

The key here is to practice a little 'Kaizen'– the art of continuous improvement.

Just get started with a decent (though not perfect) website and make small improvements when you need to as your traffic grows and builds over the long haul.

SUNDAY

MONDAY

TUESDAY

WEDNESDAY

THURSDAY

FRIDAY

SATURDAY

Look and feel

So first off you need to find your perfect 'look and feel'– what should this be?

Check out your competition to see what kind of 'look' their websites have. Take notes of what you like and what you don't.

Take a look at company websites in different sectors. Is there anything you like on those sites that your competition *aren't* utilizing?

Now ask yourself a question ... Who are you? What makes you unique in this world? What's your personality? Sarcastic? Funny? Thoughtful?

The perfect look and feel for you and your business is a combination of all these things.

It should be a reflection of what makes you unique in this world. If you're an accountant with a great sense of humour, inject a little of that into your website. Accountants don't have to all be boring (kidding).

For a perfect example of this, take Sir Richard Branson. His various Virgin websites are still very corporate looking but have enough of his personality in them to make them stand out.

Why can't you do the same?

Organization

Next your website needs to be easy to move around. Your visitors want to quickly find what they're looking for. Once they come to your site and you're able to answer their questions and show them what they need, they may want the answers to other questions as well.

So make it as easy as possible for them. Interlink within your posts to other posts at the beginning, at various places in the middle and also at the end.

Essentially be plugging your other content as much as possible without going overboard.

Lay out your navigation bar logically and make sure that your most popular pages are highlighted.

This will get people clicking around your site, which looks good to Google, which looks great to your bottom line.

If you need help with this, again check your competition and other websites not in your sector for ideas.

Landing pages and sales pages

First some definitions.

A landing page is where your visitor enters your site and a sales page is where you offer to sell them something and they make the choice to buy or not.

The two aren't necessarily the same thing, although they can be.

It depends on what you're promoting, and whether your potential visitors are likely to be offended with a gentle sales message as soon as they get to your website and so on.

The 'sales funnel'

The idea with the sales funnel is to guide your visitors through your site to eventually land on a related sales page where you can try to persuade them to buy your product or service. The question you need to ask is 'What does my visitor really want?'

How do you get them to do this? This is the main question you need to answer and the main way to answer this question is to think about what the visitor wants.

If they've just done a search on Google for 'dog grooming service Hoboken', they probably don't need educating as to the benefits of professional dog grooming, they're ready to hire, so take them to a page with a little sales copy explaining why they should hire 'you' and a 'buy' button or your phone number so they can get in touch.

If they searched for 'dog grooming techniques', then the landing page could be a nice article explaining some basic techniques that owners could use and then maybe offer a free video showing you doing the techniques in exchange for their email address (building a prospect list) enabling you to follow up with them via email, increasing your chances of getting a client or making a sale.

(I talk about email marketing on Friday.)

 Money making ninja tip

If you can also capture the visitor's state/province/county at the same time as capturing their email address, you could earn additional revenue by taking those leads you would normally ignore and selling them on to non-competing 'dog grooming' businesses in different locations.

Speak to your techie about this – it's really easy to do and could be very profitable.

Anyway, you get the picture.

The only exception to this would be if you are an online company, perhaps a software company, and all you do is sell your software and have other people educate for you and send them to your sales website.

But, in that case you are probably not reading this book anyway!

So as you can see there are essentially two main sales funnels, direct and indirect, via email. I recommend having both for your business.

A third model – the webinar

There is a third model that is a mix between email and sales and that is the webinar model.

A webinar is just like a presentation that you do online (you talking into a webcam and/or a slide-based presentation) and that can be watched and listened to by hundreds of people at once.

This works particularly well if you offer a high-ticket product or service. You promote a special event giving away some excellent information for free that solves a big problem for your visitors and then, at the end of the webinar, you make attendees aware of your product or service (with a corresponding high price tag) for those that are interested, with no pressure.

You can add the names of those that sign up to attend the webinar to a mailing list so the other email marketing rules still apply and, while the sales volume may be lower, the actual money made can be higher, depending on the business.

In the dog groomers example, this could be a week's vacation for their pooch including grooming, pampering, special training and so on.

If you sell a physical item, maybe bundle it up with other items or partner with someone who can offer a related service and split the profits.

Any businesses can offer a 'premium' version of their product or service. It just requires a little thought.

Once you know what you're selling, what next?

Tracking

Now is the time to start tracking your visitors on your website. Where do they spend the most time?

How many pages do they view?

Where do they land the most frequently and from there where do they click?

Are your visitors mostly mobile?

And of course the most important question:

What percentage of visitors buy?

All these and more are questions that you must answer to have the ultimate sales website.

Only in this way can you see what is really working and what isn't. You may be getting a lot of traffic to one page but the visitors end up leaving quickly or not going to another page. Why? Who knows but you need to find out. Go and check out that page, and see whether you can spice it up.

Actually, you can do all this by having analytics software installed on your website.

This is very easy to do – literally copying and pasting a code into every page you want to track or into your website's design template (if you have software like WordPress or Magneto eCommerce).

I recommend using either Google Analytics (GA) or Clicky.

GA is free and can directly interface between your Google AdWords and Google Webmaster Tools accounts to get the maximum amount of data possible.

Clicky is perfect if you're worried about information overload because the interface is a lot simpler.

Spend time getting to know the interface and go through the settings one by one. There are lots of settings and I could write a full book on them alone.

Google provides a couple of excellent free resources where you can learn everything you need to know to get up to speed with GA:

www.youtube.com/googleanalytics?hl=en
www.google.com/analytics/learn

You can sign up for Clicky here: http://clicky.com

There are lots of tutorials on YouTube for both Clicky and GA – just do a search for 'Clicky analytics' or 'Google Analytics.'

If you use WordPress to power your website, you can integrate both their GA and Clicky in just a couple of mouse clicks by installing related plug-ins.

Use analytics to track the changes that had a positive increase on your pages, then replicate them on others and see what happens.

Split testing

Once you have traffic and are tracking where your visitors come from, where they go on your website and what kind of conversion rates you get, it's time to start split testing your sales and order pages.

One simple way is to use Content Experiments by Google Analytics. It's pretty easy to set up and once you have done so, each of your visitors will be shown one or other of the pages in the Experiment automatically. When set up correctly, you'll be able to track right the way through to a sale or whatever the action is that you want to track.

(Again there are videos on YouTube showing you how to do this, or hire a geek on a freelancer site like oDesk.com, eLance.com to do it for you.)

When you do this, don't send them to two entirely different pages. Only make a small change to the second page, that is, change the 'buy now' button to an 'add to cart' button or change the button colour. Small changes like this can make a huge difference.

Change the font to something easier to read. Change the headline at the top of the page. And on and on.

Keep in mind that you should *only change one thing at a time*. If you change multiple things at the same time, there is really no way to know why the page is doing better or worse than the other page.

There's a great free Content Experiments tutorials video here courtesy of Google Developers:
http://lk.gs/2

In conclusion

The key is to start getting your website out there. A perfect site doesn't exist. But imperfect sites make money every single day if they get traffic.

So make a site that matches your personality and get going.

I was once involved in a project back in my beginner days with a doctor who wanted the 'perfect' website. He paid upwards of $20,000 for everything he wanted custom made. Problem is when he opened up the site he found out nobody really wanted what he offered. He eventually ran out of money and had to go back to work as a doctor.

Don't be that person.

Summary

If you go through the things recommended in this chapter today, you should have a website capable of making sales within a short period of time.

But don't just rest on your laurels. Keep tweaking, testing, tweaking and testing until it becomes second nature.

If there is one constant in marketing, it is that you and your market will always be changing!

Things that worked a year ago don't work now. Those that work now might not work as well a year from now.

So keep an eye on your website (or hire someone once it is making money to do that for you) and it will be a source of income for years to come.

So now we have the first set of questions to make sure that you've taken everything on board ...

SUNDAY

MONDAY

TUESDAY

WEDNESDAY

THURSDAY

FRIDAY

SATURDAY

Questions (answers at the back)

1. When building your site, you need to have: .
   a) The ultimate sales website right out of the gate ❑
   b) A good site to start and the ultimate site later ❑
   c) A bad site to start and the ultimate later ❑

2. Landing pages are:
   a) Pages that are fallen on sometimes, causing them to break ❑
   b) The first page your visitor sees ❑
   c) The place you sell your visitor stuff ❑

3. Sales pages are:
   a) Pages that people should come to first ❑
   b) Pages that people should come to second ❑
   c) Pages that people should come to when ready ❑
   d) Pages that are basically the same as landing pages ❑

4. How many sales funnels are out there?
   a) 1 ❑
   b) 2 ❑
   c) 3 ❑
   d) 4 ❑

5. These sales funnels include:
   a) Immediate 'buy now' pages ❑
   b) An email follow-up series ❑
   c) Webinars ❑
   d) All of the above ❑

6. The website tracker of choice is:
   a) Google Analytics ❑
   b) Anything that you can get a hold of that costs money ❑
   c) Search and find the best for you ❑

7. The best way to get to know GA is:
   a) Use it ❑
   b) Use it a lot ❑
   c) Go through everything many times ❑
   d) Watch the video tutorials ❑
   e) All of the above ❑

8. When you find a page many are going to but are then leaving, what can you do?
   a) Spice it up a bit ❑
   b) Force your visitors to visit a new page with ninja mind tricks ❑
   c) Change your site completely ❑

9. When split testing:
   a) Test only one thing at a time ❑
   b) Test two entirely different pages each time ❑
   c) Change at least two things on the new page you are testing ❑

10. There is a point at which you can just stop testing and learning new things:
    a) True ❑
    b) False ❑

SUNDAY

MONDAY

TUESDAY

WEDNESDAY

THURSDAY

FRIDAY

SATURDAY

MONDAY

SEO: The backbone of any digital marketing strategy

Today we're going to be covering the first basic step of digital marketing and that is search engine optimization (SEO).

This is the solid base that, if you get it right, will help all your other areas of marketing.

Why?

Because just as digital marketing is a holistic (complete) approach to marketing in a primarily digital age, *SEO is also becoming more and more a holistic website experience for the user.*

If you want to sell online, you need to have a good website with good SEO backing this up.

SUNDAY
MONDAY
TUESDAY
WEDNESDAY
THURSDAY
FRIDAY
SATURDAY

SEO defined

SEO can be defined as the things you do for the pages on your website so that they are found by Google and to ensure that they show in the top ten results when people search for something related to your business.

For instance, this may include being found when your customers type the keywords 'chiropractor Dallas TX', 'dog grooming supplies' or 'cute kitten photos' (if that's what you're trying to make into a business) into Google.

This in turn brings you a lot of traffic and, depending on how valuable those keywords actually are, this can then in turn bring you new customers and clients.

So yes, this is pretty awesome but, as I will show later in the week, it is not the only way that your customers find their way to your door/website. Nor is it necessarily always the *best* way for your customers to come to you. In fact, depending on your market, it might not even be the best place to start.

But SEO is an essential skill to learn and it's not that difficult (regardless of what high-priced SEO consultants may lead you to believe) so let's get into it today, shall we?

So exactly how does SEO work?

People and SEO consultants have a million theories as to how exactly to go about doing this, but what really works?

I have written a whole book on this subject, which of course I recommend you read for more info, but here is the basic idea in a nutshell.

First look at it from Google's perspective: they want their results to be the best of any search engine, because the best results mean more users of their service, which means more eyeballs on their site and more eyeballs means that more users will click the paid ads on the right-hand side.

Google is continuously fine-tuning the number and types of factors they use to determine whether a page gets into the top ten results for a certain search phrase, like looking at how long people stay on your site, how fast your webpages load, the number of people who like and share your content on Facebook, Twitter or Google+ (G+) and so on.

But when you boil it all down, essentially what Google and the other search engines are looking for is a *great user experience.*

Note

A couple of major updates to Google have been making the news over the last year or so: 'Penguin' and 'Panda'.

These updates were implemented to stop people from 'gaming' Google using webspam techniques like links from 'dubious sources' and having 'unnatural link profiles' to each of their pages (where people use the same link text hundreds or thousands of times).

If you follow the guidelines below, you really won't have to worry about them as my guidelines don't try to *trick* Google, they just aim to get its *attention.*

NOTE: I go into more detail about 'Penguin' and 'Panda' in *Teach Yourself SEO and Search Marketing In A Week*

To sum it all up there are two aspects of your site that you need to keep in mind when developing it. If one is missing, you will not have the success you want out of your website in the long run.

First, you need to think about your on-site goals.

This means that your site should load quickly, look good and be logically laid out so people can find your content in the easiest and quickest manner possible.

Next, your site needs every page to be in some way related to your site's overall theme (e.g. dog product-related if you are selling dog products) and every page needs to be optimized for just one keyword phrase (more on this later).

Third, you need to take care of your off-page criteria.

If you have heard about SEO at all, you might have heard that getting high in Google is pretty much just about getting links.

And you'd be correct. However, the real power is by getting what are known as 'authority' links pointing to your pages and your website.

'Authorities' are websites and pages that Google deems highly trustworthy on your subject matter.

So for example, if you are a website selling accessories for iPods, iPads and iPhones, the ultimate (albeit unlikely) dream would be for Apple to link to you in some way.

But even if you're unable to get an 'Apple' level of authority linking to you, if enough people link to a page then that page will be seen by Google as an 'authority' on the subject and (all things being equal) they will move it up the rankings for certain keywords and search terms.

Although this extra 'weight' is not as high as it used to be, it is still there. However, if you want your site to *last* it is not all you should focus on.

Super ninja trick

Create your own 'authority' site. How can you do this? Create pages on something that Google sees as an 'authority' already!

The best site for this right now is YouTube and another one is Google+. There are a few others out there but these two are the most effective.

Create a business page on Google+ then post good You-Tube videos using the same account. Send links to those videos and you will be amazed at the authority boost you will get now that these two authority pages are linking to you.

SEO guide

Now we know a bit more about SEO, what are you to do about it?

We see the search engines are looking for a great user experience. So what does this mean for you and your business?

Let me present to you 'Nick the geek's guide to solid SEO', the sure-fire steps to SEO that gives your website the best shot possible. (I can't guarantee anything though, since I don't own Google. I can dream though ...)

First step is your website's HTML code – the markup language used to build webpages – should be fully validated with W3C standards (speak to your techie about this).

Your website should load as fast as possible and should look good. It doesn't have to be the Sistine Chapel to start off but it shouldn't scare people away either and needs to have a good amount of content (at least ten optimized pages and five to ten optimized blog posts).

Load times can be improved by getting good-quality web hosting (it is definitely not all the same – drop me a line and I'll tell you who I use).

Keep your webpages' file sizes as small as possible to help load quickly and your images should also be optimized for the web (I tend to use JPGs wherever possible at 60 per cent compression – again, speak to your techie).

W3C compliance and load speed can both be covered by using a content management system like WordPress (free from WordPress.org) and getting a good premium theme from them that matches your business and goals (this will take care of the coding).

Premium themes average approximately $50 and will look like your website had thousands of dollars spent on it.

If you have a website already, go to http://webpagetest.org/ and test your site out for free (you want the load speed to be less than seven seconds to be good, fewer than five seconds to be the best).

Websites generally tend to have static, unchanging content on them, so to continually give Google and the other search engines a reason to keep visiting your website to index it in their huge databases, I recommend having a blog somewhere on your domain.

The search engines all tend to prefer new and timely content, so the more often new content is added to your site, the more the search engines will like it. And the more the search engines like it, the more often they'll add new pages from your site (your blog posts) into their databases and you then increase the chances of your website being shown to someone looking for what you offer.

More content = more chances to be found. Easy, isn't it?

TIP

Time saver suggestion

Do you find yourself short on time like every other business owner in the world? Keeping a blog doesn't have to be an added pressure on your time. Simply automate the process.

Blog posts can be text, images or video. Take a couple of weeks and dedicate them to content creation. Now search around and find a good plug-in that will 'autopost' one piece of content to your blog every week or so.

Content

If your website was a building, then content is the foundation that makes that website go the distance.

Not just ordinary content but great content.

Why?

Because this is what your website visitors really want, they don't really care about your super-slick graphics, or your sci-fi looking interface. They want the answer to their question. They want information they can use.

If you give it to them, you will be rewarded by Google for it.

So not only do you want good content, you want good content that will match your ideal visitors' needs and desires. If you do it well, you will meet your visitors' needs and desires at a stage before they want to buy from you.

You also want, as much as possible, for *every* page of your site to be optimized for at least one keyword. Even if it is a keyword that is only searched 100 times a month. Every page should have some key phrase that you are trying to win for.

TIP

If you want to get an idea of what your customers are actually looking for, go to Google and do a search for 'Google keyword planner'.

This is available free in a Google AdWords advertising account (less than $10 to set up) and will enable you to generate a list of keywords/search terms that users have entered into Google and also roughly how many people have searched for each term. If you enter your website address, you can see the keywords Google thinks are relevant to you, which can help spark ideas.

Definition

'Optimized' means the main keyword you'd like the webpage to rank for in Google.

So for example, let's say you want to target the keyword/search term 'Vietnamese dog brush'.

First of all, put the keyword as the filename (or the permalink if you're using a CMS) so it looks something like:

http://yourdomain.com/vietnamese-dog-brushes or
http://yourdomain.com/vietnamese-dog-brushes.html

You need the title of the page to use an H1 HTML tag (ask your techie) and contain your keyword within it but *not* be the exact keyword.

Something like 'high quality Vietnamese dog brushes'.

You should make sure that this 'close keyword' is mentioned first on the page, and once every 200 words or so in the content.

You should have at least one picture on the page that has a filename of the 'close keyword' and it is always good to have a video embedded on the page about the dog brush as well (more on this when we talk about YouTube later).

This requires a plan

First, do a bit of thinking about what your visitors want. This
is key at this point; don't think about what *you would want* but
what a *visitor wants*. These will often be two different things.
You are the expert in this area (hopefully) and as such you have
a lot more knowledge than your visitors.

For instance, say you are a chiropractor; you may search for
'chiropractor', while your prospective visitor may look for 'back
pain specialist' or 'what to do to help a sore back'.

You will use acronyms and other jargon. For example, I
would use SEO or PR (page rank), or '*ranking* a website' in my
searching but you might use 'being found by Google' or 'online
marketing' in yours.

Learn what this means for your potential customers and
you will go somewhere many other experts in your field
haven't gone.

Super ninja tip

*Google had a significant update in August 2013 known as
'Hummingbird'.*

*Hummingbird is central to Google's efforts to actually
understand question-based keyword searches and possibly
in time rank those higher in their results.*

My advice to take advantage of this: do lots of research in the Google Keyword Planner, discussion forums etc. for actual questions people are asking relating to your subject and create content around those questions.

Next, think about what your customers search for before they come to you. Looking for a chiropractor, maybe they will search for 'back pain home remedies'. Now, meeting this need may send some customers away (because the problem may be fixed), but those who find no relief or only some relief will now know who to visit for full professional help.

Say you make Facebook apps, maybe you can make a page on 'how to make a Facebook app'. People may be searching for them and a few will make their own app. But many of these just want to know the details and will then give you the money to do it for them because they can tell that you know what you are talking about.

Google Keyword Planner

Take these ideas for content and load them into the Google Keyword Planner tool. This will give you a bunch of additional ideas as it will spit out the related keywords to the phrases that you already have in mind.

What you are looking to get right now is both lower and higher demand. Look at the general search volume for the term. You should have a good mix of 100–500 per month and 1,000–5,000 per month related searches with which to begin your site (only do with less than this if you can afford to make fewer sales; if you make $1,000 per sale then you can live very well off of a 5 per cent conversion rate on 500 people).

What you *don't* want to do with your content

Don't go out and put random content on your site just because a lot of people are searching for it. If you go out and rank for, let's say, 'underwater hang-gliding' and you are a chiropractor, when people land on your site they're going to be understandably confused and will probably leave faster than you can say 'Jack Robinson'.

This is the equivalent of putting a huge '**Free sex**!' at the start of a newspaper ad and then saying 'Now I've got your attention ...' Don't do it.

What you *do* want to do with your content

Make your content high quality and every last word worth reading (or every last second worth watching if it's a video).
Some ideas for content:

- Videos – these are hugely advantageous when used creatively. Don't just post bland boring stuff; don't be afraid to show your fun side! Videos are great and can really drive people to your site (more on this later).
- Informative text content, ideally over 1,000 words long (Google likes more content on a page).
- High-quality images (like infographics) – use these as much as possible to explain what you do or an important aspect of your niche.
- Audio recordings – of you talking in a radio talk show format or interviews with other leading experts, and so on.
- Case studies of clients or customers that show their success with your product/service.

Next steps

Now you have a plan for your content, a well-designed and running site with a blog. The next step is to start getting people to the site (all the prettiness in the world won't make people visit).

One of the best ways to start doing this is going out and getting links that people click (more ideas later in the week!). But how to get these? They are actually embedded in the above content ideas.

For instance, if you create videos you can upload them to YouTube and as soon as you post them you should always put the link to your site as the first line in the video description and also encourage people to visit in the video.

If your videos are good, you will start getting clicks on this link and Google will quickly reward you for that.

This is a traffic source that I see many, many people surviving off **alone**. They don't even really need Google traffic. Though you should go after both of course!

When you do audio podcasts, you can then go out and submit your site to podcast directories, which in turn will link to your site and drive people back to your site.

When you interview an expert in your field, you'd better believe they will probably link back to you.

Building this way takes a bit of time and doesn't happen overnight but will build solid links and traffic that will last a lifetime if done right.

Another way to get links and traffic is to just be active in your niche reaching out to related businesses cross-promoting each other. This is particularly powerful for local businesses that require foot traffic to their door such as doctors.

In the case above, it wouldn't even have to be related so much as just another business in the area. Google sees those links almost as recommendations from friends.

Keep it up tip

Be constantly experimenting with and expanding the variety of your links. Don't just keep going back to YouTube or any other single source of links over and over again.

It is important to diversify and get as many different sites as possible linking to you.

After a certain point you can scale back but never stop completely.

Ignore the siren call to use software to blast millions of links at your site and then stop.

Conclusion

I hope I didn't blow any brain cells with the above and if so I apologize (a little).

The bottom line is you need to take care of two things. First what is on your page (your on-page criteria). You need to make sure that the words that you want people to find your page with are in the right places on your site.

Secondly, you need to make sure that you are being linked to from good quality places out on the web (your off-page criteria) which will bolster your reputation in Google's eyes, rewarding you with improved rankings and, all things being equal, send you more visitors.

Summary

The following is a summary of what I suggested above in the SEO area:

1 Get a fast-loading well-designed site.
2 Create great content that your customers and potential customers will love, that meets a need they have (whether they know it now or not).
3 Become active in your niche (and area if you are a local business) and reach out to the established people around you to start getting links and traffic. Comment on other blogs in your niche (giving valuable insight) and leave your link.

That is it ...That is pretty much SEO. Tomorrow we will talk about the next traffic source – social media.

So now we have ten questions to help your head remember the important things you learned today:

SUNDAY

MONDAY

TUESDAY

WEDNESDAY

THURSDAY

FRIDAY

SATURDAY

Questions (answers at the back)

1. SEO stands for:
a) Super epic organization ❏
b) Search engine optimization ❏
c) Send error out ❏
d) Search engine opposition ❏

2. Digital marketing is:
a) A holistic approach to marketing in a primarily digital age ❏
b) A great way to trick people into buying from you ❏
c) The ultimate way to make lots of money overnight ❏
d) Pure magic and impossible to learn ❏

3. SEO is:
a) A game where you learn to get one over on Google and get free traffic to your site ❏
b) The only way to get traffic to your site ❏
c) Becoming more and more a holistic website experience for the user and is only one of many ways to get traffic ❏
d) The be all and end all of digital marketing ❏

4. Keywords are:
a) Words shaped like a key ❏
b) Special magic words ❏
c) Words that you repeat three times and get traffic to your site ❏
d) The words that people type into Google/Yahoo to find your site ❏

5. There are two areas you need to keep in mind when you want to start getting traffic. These are:
a) Nice-looking websites and cool graphics ❏
b) The latest cutting-edge technology and a private server ❏
c) On-page and off-page criteria ❏
d) You should have done the Google rain dance and worn your lucky Google pin while turning around three times before sitting at your computer ❏

6. One key to reaching customers is:
a) Finding them after they have purchased from a competitor ❏
b) Reaching them before they even know they need your product/service ❏
c) Brainwashing them from birth to want your product ❏
d) Being really nice ❏

7. An optimized page is:
a) A page that looks nice ❏
b) A page that has been customized ❏
c) A page that has your keyword choice strategically put all over it (not too much though) ❏
d) A page made to trick the search engines into thinking that your page is perfect for that keyword ❏

8. You should optimize each page for how many keywords?
a) 1 ❏
b) 2 ❏
c) 3 ❏
d) 4 ❏

9. Great ideas for content are:
a) Interviews with related experts ❏
b) Videos ❏
c) Long articles (1,000 plus words) ❏
d) All of the above ❏

10. My recommendations for CMS and hosting are:
a) WordPress and a Cloud server on Hostgator ❏
b) Custom made and GoDaddy ❏
c) Custom made and a private server privately run ❏
d) None of the above ❏

TUESDAY

Social media marketing madness

Hi there and welcome to Tuesday! Hope yesterday was easy because today is going to get really tough ... just kidding!

I want to make this whole week as user-friendly as possible, which is why I don't get very technical and am trying on focus on the concepts that really work.

It's great to see you continuing to learn the tips and tricks to getting buyer traffic in this day and age and I actually have some particularly cool stuff today.

Today we are going to look at social media marketing. As this area is the focus of Week 3 'Social Media Marketing', we will cover much more ground there as well as going over some of the points made in this section.

If SEO is a lot about your relationships within your marketplace (i.e. the related but-not-competing links that point at your site), then social media marketing is more about your relationship with your actual customers.

In fact, one of its primary and most effective uses for business is as an instant online customer support centre (more on this later).

What is social media?

Social media is defined as content that is generated and interacted with by the participants and the generators of said content.

To give you an example, say you take a picture (create content), you post it on Facebook (publish it on a social platform), a million people comment on it, like and share it with their friends.

You generated the content but the other participants interacted with it and in so doing spread it all over the world. In so doing, they became *content amplifiers*. This is one of the huge potential powers of social traffic.

They willingly spread your message and voice for you, amplifying what you could never have done at all on your own.

Now getting shared a million times is a rare thing (it's what you might have heard referred to as going 'viral').

But it can and does happen many times every single day.

However, that *shouldn't* be your goal for using social media because if it is you're going to be disappointed once you find out your funny cat video only got a hundred views (which is the YouTube average).

Why you need to be on social media

1 Your customers are there (*billions* of people around the world have a social presence of some kind on a social network).
2 See point 1. That is about it.

Seriously, don't give me anything about Facebook takes your identity or anything like that. If you are a business, you need to be where your clients and customers are, and you need to be interacting with them where they feel comfortable interacting.

So, now that that is out of the way ...

What different platforms are there?

There are literally hundreds of tiny social networks out there. Some exist just for small-business people or particular countries.

The main ones that you need to concern yourself with to start are:

- Facebook (I know, big surprise right? Well it has over 1.3 billion (with a B) users so it is a pretty big deal)
- YouTube (this is the second most searched site in the world, making it the second biggest search engine in the world and is also Google-owned)
- LinkedIn (particularly good for business-to-business operations but also good for any business as a place to be found by other business people who may just want your service or you might want to use theirs)
- G+ (not only good for social traffic, also has some SEO benefits that will be talked about later today)
- Twitter (more specialized but still very useful)
- Pinterest (a social platform that is fast gaining popularity and value)
- Instagram (an image- and video-based social network popular with the tech-savvy demographic because it's a smartphone app).

If you could only choose three to start, I would choose Facebook, YouTube and G+ for the normal business; for the business-to-business company, replace Facebook with LinkedIn.

Now let us determine what social media marketing is good for and what it isn't good for so you can start to have an idea about how you can use it for your own business.

What social media is good for

1 Social media is a great place to interact with your customers on a personal level.

They can be made to feel comfortable posting questions on your timeline or as comments to updates you've posted.

On Twitter, the tagline is 'It is all about the conversation' and that is the truth, not only on Twitter but on Facebook, YouTube and all the other social platforms out there.

If you ship products as part of your business, you can be sure to get a few 'where is my package?' Facebook page posts now and then. As well as other product-related questions ...

Note:

Always, and I mean always, answer these questions publicly (whether they are bad or good). If you do not, nothing can stop your other customers from interacting with you faster.

It is really a bummer to go on a fan page and one of the first posts is, 'Where the heck is my package? I ordered it 5 weeks ago!' and the post is weeks old and there is absolutely no response from the page owner ...

The least they could do is take five seconds and go on their page and delete the comment. But no it just sits there scaring away prospect after prospect whether the page owner knows it or not.

The question is still there so as far as the person from the outside looking in knows this business owner never checks their Facebook page so why should they check it?

2 Social media is also a great place to get social proof.

Everyone always goes where the crowd is just to see what they are looking at.

It's the same for your social efforts; build up your fan base and more people will follow, just to see what is going on, and they may also end up being customers.

3 Social media is good for lead generation (prospecting).

This is not to say that social media is good at direct selling (see number 1 in the next section) but it is a great place to find people who are willing to find out more about you before buying.

4 Social media is great for product demonstrations and service descriptions.

This is where YouTube shines and, by extension, provides something you can share on Facebook and Twitter, that is, the ability to demonstrate how something works and explain it in detail. Whether this is the latest do-hickey that you came up with or how a divorce settlement really works, this is a good place and way to illustrate it and make it clear for people to understand.

What social media is *not* good at

The number 1, and I repeat, the number 1 thing you need to know about social media is that it is not a good place for:

1 Selling directly and incessantly

As you can imagine, I'm on one social media platform or another pretty much constantly and the one thing I continually see is businesses that do nothing but broadcast their latest promotion ... **all the time**!

I mean, this is all right if you're a deals site like Groupon or something like that. But if you're not, you're just going to turn your prospects off and then you've lost them for good (if you're lucky); if you're not lucky you'll get your account banned for spamming.

Just the other day I saw someone in a £185/month private Facebook mastermind group spam twice within an hour with their first two ever posts. Crazy.

No one likes to be sold to while hanging out with their friends.

That is what you are doing if you do nothing but broadcast sales messages and nothing will banish you to social oblivion faster as well.

So don't do it.

Now, thinking about the above scenario, say you became friends with a member of the staff of a company and one day they suggested to you, 'Come check out this sale my company is having'.

That is a completely different matter.

So the occasional sales message combined with good interaction skills is all right.

Just for heaven's sake don't do it all the time! Try to limit it to once a month, if at all.

2 Social media is not a place for blah content

You have to excite your users the second they lay eyes on your post.

You want them to be hitting the share button before they even know what they are doing because what you share is that cool.

They don't want the latest blah article you found via Google search. They definitely don't care about your tenth anniversary of being in business ... Really they don't care ... Seriously ...

Super ninja trick

Take what your customers don't care abut and make them care about it.

What do your customers care about? They care about what is in it for them or how their lives are affected or can be improved.

So to turn around the ten year anniversary of your business say 'We are celebrating giving dogs the best cuts in the New York area for the last ten years' – make them care!

Lead with why they should care and they will do just that.

How to get started

Go to all of the sites above and register your unique name (whether you plan on using them immediately or not).

Otherwise, you may find that the name you want is gone before you get there.

Next, choose your starting three (for this example, I will use Facebook, YouTube and Pinterest as Facebook/G+/LinkedIn are similar).

Facebook

For Facebook, LinkedIn and G+, you first have to get a personal account before you can register your business name and get yourself a page for your business.

I recommend that if you already have a personal account then great, go ahead and create a business page. See the links below for help with this.

http://goo.gl/myYYRq (How to create Pages on Facebook)

http://goo.gl/TT4eKT (How to create Pages on G+)
http://goo.gl/ZFRJFn (How to create Pages on LinkedIn)
Next you need to populate all three of these pages with as much useful information and content as possible.

No one likes walking into a ghost town page with just a headline and an 'under construction' sign.

If you are a business with any history whatsoever, it should be relatively easy for you to create content here.

Put it all down in chronological order. (They all let you do this.)

For instance, put in when certain products became available, any awards you have received, any conventions you have been to, major partnerships you have started and so on.

Anything that just shows you are a real company. Photos. Videos. Audio. Scans of newspaper clippings. Anything.

Done well, this will have your potential customer scrolling through your history thinking 'this is one accomplished company'.

Note:

Don't make stuff up. Nothing can be worse than lying on social media. You **will** be found out. A good word travels at light speed, a bad word at warp speed!

If you're a new company, that doesn't mean you don't put up information, but put up information about your planned ventures, and your accomplishments so far. Even if it is only joining your local chamber of commerce and hiring some cool people at the local job fair.

Be real and share your company's life (if ever so short) there.

Now get some fans. I recommend getting all your employees and their families, your family (even the mother-in-law if you dare) and past/current clients and customers to like your page on Facebook.

Then, run a short 'like' campaign using Facebook Pay Per Click Adverts targeting people within your local area who might be familiar with your company. Aim to get more than 25 likes as this will give you the ability to choose a 'vanity' URL for your page.

Something like: facebook.com/dog-supplies-inc.

It will also show that you are a happening place and moving and grooving company, at least in people's minds at this point. Now you need to start producing content.

Producing great content on Facebook

Creating good content on Facebook is not as difficult as it may seem but it can be a case of trial and error depending on your customers.

So how to really make good content?

Think emotional.

What gets your customers/clients emotional? Not just nice, but in an emotional moment. Do you have a pet service? Maybe some pictures of kittens ...

For instance, a day-care centre could post pictures of cute kids, have inspirational stories of parenthood, money-saving deals you've found on clothes, toiletries and so on.

Maybe, though you don't have such a specific group of people, you still have a group of people. Like teenagers or young adults. What gets them excited and emotional? (Teenage boys of course don't get 'emotional' – 'stoked' or 'blown away' maybe ...)

Those are the things you need to think of to make great content on social networks that get shared over and over again.

Your latest doo-hickey to get Fluffy's hair straight will get trumped *every* single time by that picture of a dog and cat snuggling together with 'friends forever' written underneath it.

The more that people read and share your emotion-inciting posts, the more people will remember you and see your other posts later when you mention a sale that you have just for your Facebook friends.

That being said, the three best formats for getting an emotional response for the most part are:

- pictures/other images
- videos
- everything else.

See, a picture is really worth a thousand words.

Producing great content on other social networks

For G+, you should do the same emotion-impacting things that you put on your Facebook page. But LinkedIn is a different animal. The content that needs to be talked about there needs to show people your company and you contributing in big ways to the community as a whole.

You need to start groups and contribute good content to related groups.

For example, if you are a lawyer consider starting a group in your area of expertise to answer people's questions, then *really* answer people's questions.

Many businesses start these things but then promptly forget that they did and get 'too busy'. If you want to see growth on LinkedIn, you need to be willing to contribute to the conversation.

If you aren't able to find time, consider outsourcing (covered later).

YouTube content creation

Here you need to be creating things that your customers are looking for and that really depends on your market.

'How to' videos may really work for you here or instructional videos on how to use your products. Other things that help are to create videos that talk about things that people would look for before coming to you. Perhaps 'back pain remedies' if you are a chiropractor or 'how to fill out small claims forms in your state' if you are a lawyer. Almost any business can profit from this kind of advertising, because almost everything can be portrayed by a good video.

There are some rules.

Set and follow a set flow with every video. Here is my suggested flow:

1 Introduction with music and logo with brief intro to yourself
2 Then tell them what you are going to explain/do
3 Explain/do it
4 Sum it all up with a conclusion
5 Put a call to action (Visit your site, download your report, etc.)
6 Don't be boring
7 Don't be boring
8 Don't be boring

That is about it, be yourself (unless you are boring); in that case find someone else that can show enthusiasm. I am currently working with a client who is not a naturally exciting individual, so I asked him to actually put his employee in the videos.

Don't take it personally, it is how it is. You need to show excitement or people will think you are in it only for the money (which may be the case but don't *show* them that).

It will be trial and error, at least to start with, to find the content that people want but here is a secret to success.

After producing your first ten videos, which will establish you as an expert, you can ask your viewers what they want you to talk about.

Do those things, then ask again, 'Now what do you want me to talk about?'

Some of the best YouTubers never have to 'figure out what to do' because all they do is ask their viewers what they want and give it to them.

You must remember this is a two-way street, you are not just broadcasting these videos (or those pictures on Facebook) to faceless millions. You are broadcasting them to specific people that have an interest in you and your company.

If you ask them what they want, they will probably tell you (unless you are producing such boring content at that point that they might not even be seeing your requests). Maybe you only get a few responses to your first request. Do them and you will win the business of those who requested them.

Then, when people see that you are listening, more people will speak up next time.

Success is never instant on social media. You need real people talking about you to get other real people to come.

Why you need to be on Google+

You may have noticed that G+ is in all of my recommendations and you might wonder why. If you track these things at all, you might know that there is not necessarily as big an audience there as there is at Facebook.

Well there is one reason and that is SEO.

Here is one of the places that SEO and social media intersect. The only reason that there is SEO is because of Google. Google is 67.6 per cent of the US market and 90 per cent plus of all the other markets.

Here is an example.

A little while ago I had a website where I posted a link on my G+ to a site that I own in Brazil. Recently doing a search for that term on Google, I realized that my comment for that link is *above* the actual site itself!

Being on G+ is essential for your local profile in that Google Local is now rolled up in your G+ business profile.

So all you need is one personal G+ account, one business G+ page and, optionally, one personal G+ page.

More advanced image tips

As I showed above, images are the number one thing being posted to Facebook at this time.

Now the best way to put images on social networks is to put images on two other specific networks at the same time.

These were not recommended above because it is usually best not to bite off more than you can chew to start with and posting images on Facebook alone is just fine if you want to test the waters.

To do images right and get the maximum exposure for your image efforts, post them both on Instagram and Pinterest at the same time.

Pinterest is mostly aimed at the desktop crowd (though there are many mobile users) and Instagram is almost completely aimed at the mobile crowd. In fact, without a mobile device you can't really use Instagram properly. You can view images using sites like:

http://websta.me/ (Webstagram)
http://iconosquare.com/ (Iconosquare, formerly Statigram)

However, you can upload any photos you have to Instagram by simply emailing them to your phone email address or putting them on an SD card and putting them on your phone and/or tablet.

Note

Check the Victoria Secret Instagram page (it's OK, you can tell the wife I told you to do it) ... now, tell me those pictures are uploads from an iPhone ... yep, exactly.

Anyway I digress.

So after you have tested out your images on Facebook, head over to Instagram and Pinterest and get to gramming and pinning. They are truly a match made in heaven.

Summary

Be real and interactive on your social media accounts and post things that people get emotionally involved with and you will be light years ahead of your competition.

Focus on not being boring and check your updates constantly. If you don't hire someone to be doing it on a constant basis, there are many places online like oDesk.com where you can find people who will do it for a reasonable low monthly fee (say $200).

Be involved in as many platforms as possible from Facebook to YouTube and everything in between. This gives your customers multiple ways to interact with you and also gives you authority in Google's eyes.

Be sure to include getting on Google+; whether you actually get traffic itself, this more then anything else can get your business noticed by Google and can get you listed in two spots on the first page of Google if you do it right.

SUNDAY

MONDAY

TUESDAY

WEDNESDAY

THURSDAY

FRIDAY

SATURDAY

Big things now include images and videos but mostly images are king now. The latest updates Facebook just made increase the upfront and centre position that Facebook was already giving images.

So images are not going away anytime soon.

Questions (answers at the back)

1. One of the best uses of marketing on social media is as:
   a) Sales engine ☐
   b) Direct response ☐
   c) Online customer support centre ☐
   d) List building ☐

2. One of the main uses for social media is:
   a) To make massive amounts of money from people who trip over themselves to buy in your sales ☐
   b) To be a customer support centre ☐
   c) To build an email list ☐
   d) Both b and c are correct ☐

3. Social media is:
   a) All websites in the world ☐
   b) Sites where users and creators interact seamlessly ☐
   c) Only Facebook ☐
   d) Only special sites named social media ☐

4. The main social sites are:
   a) Facebook ☐
   b) YouTube ☐
   c) LinkedIn ☐
   d) Pinterest ☐
   e) Google+ ☐
   f) Twitter ☐
   g) All of the above ☐

5. Social media is ideal for direct sales:
   a) True ☐
   b) False ☐

6. Social media is a great place for social proof:
   a) True ☐
   b) False ☐

7. The best type of social content is:
   a) Lots of related articles every day ☐
   b) Pictures ☐
   c) Videos ☐
   d) Emotionally moving pictures ☐

8. Google+ is ideal for:
   a) Social and SEO ☐
   b) SEO only ☐
   c) Social, SEO, and 'author rank' ☐
   d) None of the above ☐

9. After expanding in your top three networks:
   a) Stop there and keep going ☐
   b) Move on to Pinterest and Instagram ☐
   c) Go really deep to niche-specific ☐
   d) Work on the hundreds of other social networks out there ☐

10. The most important thing is to be 'Real'!
    a) True ☐
    b) False ☐

WEDNESDAY

Pay per click (PPC) simplified and explained

Today we are going to discuss another tool that should be in every digital marketer's toolkit and that is pay per click (PPC) marketing.

SEO and social media are great ways to get traffic for 'free' – although not totally 100 per cent free because you're spending time that not all business people have to spare to be able to create content, get links, likes and shares and so on from your marketplace.

Sometimes it is nice just to click a couple of buttons and get visitors and this is exactly what PPC can do for you, but only if you do it right.

Don't go crazy now and say I told you PPC is a magic button to make money online. Far be it from me to say such a thing. What PPC can do is make money on demand if you do it right. This, like anything, requires work plus knowledge and analytical ability to read numbers, and then you need to apply those numbers.

First, let's talk about the state of the PPC market and then get into how to do it right.

PPC ads in a nutshell

It should come as no surprise that Google is number one in this arena. Google's AdWords (PPC) system is the primary revenue stream for Google ($50 billion+ in 2013, 85 per cent of their total revenue) – well, at least until driverless cars and Google Glass 'take off' any time now...

Facebook is Google's next major competitor in the PPC space but their revenue is just a tenth of Google's and uses a different system (which I personally think is better) that we will get into later in this section.

And also you have the smaller players like Yahoo Search Marketing, and Bing PPC that all have their place.

Google search ads

When someone types in keywords, the first two to three listings are ads as well as all the links on the right side of the page.

This is Google's Search Network.

You can see a sample screenshot of those ads below in the highlighted boxes:

Also Google has its tentacles (shh don't tell them I said that, I mean its ads) on millions of websites across the web.

This is known as Google's Display Network. Website owners can apply to Google to have these ads on their websites via their AdSense Program and this is a legitimate way to help monetize a website.

You can learn more about Google's Ad Networks here: http://adwords.google.com

So how does PPC marketing work?

There are two main types of PPC – keyword related and demographically related.

Keyword related is how Google does it in their Search Network.

You bid on which keywords (search terms) your ad will show up on the right-hand side of and you pay $x.xx or just $.xx every time your advert is clicked.

You can find out the average cost per click (CPC) for each keyword using either the Google Keyword Planner or Google's Traffic Estimator tool (accessible only from within a paid AdWords account).

The price you pay is a combination of the amount of competition for the keyword and how popular your ad is. The more times your ad is clicked in your PPC campaign, the more Google rewards you by ever so slowly nudging you up the paid ad rankings.

So if your ad was initially placed fourth and ended up getting more clicks than the third, second and first place ads, it's possible that your ad will jump the queue into first place and you'll still be paying the same amount as you were when you were in fourth place.

Once again, Google rewards relevancy with ranking, and because ads in first place generally get more clicks than lower-positioned ads (assuming it does get the clicks), you'll end up sending more traffic to your website at a lower cost than your competitors!

Google's Display Network

This is a bit different from the Search Network for two reasons:

First, with the Search Network you're limited to only using text ads. But because the Display Network is made up of external websites, you can use a text ad, a banner image ad or a video ad.

Second, you don't bid on keywords shown up from a search; instead you bid to show your ad on pages Google deems relevant to a keyword.

And with the Display Network, you can either pay CPC or CPM. CPM is Cost Per Mille, the cost per 1,000 impressions. So when Google shows your ad 1,000 times, you pay $x.xx regardless of whether your ads are clicked or not.

Facebook ads

Facebook does CPC, CPM and also PPE (Page Post Engagement, more on this in a second) but they are demographic-based. Their PPC network used to only work inside of Facebook, but at the time of writing they are in the process of setting up their own 'Display Network' to compete with Google where Facebook ads show up directly on external websites.

You can already run 'retargeting' campaigns with Facebook, where each new visitor to a website gets a small file called a 'cookie' placed in their browser enabling the website to show their ads on other websites in the same network, Facebook Exchange (FBX).

Another way that Facebook is doing ads now that is totally different from Google is their PPE set-up. This is a new viral way of marketing where your update is seen in other people's newsfeed (that is where all your friends' updates are when you first log in).

You pay based on how many people you can get to engage with your ad (post). If you get more people to make it 'go viral' you pay less per engagement (an engagement is a like, a share, a click, a comment, even clicking to see more comments is an engagement). If they have to show it to a million people to get one person to 'like' it... maybe you should do another ad.

And because Facebook's PPC network is 'demographic-based', this means that instead of targeting what people are *searching* for, you can target people according to *who they are*, for instance, the things they like, their occupation, their age, their sex and so on.

Although you can do this type of demographic targeting in Google, it's nowhere near as detailed as it is in Facebook, because Google simply doesn't have the data. This might possibly be another reason why G+ was created. Maybe, just maybe ...

The problem is that some people don't even know that Facebook has ads. I mentioned to my mum recently I was running ads on Facebook and she said, 'Really, do they have those? Where are they?' Ad blindness strikes ... This new PPE model that I mentioned earlier gets around this though – they cannot miss your ad if you do it right.

The others

I have tried Yahoo/Bing ads that follow pretty much the same rules as Google as well as other small players, and I'm not very impressed by them or their conversion rates although Yahoo/Bing was OK (your mileage may vary).

Facebook and Google are where you should focus your effort if you choose this path. You want to reach as many people as quickly as possible with this method, so go with the big boys first. So why would you choose this path? Let's look at the pros and cons.

Pros

You know that people are at least vaguely interested in what you have.

They went and clicked your ad so they must be at least curious to see what is on the other side (if you wrote your ad right, that is, more on this later).

You can really focus down to the nitty-gritty for your visitors.

If you want people from North Dakota who like bubble gum and rock and roll, you can definitely find them with Facebook, not quite in such detail as with Google, though you could find people that are searching for particular terms around rock and roll or bubble gum, just not both in the same campaign.

You can say with (almost) certainty that you will get traffic.

When they're on the ball, both Google and Facebook can approve an ad very quickly – I've personally had ads approved and live in less than ten minutes before but it's normally within an hour or two.

Cons

Costs per click (CPC) are rising generally and can be unnaturally high unless you do proper research, choose your correct keywords or demographics and also point ads to a specific page on your site, not your homepage.

Both Facebook and Google are now public companies, answering to shareholders and having to go out of their way to make sure that they are profitable.

And that means extracting as much money as possible from advertisers.

CPCs can range from anywhere between 5 cents to 50 dollars *a click* and sometimes more. It all depends on the market and keywords being bid on. So you really have to do your research into every word you are bidding for to make sure that you are getting the amount you can afford.

Even this can get really expensive really fast.

Luckily, both Google and Facebook allow you to set daily budgets that you cannot go over, so you shouldn't have to sell a kidney or your first born to pay your PPC bill.

But that daily limit needs to take into account the number of clicks you want, clicks sending people to your website.

Slight aside

PPC works really well, especially if you're doing any type of testing as you can find out pretty quickly what is working.

You need to keep in your mind though that you should aim to generate at least 200 visitors a day to your test URLs so you can be reasonably sure which item you're testing is the winner.

Here's a great online calculator that will help to tell you whether your testing results are statistically significant:

SUNDAY

MONDAY

TUESDAY

WEDNESDAY

THURSDAY

FRIDAY

SATURDAY

http://goo.gl/4UMIr

Also make sure that you set your daily budget high enough so you can get at least 200 daily visitors.

PPC requires a lot of research and tracking

Some keywords may be expensive but might end up converting less well than other cheaper keywords for you or vice-versa.

So you need to do research combined with a lot of tracking. Tracking is where you see where the traffic is coming from and how well it converts (how many people do what you want them to). Compare the keywords to other keywords and narrow down exactly what you need.

Both Facebook and Google have free tools that will allow you to track sales, leads or other outcomes and so on.

That is the list of pros and cons. Now you may wonder why anyone would go through the hassle. When would it be a good idea to do PPC?

When to do PPC

First when **not** to do it (so we get it out of the way): don't ever do PPC just to get visitors to your homepage. You need a real reason and purpose for your visitors to put together any kind of PPC campaign that has any sort of effectiveness because you need to know exactly how much is going out and how much is coming in. Here is my list of services and products to sell via PPC (along with some exceptions).

Subscription services

One situation is if you have a product that is a monthly paid subscription, a service to which customers will be loyal or is a high converting high-ticket item that you don't spend a lot of money to get.

For instance, say you are an online service writing press releases for companies. You have a monthly service that releases a certain amount per month or you know that, when you write for companies, they tend to stick with you because you do such a good job. Either way, depending on how much you charge, you now have an idea how much you can afford to spend to get one customer (this is called the client lifetime value).

So if you charge £49.95 a month for your subscription and you know that on average a customer will stay with you for 12 months, then the lifetime value of that customer is 12 × £49.95 = £599.40.

Why is this important? When you know how much each customer is worth to you, you can figure out how much you're prepared to spend to acquire each new customer.

If you're just starting out with a new business and website, you won't have this initial data, so just concentrate on coming up with a compelling offer with a great price, make a great looking site, and direct traffic to a landing page that presents your offer well (more on this in the next section about landing pages), and see whether anyone is interested enough to buy.

Keep track of your results and as you discover over time how long customers stay with you, you'll be able to gradually increase your spending to acquire new customers.

Big ticket items

The next area this could help with is if you have a big ticket item, which could be consulting of some sort or even a high-ticket physical item, like a swimming pool. Either way, let's imagine the item is priced at $5,000.

If it costs you $1 per click to get people to your sales page and if one out of every 500 buys what you're offering (which is an awful conversion rate, but still) it might have cost you $500 to get that new customer, but you still made $4,500 gross profit and you now have that person in your customer database to sell more to down the line and maybe get referrals so more caching!

Social experimentation

Another place it could work in the short term is getting people's opinions.

For instance, say you are writing a book and you want to know if people are interested in your subject of hang-gliding in the Andes mountains. You put together a little $50 campaign that has hang-gliding and Andes mountain-related keywords with its title, 'Hang-glide the Andes mountains?' You can then judge by how readily people click on the ad whether they are interested or not.

Expert marketing tip alert

You could also put on the landing page a place for people to ask their most burning question about hang-gliding in the Andes mountains and now you know exactly what people will want to see in your book (that isn't even ready yet) and you'll have a list of people to email when your book is ready for a quick burst of sales.

The same theory applies to product retailers and service providers. If people often ask the same questions before they purchase what you're offering, put up a Frequently Asked Questions page answering them.

Book titles

This tip can also work if you are writing a book and are wondering what the most effective title is. Take the best ones you have come up with, put them together on a landing page and send people via Facebook PPE or Google PPC to vote on the title they like best.

You could also have them enter their email address to get the results and also add them to an 'early bird' notification list where you give them a substantial discount (or even a free copy) as a thank you.

Getting subscribers

One other place you can use PPC is for a small niche product to get subscribers to your email newsletter.

This is where you can really use the fact that you are a small site to your advantage. I heard about someone who once did a small Facebook PPC campaign to their niche bulldog website. It had one focus, getting newsletter subscribers; they spent $20 but ended up with 100 subscribers, several comments on how nice their site was and even a couple of sales.

Likes to Facebook fanpages

As said earlier in the social media section, it is sometimes good to get those first few fans with a quick campaign targeting people that will be interested in your page in the first place.

I've done this very successfully with many, many fanpages. On one video-game related fanpage, I've added nearly 200,000 fans in just a couple of months for less than $200. (For more social media strategies see below.)

PPC advertising strategies

So now you have a focus, how do you set up your campaigns?

First you *need* to watch the relevant tutorial videos provided by Google and Bing to show you the *mechanics* of creating campaigns and ad groups:

http://google.com/adwords/onlineclassroom
http://advertise.bingads.microsoft.com/en-us/new-to-search-marketing

(Click the Getting Started tab on Bing for even more video tutorials.)

Now you've watched them, let's talk about structuring PPC ad campaigns on the Google and Bing search networks.

The most common way is to use the 'long tail keyword' approach by creating multiple ad groups, each revolving around a main root keyword and having similar keywords in the same group.

If we go back to the dog grooming example we used previously, and I type the keyword 'dog grooming' into Google's Keyword Tool, I get a series of keywords all grouped together by theme like:

KIT:
dog grooming kit
dog grooming kits
grooming kits for dogs
dog grooming kits for sale
dog grooming starter kit

TUBS:
dog grooming tubs
dog grooming tub
dog grooming bath tubs
dog wash tub
dog grooming tubs for sale
used dog grooming tubs
dog bath tub
dog grooming baths

CLIPPERS:
dog grooming clippers
best dog grooming clippers
dog grooming clippers reviews
wahl dog grooming clippers
clippers for dog grooming
dog grooming clippers australia
best dog clippers
dog grooming clippers for sale
clippers dog grooming
dog grooming clippers uk
Plus a lot more ...

Once you've selected the keywords and ad groups you want to use, you can transfer them into an existing campaign in your Google AdWords account (if you're already logged in) with a couple of mouse clicks by selecting the Add To Account button.

Bing doesn't use quite as refined a process as Google so what I generally do is to use the exact same keywords and ad grouping in Bing.

If you use the free Google AdWords Editor and Bing Ads Editor software programs, you can easily export your Google campaigns and import them into Bing quickly and easily.

Just search in Google for 'Bing Ads Editor' and 'Google AdWords Editor' to get the download links for your country.

Some quick dos and don'ts.

Do:

- Set a daily amount you can afford even if it doesn't convert at all.
- Have an open mind and test out different headlines and bodies of your ads and see which work out and which don't (this could be the exact opposite of what you think will happen sometimes).
- Try to focus on the *exact* keywords that you want to get clicks on. The more specific these are, the cheaper and more effective the click becomes.
- Wherever possible, point an ad to a landing page on your website that is related to your ad.
- Always try to get at least an email address for your efforts.
- Follow the search engine or social network's guidelines to the letter.

Don't:

- Make the click go to a one-page website. This will never be approved by Google, Bing or Facebook. Instead have it focused on a landing page somewhere in your site where the focus is what you want the visitor to do.

- Try to get clicks so that you can send the visitor to a page where you try to get them to click another ad. This is known as 'arbitrage' and sooner or later you will end up having your account banned.
- Make low-quality landing pages that are not directly relevant to the ad text. For more information on best practices for landing pages, refer to this guide by Google: http://bit.ly/ReH2nd.
- Write headlines or body that is written just to get clicks. Clicks is not the point; the point is to get people that are already interested in what they will get on the other side.

PPC/PPE strategies for Facebook

As I mentioned before, Facebook is a different beast because there are no keywords as such to bid to show your ad for.

Instead, you need to target people interested in related subjects, located in a certain geographic area, by the college or university they went to, their sex or any other combinations of demographic information.

Based upon my own experiences with Facebook PPC, here's how I recommend you structure your campaigns.

Where possible, link your ads to a post on a Facebook page. People don't really like it when you take them outside of Facebook. In my tests, the costs per click of my campaigns halved when I sent people to a Facebook page instead of an external URL.

If you intend to run a PPC campaign to generate likes for your company's Facebook page, also consider creating a Facebook page for a celebrity or subject that has a broad appeal and is somehow related to your product or service *and then* running a PPC campaign to generate likes for *that* page too.

For example, if you were a weight loss consultant who specializes in helping women lose weight and get fit, you might create a fanpage around a female celebrity who has successfully lost weight and now looks great, for instance Jennifer Hudson if you're in the US or maybe Davina McCall if you're in the UK.

Piggy-backing on a celebrity or broad subject like 'weight loss' should make it easier to generate likes for *that* page, targeting people using your criteria (local area, sex, age, etc.) and then you can send occasional 'promoted posts' to your fans with special offers on your company Facebook page.

> ## Something to ponder
> If you have a lot of fans/likes for your broad subject Facebook page, you might be able to sell 'promoted posts' to other companies not in direct competition with you, generating another revenue stream. Just a thought ...

Boomerang Ninja PPC Trick

This is a technique that few marketers will share with you because it is so powerful and that is retargeting or what I like to call 'boomerang ninja marketing'.

What this means is that if someone visits your site they are automatically given a little code and when they go other sites on the web they will start seeing your display ads. This can be on everywhere from other Google sites, on Facebook, as well as Yahoo.

As give or take 98 per cent of those people that visit your website through social media/SEO and PPC will not actually buy, this means that those potential customers will now have a chance to come back when they are ready to buy without having to actually remember your website's name.

This tool is Ninja-like in that, whether consciously or unconsciously, your visitors suddenly start seeing your ads at their favourite web news site and the sites they visit every day like Facebook.

This causes them to slowly but surely begin to trust you more and more and see you as an authority if only because they saw your ad on the New York Times website ...

The services I use for this are:

http://adroll.com.
http://perfectaudience.com

Both of these offer simple and elegant solutions and reach a lot of websites around the world.

October 2014 update: Facebook has just launched 'Atlas', which can track users anonymously using a unique ID linked to their Facebook account and across multiple devices – web, phone, tablet, even apps – enabling businesses to serve ads to individuals who are on different websites outside of Facebook so long as they are still logged into Facebook on the machine. It should be rolling out to all advertisers in the coming weeks and months – so keep your eyes open.

Video PPV on YouTube and Facebook

As I have stated in other places in this week, YouTube is the second biggest search engine in the world and it is totally worth your time to create videos to get traffic. Now though, with their new pay-per-view program (PPV), they have become even more potent.

Say you create a video but you are wondering if it converts real fast.

Spend $20 and get a bunch of views to it and see!

Out of those views, how many clicked through to your page? How many of those became customers?

At this point you might want to optimize it more and edit it a bit. With YouTube's average view time, you can see where people start to drop off and it might give you an idea of what to change.

Or it might make sense to leave the ad up and continue to pay for views.

Otherwise, if it still converts and retains your audience but not enough to make sense continuing the ads, just keep it up on YouTube and get natural views.

Either way it is a win-win for you by saving time and helping you improve at the same time.

Once you get a few good videos converting well on YouTube, consider setting up a campaign on Facebook as well, driving dirt-cheap clicks to these.

This way you can get multiple uses out of your successes.

Ninja tip:

When a potential customer watches a video, they become an 'educated prospect', that is, they know about you, what you do and what problem your product solves.

They will still not convert 100 per cent but some studies have shown educated prospects to be worth 10 times what an uneducated click is worth.

Now combine this with the boomerang marketing technique detailed in the section before this (targeted just to those educated prospects that land on that page) and you may just have an unstoppable PPC force!

Summary

PPC can be done on the cheap or it can be expensive if you don't have a specific goal. Either way if you keep the focus right you can make it profitable.

The key is to make everything measurable. If it's not measurable you are spending money without any idea of whether you're making a profit or losing your shirt.

Focus on your keywords and get ads that get clicks and make sales. Once you determine those and get your percentages, you can pour money into them as you know how much you can afford to spend to get one person to buy.

Then you can branch out and start experimenting with different keywords where the return is not so guaranteed.

And on and on it goes.

Experiment – do 'split tests' (i.e. run two different landing pages targeting the same keyword and see which does better).

SUNDAY

MONDAY

TUESDAY

WEDNESDAY

THURSDAY

FRIDAY

SATURDAY

Test run 'boomerang' (retargeting) ads and definitely give video PPV marketing a spin (huge potential).

In everything start small (100–1000 clicks/views) and make sure it is profitable before you commit your life savings to the Google gods.

Questions (answers at the back)

1. PPC stands for:
   a) Perfectly politically correct ❏
   b) Payment potentially considered ❏
   c) Pay per click ❏
   d) Panning people consolidated ❏

2. The main PPC giants are:
   a) Facebook ❏
   b) Google ❏
   c) YouTube ❏
   d) Bing ❏
   e) Everybody else ❏
   f) Both a, b, and c ❏

3. Be sure to place a daily limit based on:
   a) How much you expect to make ❏
   b) The size of the market ❏
   c) How much you can afford to completely lose ❏

4. Subscription services:
   a) Are a good service to use PPC to get clients ❏
   b) Are a bad idea to drive PPC traffic to ❏
   c) May or may not work ❏

5. Your homepage:
   a) Is a good page to use PPC to get clients ❏
   b) Is a bad idea to drive PPC traffic to ❏
   c) May or may not work ❏

6. When you do PPC, it is good to have the focus of those clicks to be:
   a) Four different options ❏
   b) Three different options ❏
   c) Two different options ❏
   d) One measurable thing that you want them to do ❏

7. Before you start some PPC campaigns, you should know:
   a) Your lifetime client value ❏
   b) How much you are willing to spend ❏
   c) What you want the click to do ❏
   d) Have a plan for what to do with the information you are going to glean ❏
   e) All of the above ❏

8. Always try in your PPC campaign to:
   a) Make sales for your efforts ❏
   b) Learn everything about your clients for your efforts ❏
   c) Get at least an email address for your efforts ❏

9. Landing pages are:
   a) Where the potential client 'lands' after clicking on your ad ❏
   b) One-page sites that your clients want to visit ❏
   c) Only for users of private planes ❏

10. Retargeting ads mean:
   a) Someone visiting your website will now see targeted ads on other pages ❏
   b) You will know where they live to set up your sniper nest ❏
   c) You can now find out everything about this person ❏
   d) b and c are correct ❏

THURSDAY

Mobile optimization and getting mobile users

You cannot miss this, the Internet world is changing and it is changing quickly. Times are changing so fast, that today is the day you need to make the changes I am going to be talking about.

This is not something to do next month, this is not something to put off till you have time. This is something that you must do if you want to have a digital marketing business at all.

What is this essential bit of tech?

Mobile technology

I'll give you some stats to back up my statement above in a minute, first though, what are the immediate steps you need to take today?

Making your website ready for the mobile generation

First, your website needs to be ready for mobile users. (Yeah great, thanks Captain Obvious!)

Sounds stupid, but according to one survey by Adobe and E-consultancy, just 45 per cent of marketers polled have a mobile-optimized website.

My personal feeling is that this figure is actually much lower but I don't have any data to back this up, it's just a hunch from the many websites I have visited; many of those that think their website is ready probably don't know what 'mobile optimized' means.

Regardless, if you're optimized for mobile your **whole business** will gain a *huge* advantage over your competition just for being first in line for mobile users.

Now you need to know some numbers to get this into perspective and understand why I sound so serious.

Currently there are 2.4 billion Internet users worldwide.

When it comes to growth, the most is now happening outside the West. China, in the last four years, added more Internet users then there are people in the USA.

But the Internet penetration of the USA still stands at an all-time high of 78 per cent, while China is only at 40 per cent at this point.

What does this mean?

This means that the Internet is still growing, and still has plenty of space to grow further, being only about 25 per cent of the total population on the planet.

This also means that having international visitors will become more and more commonplace.

Great but what does this mean to you as a small business in Bithlo, Florida?

What you need to focus on are the numbers in the USA. While still growing slowly, nearly 78 per cent of the US population has an Internet connection.

This means that if you don't have a website, you are missing out big time.

Now let me qualify that statement above: if you don't have a high-performing, quality website that is optimized for getting traffic, you are missing out.

If all you have is a website with contact information and a little bit about who you are and a place to sign up for a newsletter that you never really put out, then you are missing out nearly as much as those that don't have a website at all.

But this is only the beginning. Let's get into the rest of the data. While the Internet market is still growing steadily, the mobile market is simply exploding.

The venture capital firm KPCB published a report called 'Internet Trends' and in it analyst Mary Meeker says that mobile devices now account for 45 per cent of all Internet browsing.

The report also says, 'Mobile is huge, it's going to get tremendously larger, and will soon become... The Primary Way Most People Experience The Internet!'

It even goes so far as to say 'the Mobile Internet is becoming THE Internet.'

The mobile market in the USA is currently at 172 million people compared to 244 million regular Internet users. That means that mobile use is up to 70 per cent of the size of the regular Internet already.

Mobile Internet traffic is currently 15 per cent of all Internet traffic and is expected to continue growing one-and-a-half times per year.

With the explosion of smartphone and tablet ownership, how long do you think it will be before there are more mobile users than desktop users?

Research firm IDC projects that there will be more tablets shipped in quarter 4 of 2013 than desktops and laptops and that on an annual basis, tablets will be winning the war by the end of 2015.

So it's only a matter of time before the majority of visitors coming to your website, Facebook page, or whatever presence you have will be via one mobile device or another.

What exactly this means for your business

This means that you need to start thinking about how best to cater to these visitors. We recently had a real estate client that said that 40 per cent of his traffic was mobile!

And it's now common for sites to experience nearly 20–35 per cent of their traffic coming from mobile platforms.

Some points to consider:

Data from Google shows that 79 per cent of US smartphone users (iPhone, Android, Blackberry, etc.) use their browser **daily**.

Also from Google, nearly a third of all UK page views are from mobiles and tablets.

And people are not just searching and reading with their mobiles and tablets ... they're buying with them.

According to ComScore research, Amazon (the Internet's largest retailer) has had year-on-year growth of sales made via mobiles of 87 per cent and Apple is seeing a 75 per cent growth of sales made via smartphones and tablets.

If you sell a product or provide a service, you need to make sure that your website can be easily viewed on a smartphone and tablet.

How do you find out whether you're already getting mobile visitors? Check your analytics software (or speak to your geek and get them to find out).

All right so, maybe you are getting a lot of mobile traffic.

Do you know what to do with it?

Of course, if your mobile visitors aren't staying as long, you might need a better website with 'responsive design'.

This is when your website design files contain special code that detects what size screen and operating system the visitor is using. If it's one that could match a mobile device, it automatically gives that device the 'mobile' optimized version of the site.

Besides that, you might be tempted to treat them as just any other visitor to your site.

Why this is a bad idea

While a few of these visitors are probably browsing from home on their iPad, many of these (particularly those on their phones) may be checking out your site from across the street! Or while they are out and about and looking to purchase. These users then have massive potential for you and your local business.

For my real estate client, this meant that many people were seeing his 'for sale' signs and they were searching that address while looking at his sign.

Creating ads for mobile users

Create offers just for these visitors and pages that only they can see perhaps.

Think about what these visitors want from you and your business. Maybe you are a dog grooming business and you have a lot of mobile visitors. These visitors might have their mangy pooch sitting next to them in the car looking for a good service.

At the top of your mobile page should be something like 'Come to our location today, check in with Foursquare (or Facebook) on your mobile and get 20 per cent off!'

How likely would those visitors be to go and do that? How many dog owners do you think will come just because of that little ad? They might sign up for a Foursquare account just to get the discount ...

Well you won't know if you don't offer the option. Have a brainstorming session with your staff, and think about what someone that is sitting across the street would need to take action and give you a chance.

Another necessity of the mobile market

As well as your website needing to be mobile ready and having specific mobile ads, you also need to be checking your reputation on places like yelp.com and other local sites like Google Places.

These are most (if not all) mobile users' places of choice when it comes to finding a lot of businesses within a specific area from which to choose. With the right amount of SEO and some good reviews, you will be at the top of the search in no time.

Some of the key points on these sites are the following.

1 Make sure that you define the area you serve well.

Don't target everyone within 1,000 miles (at least in the beginning). Aim for everything within 20–30 miles of your place of business.

You do this by working on your site first, putting a page on your site targeting each area or sub-area within that bubble.

Also in the footer of your site, add all the zip codes (or post codes) with city names of the areas that you cover.

2 Next, register with Google Local, Yelp, Yahoo Local and Bing Local and set your area of service to the same 20–30 mile radius.

3 Next, start getting good reviews.
   How to do this? Well asking for them helps. The tip is here, right after giving great service, as customers are on their way out the door, train your personnel to say that if they appreciated your service you would appreciate a quick review on X (where you need reviews at that point) service.

If you did a good job, many may whip out their smartphone right there and give the review.
   You can also ask for these reviews via your email and address list as needed.

Start expanding

As you get a solid grasp of your core area, start expanding 10 miles or so at a time. Each time you do this, you will find it easier and easier to find new business. All the work you have done before will be building behind you.
   These local strategies above, combined with a big social push on Facebook/LinkedIn with YouTube and a blog are absolute gold for your business as those services are very mobile-orientated as well (so everything you are learning in this week builds on this).

Run mobile ads/contests

If mobile ends up being big for you and your business, consider running ads targeting mobile users only on Facebook, Google Adwords and more. These customers, compared to how much time they spend on their mobiles, are only **10 per cent served**.
   This means that mobile ads have little to no competition. Compared to the other areas of advertisement, this is almost the only area of real opportunity.

For instance, in newspaper advertising, compared to how much time people on average spend in the medium, it is saturated with over ten times more ads then the time warrants.

> **Note**
> A note for you if you are running newspaper ads. Now is probably the time to drop them unless you know that they are bringing in more business than they are costing.

Taking this to the next level

Okay, so you now have some ideas to start engaging the mobile user but there is a whole other level of integration that takes place when you enter a mobile user's life.

First some more stats to chew on:

- Mobile units (smartphones/tablets) overtook desktop/ notebook computers in total amounts of shipments in 2010.
- The installed base (i.e. how many of these devices are actually in use) of mobile units is predicted to beat desktop/ notebooks **this year** and nearly double the desktop/laptop market by 2015.
- This means that in only two years there will be twice as many mobile devices to check your site out than there are computers.
- With the resurgence of mobile operating systems, Android and Apple are now shipping more operating systems per year than Windows.
- This doesn't mean they are going to overtake Windows in installed bases soon but what it does mean is that Windows has a long way to go to break into the mobile market (as they have tried and so far failed to do) and even buying up Nokia's smartphone division may be too little too late.

With this mobile marketplace, people are now taking everything mobile. Now I want to talk a bit about where we see this shift in culture today.

Knowledge is now mobile

A recent study showed that while people were unlikely to know certain well-known facts, 90 per cent of the people that didn't know those facts knew where to find the answer online quickly if they had too.

This is also happening in the mobile world. People increasingly don't know where your business or others really are. But they do know where to go to find that information.

Now, instead of having to know everything they can whip out their mobile phone and do a search for up-to-date information.

Do you remember the last time you looked at an Encyclopedia Britannica?

Nope, me neither. They don't make them anymore. They went the way of the dodo with the advent of Wikipedia and Google.

Photographs have gone mobile

Instagram, Facebook, Flickr and more all cater to a market that uploads photos on the go.

In fact, every smartphone produced now has a camera in it that can take high-quality photos just like digital cameras.

In fact, stand-alone digital cameras are becoming more of a professional product then a consumer product as shipments of all stand-alone cameras peaked four years ago and have yet to recover.

Super ninja tip
Create a contest with photos where people put in a tag and do something with your product. For instance, taking the example of a pet grooming service, it could be take the best photo you can of your freshly shaved pooch and get the most likes on Facebook and Instagram and your next shave is free!

Books are going mobile

Kindle e-books now outsell print books on Amazon nearly three to one. In the first quarter of 2012, e-books outsold hard cover books in dollar terms!

As nice as it is to snuggle up with a book, people find it just too much to cart around many hardcover books. It is much easier to buy a book online and download it on any device they happen to have handy.

Navigation is becoming mobile

Just as stand-alone digital cameras are dying so are stand-alone GPS systems. Waze (which is a program that crowdsources mobile devices such as Android and iPhone), recently added more users than there were individual GPS devices shipped.

This is not counting mobile technology or people using Google or Apple Maps as a whole but just one app that helps with directions.

Notebooks/cabinet files are going mobile

Not only are the obvious things going mobile but even note-taking via Evernote, Dropbox, and other services are making documents and notes you have made accessible by just a few taps of your finger.

Wonder if that invoice has been paid? Check your Dropbox ...

Magazines/newspapers are mobile

Print is dying ever so slowly but pretty much everything is going online and by extension everything is also going mobile. Why wait monthly to find out the colours for this season if you can log on right now and find them out as you are putting on your make-up at the mirror?

Why wait till tomorrow morning to find out what is happening in the news today when you can find out instantly on Twitter from the very people making the news? Or via the online versions of the newspapers?

All brought to us by mobile technology.

What this really means

The reason I have gone to such great lengths is to show that everything that can go mobile is going mobile. So what does this mean for your business?

This means that you should go mobile as much as possible. Position yourself early or you will find yourself playing catch up.

As you hopefully see by now, this means much more than just having a mobile-enabled website.

Level 1 Mobile integration with your business

This means, using the example of the dog grooming service, that you might consider doing an on-demand service actually going to your clients' homes. To make it even easier, provide a subscription service for those that want it and set times when you will come to their house to shave their beloved pooch.

These are the things that the mobile generation desire. They want something that does what they want when they want it. They want something that does everything in one thing, that is, the iPhone.

For those businesses without a physical service, you can start meeting your customers and demonstrating your services and products while they are on the go. Using such methods as GotoWebinar or Google Hangouts, you can meet your customers online and give them a presentation, with you and them being located anywhere in the world.

So, how you can start doing something now can be summed up in one sentence: Find out how you can go to your customer where they are now – without them having to come to you.

Level 2 Mobile integration

This involves getting involved in your clients/customers lives on a very real level without having to 'do' anything.

This involves a few different working parts that automate your business to the point of absurdity almost.

For the physical service

For instance, with the dog grooming service, create an app, that:

1 Reminds the customer that it is time for a hair cut for their dog.
2 Gives them a place to choose which cut they want on their dog this time. It should also give an option to write in what they want if the pre-selected options you have don't quite fit.
3 Gives a way to order right from their phone (if they aren't subscribed already).

See how this integrates you into their lives? They never have to see it done; they could be off in Africa for all you know but you have the order, the payment and what to do without doing anything but having an app made.

For the service provider

Let's say you are an accountant. You could create a similar app that could:

1 Remind clients to send in their monthly figures.
2 Notify them of upcoming changes to laws.
3 Give them the ability to upgrade/downgrade their service level directly via the app.
4 Publish exclusive special reports or white papers to only those people with the app. Use titles like '3 Ways To Legally Keep An Extra £5,000 in Your Pocket At Year End'.

I mean who wouldn't want to download an app just to read that?
Once again, you integrate yourself into their lives so that it becomes seamless.
This is just the tip of the iceberg. Sit down and brainstorm this hard until you figure out how you can position your business for the mobile explosion before it is too late!

Summary

Mobile is here and it is exploding at an incredible rate that may make the Internet explosion look like a firecracker in front of a nuclear bomb (OK a little over the top but give me a break, I thought it was cool).

You need to get on the band wagon right now otherwise you will be one of those that get left behind scratching their head wondering at other businesses' success.

Get moving, start looking around at all the things that are going mobile and align yourself and your business to cater to mobile users. They want things right now and on their terms. They want to push some buttons and forget about it. They don't mind paying a little more if they have to think a little bit less and get the job done.

Take these underlying themes and run with them. If you position yourself just right at this point you can ride this wave for many, many years ahead.

Let's consider ten questions again shall we?

SUNDAY

MONDAY

TUESDAY

WEDNESDAY

THURSDAY

FRIDAY

SATURDAY

Questions (answers at the back)

1. Mobile technology is:
   a) Essential ❏
   b) Optional ❏
   c) Boring ❏
   d) Rude ❏

2. You should put off changing to meet the mobile wave for:
   a) Months ❏
   b) Years ❏
   c) Days ❏
   d) Minutes ❏

3. In the next 1–2 years:
   a) Things will be about where they are now ❏
   b) Mobile users will outnumber desktop users ❏
   c) There will not be desktops anymore ❏

4. Amazon's purchases via a mobile device have increased:
   a) 25 per cent ❏
   b) 52 per cent ❏
   c) 60 per cent ❏
   d) 87 per cent ❏

5. You should treat mobile visitors like any other visitor to your site.
   a) True ❏
   b) False ❏

6. Mobile ads are only how many per cent served:
   a) 5 per cent ❏
   b) 10 per cent ❏
   c) 30 per cent ❏
   d) 50 per cent ❏

7. Foursquare and Facebook are both:
   a) Social media ❏
   b) Good for getting people to check in at your location ❏
   c) Places that your business should be findable on ❏
   d) All of the above ❏

8. 90 per cent of people didn't know basic information but those same people:
   a) Had no idea where to find it either ❏
   b) Knew where to find it online ❏
   c) Guessed good and got close ❏

9. What has gone mobile in one way or other?
   a) Navigation ❏
   b) Notebooks ❏
   c) Books ❏
   d) Notes ❏
   e) Knowledge ❏
   f) All of the above ❏

10. What should you consider to get mobile clients?
   a) Meetings with Gotowebinar ❏
   b) Creating an app ❏
   c) Being more 'on demand' ❏
   d) Being more flexible and going to your customers ❏
   e) All of the above ❏

SUNDAY

MONDAY

TUESDAY

WEDNESDAY

THURSDAY

FRIDAY

SATURDAY

FRIDAY

Email marketing – why you should do it no matter what

Ok so that title may seem pretty bold but it really isn't.

Email is often overlooked as an effective marketing medium because it just isn't as 'sexy' as tweeting or Facebooking, Instagramming, or whatever other social network updates you do, but the truth is email marketing is far and away the best way to reach consumers on a personal level.

If you call your customers, they hate you for bothering their day and if you write them a letter, while cool (and a great potential way to break through the 'noise'), it costs actual real money to send to large numbers of people.

If you're targeting potential clients to offer high-end services, I recommend using personal letters or even FedEx to really get their attention, but for the average value client or visitor, I recommend email every time.

Email

Some facts on email that could blow you away (from 2013, the latest year that we can get data on):

- 838 billion marketing messages were sent in 2013 (*more then there are stars in the Milky Way Galaxy*)
- 91 per cent of consumers check their email daily
- 74 per cent of consumers prefer to receive commercial communications via email
- The average click-through rate for B2B marketing emails in Q2 2013 was *only* 1.7 per cent
- 60 per cent of marketers believe email marketing produces positive ROI
- 66 per cent of consumers have made a purchase online as a result of an email marketing message
- The average email marketing has an ROI of 4,300 per cent
- 59 per cent of companies are integrating email and social channels together
- 76 per cent of email opens occur in the first two days after an email is sent
- 48 per cent of emails are opened on mobile devices
- Only 11 per cent of emails are optimized for mobile
- 69 per cent of mobile users delete emails that aren't optimized for mobile
- 25 per cent of emails are opened on iPhones
- A 2012 survey of consumer channel habits and preferences found 77 per cent preferred to receive permission-based promotions via email; 6 per cent preferred such messages via social media. A similar survey of UK consumers found 69 per cent with a preference for email as the channel for brand communications
- The 2012 Marketing Channel and Engagement Benchmark Survey found 63 per cent of respondents cited email as the channel offering the best ROI

As I hope you can see from the above stats, email needs to be done right for it to be completely effective. And as we talked about yesterday, it needs to be done right focusing on mobile marketing.

If it's done incorrectly, in fact it's almost worse than not doing it at all. It really breaks down into two separate categories:

1 Make sure that your email is received
2 Next, make sure that your email is read *and* responded to.

Making sure that your emails are received

If you go to all the trouble to write emails, you had better make sure that they actually hit your prospects' and clients' inboxes.

While this isn't so much of an issue when emailing directly from you to them, when you want to send messages to multiple respondents at the same time (for example, if you're sending out an email newsletter), then things get a little sticky.

Most Internet service providers (ISPs) will limit the number of emails that you can send out per hour and per day, so you can't just repeatedly blind carbon copy the

SUNDAY
MONDAY
TUESDAY
WEDNESDAY
THURSDAY
FRIDAY
SATURDAY

5,000 people in your prospect email database and hit send in Microsoft Outlook.

Even if you manage to get the emails sent, if you keep doing it you run a very good risk of having your company's domain name (the one you use in the From: setting in your email software) added to email spam blacklists that ISPs use to block emails from reaching their customers.

You also run the risk of your ISP thinking that you're spamming and simply disconnecting your Internet access.

To eliminate this possibility, you have two real choices.

Sign up with a dedicated email marketing service provider like Aweber.com, GetResponse.com, iContact.com, Mailchimp.com. They have arrangements with the major ISPs that enable you to increase the chances of your email getting to your prospects and clients.

You benefit from the trust that the ISPs have with these email marketing service providers that they monitor and will stop as much spam as possible from being sent in the first place.

With most email marketing service providers, every email you compose will be evaluated for trigger words and phrases that could unintentionally flag your email as spam, enabling you to rewrite them accordingly.

You will also be evaluated by the number of 'spam' reports your emails generate from users, which will see your deliverability numbers diminish and then, ultimately, your account will be shut down.

Roll your own email marketing solution.

There are a number of software programs out there that can be installed onto your website or separate server that will enable you to run your email marketing system.

Two excellent programs I can recommend are ARPReach and Interspire Email Marketer. Both of these are very high-quality offerings with lots of features and functions with excellent support and installation help.

In years gone by, you would have needed a very high-end server set up to be able to run an email marketing system using this type of software but now with the advent of third-party email sending services like SMTP.com, Amazon SES and SendGrid.com, you can get the best of both worlds.

Both ARPReach and Interspire Email Marketer are able to directly interface with these external email sending services so you have 100 per cent control over the data, services like Amazon SES handle the server-intensive tasks of actually sending the emails and you get to benefit from their similar arrangements with the main ISPs.

Which route you take, email marketing service provider or roll your own, is up to you. If you don't have technical people on staff or you're not technically minded, go with option 1, otherwise take a serious look at option 2.

Mobile optimization

How would you optimize your emails for mobile? This is thankfully not too complicated. If you have some tech knowledge this post sums it up: http://blog.hubspot.com/marketing/optimize-email-mobile-list

Or if you are using Aweber or some comparable service just use one of their mobile templates to be sure.

How to minimize your undeliverable emails

One way is to make people confirm their subscription request (sometimes known as 'double' opt-in).

This is when a visitor submits their details and then is told to click a link in an email just sent to them to confirm that they want to receive your emails.

Confirmed opt-in email subscribers have much higher engagement rates and email open rates, not to mention deliverability.

However, there is a drawback. In my experience only around half of the people who are told to confirm their request will actually do so, so you *will* lose some subscribers, either because it's 'too much effort' to go back to check their email and click a link, or they just never receive that confirmation email.

You can't really do anything about it if they never receive the confirmation email but another way to stop them from *not bothering* to confirm is to make sure that they have something significant to *gain* by subscribing.

My advice is don't bother with trying to get people to subscribe to receive an email newsletter.

Newsletters are seen as 'boring' and unless yours has amazing information in it every issue, people just won't subscribe. Better to just send them great, actionable information on a regular basis.

Send reports, white papers with cutting edge info and links to YouTube videos you've uploaded with ground-breaking news that directly affects them.

Think about how best to stand out from others in your industry and make sure that whichever method your 'ethical bribe' content is released by, it's not just vague, general information but very *specific* to the kind of client or customer you're looking for.

Marketing tip

One tactic that some business owners are beginning to use is to write a quality report on their area of expertise and publish it in Kindle format on Amazon.

There are lots of videos showing you how to do it on YouTube and it can be done totally free (if you're doing it yourself) or you can hire someone from a freelancer website like oDesk.com or eLance.com who will format and set up the book on Amazon.

Why go to the trouble to do this?

Because then you can give the book/report away for free with a 'As sold on Amazon for $x.xx' statement on the page.

Do you see the power of this? First, it uses Amazon's credibility to build yours (you're a published author now) and at the same time gives the information an actual $$ value, regardless of the value the reader will get from the information within.

Whether you actually sell books on Amazon is irrelevant. Your visitors now have a good reason to jump through one extra hoop to get your book.

SUNDAY

MONDAY

TUESDAY

WEDNESDAY

THURSDAY

FRIDAY

SATURDAY

Aside: Single opt-in or confirmed opt-in

Some marketers (including myself I have to say) never make people confirm their subscription.

If you would prefer to have a higher quality of subscriber and accept the inevitability that you'll lose half of all sign-ups to apathy or deliverability issues, then go with confirmed opt-ins.

If you want to maximize the number of subscribers into your prospect list (which should be the beginning of your sales funnel), then stick with single (non-confirmed) opt-ins.

There's no right or wrong approach with this, it's all down to personal choice.

Getting your emails read

So now you know your preferred clients got your free 'ethical bribe' with $x.xx – now what?

Ask them to buy something!

Noooooooooo! Don't do it! (reaches out hand in slow motion) Resist this temptation like the plague – this just isn't cool.

You don't propose to someone on the first date. You need to build up a relationship with the other person before you go down on bended knee, so to speak.

Give even more quality, useful and helpful information for free to your potential clients. With the email marketing service providers and the two software programs I mentioned before, you can pre-load entire sequences of emails to be sent automatically over a period of time, each and every time someone signs up.

Don't worry about giving away too much information. There's no such thing. If you're a service provider, you may be concerned that all your subscribers will simply take all the information you give them and do it all themselves.

They won't. Not everyone has the time or the inclination to figure stuff out on their own, especially if you're marketing to business owners. Of course some will, but most won't and those are the people who will seriously think about contacting you for help. (Kind of like me and this book, some might say.)

Fill in the holes and give further advice regarding the issue or good idea that you solved in the first give-away product.

TIP

If you're still not 100 per cent sure about giving away lots of free information, don't go into deep specifics – just tell them 'what' has to be done to get the benefits but not exactly 'how' to do it.

Make them look forward to seeing your brand name in the inbox. This 'trains' them to always open your emails. Now when you send them that offer for a discount on your product or consultation, they will hear you out.

Don't stop sending good information. Make it a habit to continually be sending out good information to your email list.

One publication I follow sends out a 'reading list' of things across the web that he has found during the past week that are good reading for his particular audience.

It is a mixture of stuff from his own hired bloggers and other websites and is usually pretty informative.

Marketing tip

If you happen to find a sale or an offer that works really well for your list, don't keep broadcasting it. Make it an occasional email in the pre-loaded automatic follow-up sequence that new sign-ups see. When you keep broadcasting your offers, it has the faint whiff of 'desperate' and also begs the question, 'When is your stuff not on sale?'

Other ideas for fun and profit

Depending on the type of business you have and who your customers and clients are, you might be able to build up engagement and rapport with your subscribers by:

- Running competitions like 'xx of the Month' or 'Funniest xx' and share the results on your Facebook page.
- Posting links to interesting videos you find on YouTube created by others (who aren't in direct competition with you) and explain exactly why people should watch them.
- Finding other people offering similar services that don't directly compete with you who might want to reach your subscribers and try to cross-promote one another to each other's lists by offering useful information.

If I had to start over

If Google blasted my websites into oblivion, Facebook banned my fanpages, and my dog abandoned me the only thing I would really need are my trusty email lists.

Those lists are all I really need to generate revenue because they are people who are interested in the things I am interested in.

I know what they probably want and from that list I could make money to keep me going until I got a new website and a new fanpage.

Your prospect and client email lists are an essential business asset that you should be building, because they really are the foundation of digital marketing and where all the money is at.

Summary

The difficult part is finding the perfect mix of information and sales pitch. Try to lean as far you can to information first and test out various levels of 'sales' to make sure that you don't overdo it with your particular market. Each one has their own tolerance level for sales but can never get enough good information from an expert for free.

Don't worry if you slightly overdo it; just go back into educational mode and people will quickly remember why they joined your list in the first place.

Remember: good information, good information, good information, sell.

Wash, rinse, and repeat.

The thing about lists is if you treat them right they can be responsive for years and years.

If you treat them or neglect they will quickly unsubscribe and spam folder your emails (simply because they might forget signing up to get your emails).

And here are some questions to make sure it sinks in:

SUNDAY
MONDAY
TUESDAY
WEDNESDAY
THURSDAY
FRIDAY
SATURDAY

Questions (answers at the back)

1. Email is often overlooked because:
   a) It isn't 'sexy' ❏
   b) It's boring ❏
   c) People think it bothers people ❏
   d) All of the above ❏

2. ____ per cent of people prefer email though (according to some studies):
   a) 73 ❏
   b) 35 ❏
   c) 56 ❏
   d) 96 ❏

3. You need to be sure with email that:
   a) Your email is received ❏
   b) Your email is read ❏
   c) Your email is responded to ❏
   d) All of the above ❏

4. It is recommended that you get the following if you don't have a tech team:
   a) Aweber or equivalent ❏
   b) ARPReach ❏
   c) Interspire ❏
   d) All of the above ❏

5. The best opt-in is:
   a) Double opt-in ❏
   b) Single opt-in ❏
   c) Personal preference ❏
   d) Secret opt-in ❏

6. Giving something away of value to get people to opt-in is:
   a) A bad idea ❏
   b) A waste of time ❏
   c) Smart ❏
   d) Sort of cool but not that cool ❏

7. After people opt-in:
   a) Send them an offer ❏
   b) Send them 500 offers one after the other till they buy ❏
   c) Never send them any offers, just wait till they ask to buy from you ❏
   d) Send a bunch of more free amazing content, then an offer, followed by more free content and another offer ❏

8. Free information (including telling your clients exactly how to do what you do):
   a) Is a good idea ❏
   b) Makes them less likely to pay you ❏
   c) Makes you appear to be the expert ❏
   d) A and C are correct ❏

9. If they don't buy the first time you email them:
   a) Take them off your list ❏
   b) Keep sending good info ❏
   c) Curse them ❏
   d) Send them a virus ❏

10. If I had to start over, I would need:
    a) SEO ❏
    b) Social media pages ❏
    c) My email lists ❏
    d) A website ❏

SUNDAY

MONDAY

TUESDAY

WEDNESDAY

THURSDAY

FRIDAY

SATURDAY

SATURDAY

Other marketing tricks and tips in the modern world

Up till now, we have talked about the basic foundations of digital marketing today. First, build a killer sales website, then get traffic to your website with SEO, social media marketing and then pay per click paid traffic.

After that, we talked about the two other ways to reach your customers – leveraging the huge growth in mobile usage and, possibly one of the most overlooked ways, email marketing.

Today, I want to talk about several other methods you can use to get traffic that, when combined, can really generate a ton of traffic.

SUNDAY

MONDAY

TUESDAY

WEDNESDAY

THURSDAY

FRIDAY

SATURDAY

Online press releases

Many people will tell you that these are old-fashioned and to leave them alone if you want to reach people.

This is not the case.

People still want news, they want to know the latest gizmos, gadgets, and trends.

As such, press releases might not be for every business, though you are probably different as you are reading this book.

If you follow my advice from yesterday, you may create an app. If you have created an app, why not create a press release 'Want to pamper your pooch by phone? NY dog grooming service says "There's an app for that!"

This is news that is worth reading and worth spreading around. Other people will read this even if they aren't dog owners, just to see the latest trend. You could even end up in the *New York Times* if you play your cards right (see instructions below).

Press release best practices

1. Always be newsworthy

When you start talking about online press releases, there are many SEO benefits as well. Do your best to ignore these and just produce real news.

Feature other related businesses to highlight a trend or do something a bit crazy to get publicity or maybe broadcast how you are giving back to your community with free dog bath Saturdays or something.

Be unique but, most of all, actually *be* interesting news. This will come in handy later.

2. Keep it short and also have video and pictures

This is the best way to make your press release stand out and get attention.

- Make it about 300 words but then include great images (worth a thousand words) and a short video less than three minutes long (worth a million words).
- Newsreaders and more importantly reporters have incredibly short attention spans and you will lose them really fast unless you write short and to the point and include attractive photos. If they are really interested, they can then watch your video.
- Even if they don't use the video and pictures should they cover your story, it can be worth it just to get their attention.
- If you need help writing and promoting your press release, you can Google search terms like 'press release services' or go to a freelancer site like oDesk.com or eLance.com and hire someone to write and promote it for you.
- If you fancy taking a crack at it yourself, there are tons of books on Amazon on press releases and getting free publicity and you can search on Google for terms like 'free press releases templates' and 'how to develop a press release hook'.

3. Release at 10 a.m. on Tuesday

Why then? Because it is most likely to be noticed at that time due to the lack of other news going on. This time is usually when 'the lag' hits in the week, despite the fact that news is a 24-hour business.

4. After the release do a little leg work

Sometimes, even if you make your press release interesting and do the above, it still won't get noticed because of all the 'noise'.

Have a list of the top publications that your customers/clients will most likely read, for example, for our company in New York, their clients probably read the *New York Times* and a few other local papers.

Literally call these places, right after the release (remember it is during a lull, you should get through).

Go directly after the most relevant reporter (for instance, if you're an independent financial advisor, the reporter will be the one that writes about personal money matters).

Call attention to your press release and tell them what it's about. If they want to look at it right away, then be sure to have the release already featured on your home page. So all you have to do is give them your cute URL for them to see it immediately.

Be sure and get their email during this exchange as well (for the future).

Whether they end up publishing or not, you now at least have an email address to send to the next time you have a release.

In conclusion to press releases

Doing the above can bring massive traffic and credit in the eyes of the world and Google.

Only do it when your website is in good shape with lots of content and you have all the other foundation pieces in place that we have mentioned in previous days.

Otherwise your well-earned traffic will be wasted.

Yahoo Answers and Quora

These are both places people go for answers to questions and a great place to establish yourself as an expert.

Quora in particular is becoming more and more the mobile and social media answer of choice and the best place for you to really customize your image because they allow a lot to be placed in your profile page, though Yahoo Answers is still often at the top of Google for many searches.

Both are still valuable and worth looking into for your business.

How to use them

Give insightful and detailed answers only to questions in your specific niche. Use your equally insightful and relevant blog post as a source on Yahoo Answers (be sure and write out the link with http:// included) or as a 'for more info click here' link on Quora.

That is about it.

Pros and cons

If you look at the most popular posts on Quora, you will see that they use mostly images, and long detailed answers to get to the top. But getting yourself to the top is well worth it.

When a post gets popular on Quora, there is an email that goes out to everyone that has expressed interest in that subject and you will be amazed at the traffic you can achieve to your site.

Yahoo is not so drastic or immediately evident but requires less of an investment in time (the questions are usually very much to a specific solution, not so broad and deep as Quora questions).

Sample Quora question:

What is love?

Sample Yahoo Answers question:

How do I get rid of this zit on my big toe?

This is a bit of a generalization because there are bigger questions on Yahoo Answers too!

In my tests and former projects, however, I have seen ten visitors or so a month per question answered.

This may not seem like much but if you answer 100 questions (not hard to do) this means around 1,000 visitors a month.

Plus there are even ways to outsource Yahoo Answers as there are established and professional 'answerers' out there willing to plug you into their answers. (This is not something you would want to do on Quora however.)

In conclusion

These two sources of traffic aren't good for every business. Be sure and check them out if you decide to use them. Give incredible content and answers and you will have fantastic results, both with real quality traffic *and* your SEO efforts as the links do count despite the fact they are 'no follow' (at least according to my tests).

Guest blogging

This is all the rage right now – both rightly and wrongly so. The idea is essentially finding an authority blog in your niche and then writing a high-quality post for that site to get a link and bring traffic back to your site.

This is good when starting out and even better with G+ authorship now available but they aren't everything to traffic and SEO that others make them out to be.

So you do get credit for the post both in Google's eyes with G+ and the readers there. But it still also gets credited to the blog you posted on and the click through rates on blog posts tend to stink. (They are not that much better than Yahoo Answers.)

They require a lot of time and effort both to get the post and to create the perfect content. And wouldn't it be better if you spent that time on your site and business? Just a thought …

The best way to make this work I would think is to outsource it. Have 5–10 fantastic pieces of content created with pictures and everything. Then have someone look around for a blog willing to post them.

That should be all you need for credibility in this arena with Google and should let you know whether they are worth it (use Google Analytics to track which authority blogs are sending you traffic and which aren't – concentrate on the ones that are).

HARO (help a reporter out) http://helpareporter.com

This is a great site that allows you to sign up both to be a source for a reporter's story and also a place to find people to write stories about on your site.

How does this work?

Well first you go and sign up. Once you reach a certain level of traffic (lower than a million on the Alexa.com scale at the time of writing), then you can be a reporter.

There are no restrictions for being a source.

What happens is that there will constantly come into your mailbox 20–30 reporters that ask for a certain type of people to be 'sources' for their stories. This is one of the many places that all the experts end up with lines on online stories.

Becoming a source is good if you are dedicated to it. Essentially you will have to constantly check the emails as they come in and apply to each one that you are suited for. It is usually good to offer your services on one unique subject as well, as otherwise you will not stand out to the reporter (they get hundreds of responses).

They usually then ask you a set of questions and you get a mention in their article with a byline.

Cool.

But the most power comes from actually being the reporter. I once had it set up with one of my projects that I would put out a call for a certain group of people and suddenly I had my pick from all sorts of well-qualified people to appear on my blog.

The way I set it up was to give them a full interview either over the phone or just via email.

This got me absolutely tons of exposure, not just for my website (where I started ranking for these peoples' names); but also exposure on their websites, as many of them promoted my website as a place where they were featured.

I ended up interviewing one of the biggest names in this field with this technique on the first try, and ended up getting a free pass (retail value $1,000) to a conference in my area.

So, once you get the traffic, start running interviews on HARO – you'll be amazed where it can get you.

Rolling with the Twitter giants

Twitter is a great place to get people following your brand but it is an even better place to find big names in your industry with which to interact and get them to literally promote you to their followers.

So how this works is, first of all, research your niche. For our usual example of the dog groomers in New York, they might look for dog trainers in New York, or reporters that write about pets and/or the home, or even celebrities that have dogs in New York.

Find them and start following them (don't start spamming them or anything – nothing will get you removed faster).

Get to know them and the things they tweet. During this time, be sharing your own musings and good content as well connecting with your followers (i.e. keep it real).

Then when you see something pretty cool or related to you, retweet it, or write a comment to it. Do this consistently and do it well and you will see them eventually check you out and, if you have good content, they will follow you.

Now as the relationship deepens you can @ sign them on things that you know they will find cool (remember, you have been watching them, you little stalker you).

Eventually you will be landing deals, getting retweets and getting featured in newspapers that you would never believe possible and wouldn't be possible any other day except today.

You may end up like the guy who asked Kate Upton to the prom and actually got a call, only cooler because you will make money off of it, not just high fives from all your friends.

Viral marketing

Ah, the holy grail of digital marketing, how we all long for our material to go 'viral'. For those unsure of what this means, it means that your stuff gets shared, then shared, then shared some more and next thing you know you are on *Good Morning America* yucking it up with Oprah.

While there is really no way to know if something is going to go viral or not, there are some things to do to give it your best shot. (Below I will use the example of videos, but the things talked about can be any medium, from a blog post to an image you produce that gets shared a million times on Facebook.)

Looking at the list of most viral YouTube videos of 2012, you can note that most of them were well-produced videos.

SUNDAY

MONDAY

TUESDAY

WEDNESDAY

THURSDAY

FRIDAY

SATURDAY

In other words, they were professionally produced pieces that appealed to the video maker's followers immediately.

This is a good place to start. Don't try to make something that goes viral by being stupid and putting up junk funny videos unrelated to your niche.

Make sure that your videos will appeal to your kind of people first. This way, if it does go viral your kind of people will like it and want to visit your website.

Also, even if it doesn't go viral the views/traction you do get will only build your brand more for the next try.

Next, you will note that many of the videos that went viral were funny. Particularly the number 1 most viewed video of all time.

Humour really gets people to take notice and everyone likes to share something that makes them laugh.

As long as it isn't racist, sexist, or anything with else with '-ist' at the end of it, let your sense of humour be on full display. Don't be that boring guy that takes everything so serious.

If humour is not your style, then hire someone who can be more light-hearted if you want any chance at viral success.

TIP

Go to your local comedy club and watch a few of the acts. See who you like and see whether you can have a quick chat with them afterwards. You'll be surprised how cheaply you can hire someone to help you come up with a funny approach.

Next, make quality content to the right length. This can't be overemphasized. Make them as long as they need to be; there is no magic cut-off point for length. One of the top ten videos from 2012 was over 30 minutes long! So this could mean making your viral blog post 2,000 words long.

If you follow the above steps, it will not guarantee that you will go 'viral' but it will guarantee that you resonate with your fans/followers and so on – which is never a bad thing. Eventually, no matter how you slice it, you will get traffic from it.

So at the point that you finally go viral, it might just be icing on the cake and not so much a necessity for fame and fortune.

Summary

These were my super tips for building your brand and name. Use them for good and not for evil!

There will always be more and possibly better websites that may replace those that I have mentioned today. If you find them, jump in with both feet when you get a chance.

'There is no such thing as bad press' rings true even here. The more you get your name and brand out there the better.

For those new sites you may find and for the sites I mentioned above, remember it is always good to give a lot of good content and link to your website when it calls for it and always in context. You never know where some of these rabbit holes will lead, but I can say with certainty if you don't go out and promote yourself on these places and others, no one else will do it for you.

At least to start you are your own best promotion machine. Depending on how well you do it, it will pay off for years at a time, because most of what you do on the sites

SUNDAY

MONDAY

TUESDAY

WEDNESDAY

THURSDAY

FRIDAY

SATURDAY

I mentioned will stick forever, continuing to drive traffic till the web collapses due to nuclear apocalypse (or whatever).

Here are some questions to help them stick a little bit better:

Questions (answers at the back)

1. Today is all about:
a) Getting traffic from Google ❑
b) Getting traffic from outside
   Google ❑

2. Press releases are:
a) Still effective today ❑
b) Old fashioned ❑
c) Useless ❑
d) Nice but too expensive ❑

3. Yahoo Answers and Quora are
   exactly the same.
a) True ❑
b) False ❑

4. Yahoo Answers is more for
   specific questions about
   how to do something.
a) True ❑
b) False ❑

5. Quora usually requires more
   thought and care in how you
   answer than Yahoo Answers.
a) True ❑
b) False ❑

6. Guest blogging:
a) Is the best traffic source
   imaginable ❑
b) Is not all it is cracked up ❑
c) Should be outsourced ❑
d) Both b and c ❑

7. HARO stands for:
a) Hi are you rolling OK? ❑
b) Hold already ramping one ❑
c) Help a reporter out ❑
d) Handy Arnold rounded over ❑

8. When you start following
   someone on Twitter you really
   want to:
a) Be cool and get to know them
   first ❑
b) Spam them with all you got ❑
c) Get to know them, then spam
   them ❑
d) Spam them and all their
   followers ❑

9. One type of person to follow is:
a) Experts in your niche ❑
b) Reporters in your niche ❑
c) Celebrities that like
   your niche ❑
d) All of the above ❑

10. To turn a piece of content viral:
a) Put it into a viral machine ❑
b) Turn around three times and
   wiggle your nose ❑
c) Be humorous and resonate
   with your existing audience ❑
d) Spam people with junk videos
   of your kids playing on the
   playground ❑

SUNDAY
MONDAY
TUESDAY
WEDNESDAY
THURSDAY
FRIDAY
SATURDAY

WEEK 3

Social Media Marketing In A Week

Introduction

Welcome to Week 3 and social media marketing!

My goal is to teach you everything you need to start, as well as guidance on avoiding the minefield of social media so your first jaunt into the woods does not end in you losing an arm or leg in the process.

I will use all of my wit, charm and sense of humour (such as it is!) to communicate this to you so hopefully it will never be dull. I know what it's like to read a boring, dry textbook and that's the last thing I want for you.

I want to make learning fun, or at the very least not make you fall asleep while you're reading it.

Who is this week for?

If you are new to the world of social media, then this week is for you. If you are more of a jaded professional, this week is not so much for you, though there are some pretty cool marketing tips here that you might not find in other places.

I particularly geared this week for you, the social media newbie, because I know it can be a scary experience when there is just so much to learn. I mean, Facebook is the biggest website in the world. Where do you begin?

This week will show you how to get started with social media and give you the ability and best practices to guide your interactions with your fans and subscribers pretty much forever, even if I can't advise directly on your exact situation or sector you are part of.

In the coming weeks, months and years you'll constantly be assaulted by self-appointed 'social media gurus' telling you about the latest software or course, but in this week I will teach you the principles that will let you know if that latest gadget is a good idea or not.

To paraphrase the famous quote: 'Gimmicks are fleeting but principles are forever.'

I hope you decide to enter the training and get started today because social media is just getting too big to ignore.

In fact, according to one survey, 70 per cent of small businesses interviewed said they were active on Facebook and if you are not one of them, you will be left behind. Every day you put it off makes it that much harder to catch up with them!

Don't get left behind. Get started right now on your way to your social media success.

SUNDAY

Introduction to social media

Welcome to the beginning of your training. Grab a cup of your favourite beverage as we're heading off into the wilderness that is social media.

This wild world can get a little tangled and well a bit crazy really, but don't panic, I'll hopefully clear up any confusion.

SUNDAY

MONDAY

TUESDAY

WEDNESDAY

THURSDAY

FRIDAY

SATURDAY

What is social media?

Before embarking on our trip to understand social media marketing, it's important we first establish what social media is. Let's face it, social media is a term that is thrown around a lot and everyone is talking about how important it is for businesses.

If Facebook is a social media site and Twitter is a social media site and YouTube is a social media site, doesn't that make pretty much everything on the Internet a social media site?

Not really. Let me explain...

The best way to define what social media is exactly is to break it down. Any method that is used to broadcast to the masses (i.e. the population at large) is considered media. Think newspapers, magazines, TV and radio. If we add to that 'social' then we understand that social media is simply a method of social communications.

This means that social media isn't just a form of media that provides you with information: it also lets you interact with the information, while at the same time providing you with that information.

The interaction can be simple or complex ranging from liking a status on Facebook, leaving a comment on a blog or voting for a video on YouTube, to something more complex like viewing content recommended to you based on your Facebook interests or what your friends on social media have watched recently.

Social media simplified

A good way to think about it is this. Traditional media is a one-way street. They (the media moguls) produce the content and then you can read, watch or listen to it but your ability to provide feedback on the subject is very limited (unless you really have time to write or make a phone call).

Social media, on the other hand, is a two way-street, where the users (be they a business or an individual) can also create the content while they all interact together (not just by providing comments but also by creating videos, taking pictures and more).

This is where the real power of social media is for a business: getting others to create your content or advertisements for you (more on this later).

Social networking, social news, social bookmarking

A source of major confusion for people who are just starting out in social media marketing is thinking that sites such as Facebook or LinkedIn are all that social media is, or, they think that social networking, i.e. Facebook, is all there is to social media.

Social networking is just a part of social media, though it is a massive part. Social networking allows you to connect with fellow industry insiders, co-workers, clients and customers and to build a relationship with your target audience. Social networking sites include Facebook, LinkedIn, Friendster and MySpace.

Social 'news' is not the same as social 'media'. Social news is rather a tool of social media (which is the umbrella term so to speak). This will be talked about at length later. A few samples of social news sites include:

- Reddit
- Digg
- Propeller
- Gather.

Social bookmarking is also a tool of social media. This is a tool that allows people to tag websites and search through websites that others have tagged. A few social bookmarking sites include:

- Diigo
- Folkd
- Delicious (formerly http://del.icio.us now http://www.delicious.com).

Other social sites are used to share music, videos and images, such as:

- Flickr
- YouTube
- Pinterest.

There are 'Wiki' sites that also allow interaction (all started by Wikipedia) where readers submit the content and interact on that content through edits. (The TARDIS Index File is my favourite. Yes, I am a Doctor Who geek and proud of it!)

What is social media marketing?

Now we come to the core: social media marketing. In its broadest sense social media marketing is a form of marketing that entrepreneurs and companies can use to establish, maintain and expand an online presence and reputation. The key to social media marketing is to build a relationship with your target audience.

This is where many businesses go 'off-piste'. They make the mistake in thinking that social media is a place to sell their product or service. Social media marketing is a process and the very first step in social media marketing is creating engaging and informative content that readers will want to share with their circle of friends, i.e. their social network.

The content that you create (your message) will spread as your target audience shares it. That content needs to present you as an authority in your field so that it establishes trust. A reader will share the content you create if it is informative, well written and gives them something of value. That one reader will then share it with everyone they know and those people will share with their friends and on and on. This is what's meant when you hear something goes 'viral'.

In the dinosaur days before the Internet, this was known as word-of-mouth marketing. Word-of-mouth marketing is still one of, if not the, most powerful forms of marketing out there and it is what social marketing is geared around and what makes it tick.

This is because people always trust their family and friends more than they trust an organization. After all, if your best friend recommends that you go and see a specific film you are more likely to go to watch it because your friend gains nothing out of referring you and they know what you like. The weight of their word and knowledge of you is greater than a paid actor on an advertisement.

Social media marketing tools

It is fair to say that social media marketing has been around as long as the Internet. Any time information is shared there is almost always word-of-mouth action that accompanies it although, in the past, it was more likely to be done using email and discussion forums.

As of 2012 there is a vast array of social media outlets available to companies to help them 'spread the word'. Here is a brief list of some of the most popular social media marketing websites today:

- Facebook
- Twitter
- LinkedIn
- Google+
- YouTube
- Delicious
- Flickr
- Pinterest.

Collectively, they represent billions of connections globally. Facebook has over a billion users and Twitter's network delivers 350 million tweets a day from its 140 million users. YouTube has 72 hours of video uploaded to it every minute and 800 million unique hits every month.

Another mistake that is commonly made with social media is to believe that all social media sites are ideal for everything. The key to effective social media marketing is going to the sites that your target audience frequents. There are dozens if not hundreds of social networking sites for specific niches and markets. Facebook is not the be-all and end-all, and it isn't always the best option for your marketing efforts.

Along with the various sites out there, there are numerous methods that entrepreneurs and businesses can use. Later in the book we will go into greater detail on the tools you can use for social media marketing but here is just a small sample:

- Blogging
- Copywriting
- Social networking

SUNDAY

MONDAY

TUESDAY

WEDNESDAY

THURSDAY

FRIDAY

SATURDAY

- Podcasting
- Videos
- Bookmarking
- Reputation management.

Why you need to care about social media marketing

The Internet has made customers (potential, current and future) educated consumers. People now have access to businesses, products and services from all over the world. You are no longer just competing with the business down the street. Today, depending on your product/service, you may need to beat the world. Social media marketing is one of the main tools for that.

If you are a company who just markets and services in your local area, you should still use social media marketing but you don't need to beat the world, just the marketing efforts of the guy down the street.

Think about all the time you spend on your favourite social networking site, or the blog posts you read and comment on. You are probably doing it from a personal perspective every day. Now all you have to do is think about it and take action from a business perspective.

What is it about that blog or Facebook page that you liked that makes them stand out? Why did you reach out and interact?

From a business perspective social media marketing will allow you to become a social business. This means courting your prospects through the entire process of buying your product or service. We are talking about total customer care. While the Internet has made business overall less personal because you have the ability to reach customers worldwide, social media marketing offers you the opportunity to connect with your prospects on a personal level. You don't have to bring them into your store. You can reach them where they are at times that are convenient to them.

Social media marketing can also be used to grow your business. Where else do you have instant access to your target audience for free? Pay attention to what they are talking about and what their needs are as this opens doorways to new products and services. Perhaps you have an idea for something new already? Your followers on social media are your test market or unofficial focus group.

The question really shouldn't be 'Why should you care about social media marketing?' rather, 'Why aren't you actively pursuing and using social media to its fullest extent?'

Still not sold on the idea?

Here is a list of ten reasons why social media is the key to building and growing a profitable business.

1 Social media is the No. 1 of all online activities, surpassing email, porn and even fantasy football and baseball.
2 More than 60 per cent of people on the Internet visit social networking websites daily.
3 The average budget spent on company blogs and social media has tripled in three years which means your competition are getting ready to steal your lunch!
4 Up to 57 per cent of companies have acquired a customer via a blog, 62 per cent via LinkedIn, 52 per cent via Facebook and 44 per cent via Twitter.
5 A huge 74 per cent of consumers rely on social networks to guide purchasing decisions.
6 Facebook has over 1.3 billion users (if it were a country, it would be the third largest in the world), with half of them checking in every day.
7 As of the 2nd quarter 2014, Twitter had 271 million active accounts.
8 The Google+1 button is used **5 billion** (yes, that's billion with a 'b') times a day.
9 Pinterest is driving more referral traffic to websites than YouTube, G+ and LinkedIn combined.
10 And the No. 1 reason is... access to, and marketing with, social media is predominantly free.

SUNDAY

MONDAY

TUESDAY

WEDNESDAY

THURSDAY

FRIDAY

SATURDAY

Social media marketing done the right way

As with most things, there is a right way and a wrong way to use social media marketing. There are a few very common mistakes that marketers make in the social media world, and there are a few best practices that you need to know about before we go through the rest of the week.

- **Make the right first impression:** it is far easier to take your time and make the right first impression than to spend time fixing the wrong one. Remember the basis of this type of marketing is word of mouth. It only takes one dissatisfied or unimpressed customer to ruin an entire marketing plan. One blogger managed to shut down an entire new product line at lingerie store Victoria's Secret when she offered her opinion that a certain new piece on sale was 'overt racism masked behind claims of inspired fashion'.
- **Have a unified marketing message:** social media marketing should not be seen as something separate from the rest of your marketing. It is an integral part of your marketing plan. Every marketing tool you use should drive your business towards the same goal. Yes, you can use social media marketing for branding, but don't stop there. Don't let that be all you are using social media for.
- **Social media marketing strategy:** don't make the mistake in thinking that you have to use every social media marketing tool out there. Likewise, don't use the tools without having a strategy to what you are doing. If you are creating a Facebook group, are you also engaging people in forums and are you creating informative content for sites like YouTube? What is the aim of the social media tools you are using? Are you just trying to get out there? Do you want to introduce a new product? Bottom line? Know exactly why you're doing social media marketing.
- **Know where your audience is:** there are hundreds and thousands of social media sites out there, all of which have a different audience and serve a different purpose. Go to the sites that your target audience populates. Take the time

to do the research to find out where they are. Facebook isn't the only answer, and it isn't the right answer for everybody.

- **Engage your audience:** do not sell through social media. Social media marketing is about building your reputation, building relationships with your customers and giving them information they can use. If you have a Facebook page, that is **not** where you sell your services. You post content that provides value and directs them to another source of good content that will direct them to a capture page (where you can get names, emails and so on) and *then* you sell to them. Selling is never the first part of any effective social media marketing plan.

- **Sharing too often:** just as there is email spam, there is social media spam. When you post too often on social networking sites people tend to stop paying attention to what you are saying. It isn't that if you have ten excellent tips to help your customers or clients you can't post them, but it is better to schedule those posts to come out perhaps two a day over a week. Remember you want people to pay attention to what you have to say, not roll their eyes and click right past your post.

- **Avoid self-proclaimed social media experts:** OK, so I get the irony of this point since you're learning how to become an expert with social media by reading a book written by a social media expert. The bottom line is this. With hundreds or thousands of different social media sites out there, it's impossible for any one person (even me) to be an expert at all of them. Can they specialize in a few? Absolutely! Can they be an expert at one? Absolutely! Is there a be-all and end-all social media guru out there? Unlikely!

- **Reputation management:** building a strong, well-liked brand using social media marketing can do much more than help sell your products or services. Strong brands with a loyal following cultivated by engaging your followers can help you bounce back from any negative comments or reviews your company has received. It's one of the reasons why global brands like Toyota and US brands like Martha Stewart have bounced back from some really awful press.

If you're new to social media marketing it's best to start out with just one outlet used most by your customers. You need to make sure the outlet is appropriate for your business as well. If you offer a service for professionals, social networking sites like LinkedIn are better suited for business. Once you become familiar with how social media works, you can start repurposing your content to other outlets.

Building a strong brand founded on deep-seated relationships is the name of the game. Listen to your customers' needs, wants and concerns, and respond to them accordingly. They have to trust you and be willing to back you up should something arise that challenges your good standing. The thing is, people are ten times more likely to buy your offerings if they have faith and trust in you. They will also be the first ones to have your back covered when any negativity comes around.

After you get the hang of using social media marketing, it becomes easier and easier to manage your reputation. Not only that but it gets easier, and more fun.

Summary

Today you learned that social media is not the web as whole but a media conversation platform that goes both ways from producers to consumers and vice versa. Social media also does not only equal Facebook. While Facebook is a big part of social media there are really hundreds of social sites that all have their uses and particular aims.

You also discovered that there are three forms of social media: social networking sites like Facebook, social news sites like Reddit, social bookmarking sites like Diigo, and other huge social sites that have other specialties that are very useful like YouTube, Flickr, and Pinterest.

One thing that is worth repeating is that the key to social media is not to sell but to build a relationship with your customers. Do not miss this, and say this every time you wake up when you first look in the mirror: 'I will not be salesy on my social pages...' (OK, maybe you don't have to do that, but you get the point).

SUNDAY

MONDAY

TUESDAY

WEDNESDAY

THURSDAY

FRIDAY

SATURDAY

I then showed you how much you need to be on social media (many of your competitors are already there), plus the fact that it is mostly free! Then we went through a checklist of seven things you need to do social media the right way (these warrant repeat reading, so be sure to bookmark that page and highlight the ones that you will need the most).

Questions (answers at the back)

SUNDAY

MONDAY

TUESDAY

WEDNESDAY

THURSDAY

FRIDAY

SATURDAY

1. Social sites are:
a) Facebook, because it is the only social website ❑
b) Social sites are where users provide feedback on the experience ❑
c) Social sites are where users create the content for the site ❑
d) Both B and C are correct ❑

2. Traditional media:
a) Is a powerhouse of interactivity with fun stuff around every corner ❑
b) As stale as month old bread and trying to catch up ❑
c) Is boring ❑
d) Both B and C are correct ❑

3. Something going 'viral' means:
a) Lots of people are sharing and interacting with the content you produced ❑
b) You need to hide inside and don't shake anyone's hand ❑
c) You also need to get a vaccine ❑
d) A marketing campaign aimed at healthcare ❑

4. Social media is:
a) The number 2 destination of all traffic online ❑
b) The number 1 destination of all traffic online ❑
c) The number 3 destination of all traffic online ❑
d) Not very important ❑

5. You need to be on social media because:
a) Your customers are there talking about you. ❑
b) Your potential customers are there ❑
c) It's just what everyone else does ❑
d) Both A and B are right ❑

6. Social media costs:
a) Tons of cash ❑
b) Lots of dough ❑
c) Is mostly free to get started (though it costs time) ❑
d) Many moolah ❑

7. You need to be very careful:
a) To make the right impression ❑
b) To engage your audience ❑
c) Not to share too often ❑
d) All of the above ❑

8. If you have very bad press:
a) With a good running social campaign anything is possible ❑
b) You will never be able to get back to where you were, go back to your day job ❑
c) It is tough but doable to get back to where you were ❑
d) Ignore it ❑

9. The name of the game is:
a) A strong brand built on deep-seated relationships ❑
b) Monopoly ❑
c) Being really good and never messing up ❑
d) Getting people to buy bunches of stuff ❑

10. People are more likely to buy from you:
a) When you make them a good offer ❏
b) When you make them the same offer over and over again ❏
c) When they like and trust you ❏
d) When they are amazed by your special sales copy ❏

SUNDAY

MONDAY

TUESDAY

WEDNESDAY

THURSDAY

FRIDAY

SATURDAY

MONDAY

Successful case studies

Here we are on day two of your week to social media marketing success.

Hopefully you are still with me, because today we get a little breather. On day one we went over what social media was and the different tools that make up social media marketing. Keep these various tools in mind as we move forward. We will be talking more about creating a social media marketing plan and different strategies that you can use, and this will be important as you answer the questions to figure out what tools will work best for you.

The goal for today is to reveal to you the potential that social media marketing has for your business when it is done well. We are going to peruse a few case studies and discuss why you can't focus on the return on investment (ROI) of social media marketing right away.

SUNDAY

MONDAY

TUESDAY

WEDNESDAY

THURSDAY

FRIDAY

SATURDAY

Case studies

It is rather incredible that with the relatively short history of social media marketing in the online world that companies, both large and small, have found great success using social networking platforms to enhance their brand, boost business and provide customer service. A couple of the most successful social media marketing campaigns have involved the creative use of social networking sites such as Twitter and Facebook.

Fiesta Movement by Ford

Probably one of the very first and most successful social media campaigns was launched by Ford in April 2009. It was called the Fiesta Movement. The tactic that Ford used was very innovative and sort of cool. What they did was to loan a Ford Fiesta to 100 of the top bloggers to use for six months. In exchange, all that Ford asked of the bloggers was to upload a video to YouTube about the Fiesta and post an independent account of their experience with the car on their respective blogs. (Why I couldn't have been one of those bloggers I will never know. Oh well, maybe next time.)

The campaign was a massive success. There were more than 700 videos created by the bloggers, which generated over 6 million views on YouTube (this is a major amount as the average video only gets 100 views), more than 3 million Twitter impressions and Flickr was flooded with more than 670,000 photos of the Ford Fiesta. There was so much buzz created about this vehicle that 50,000 consumers in the United States alone wanted more information about the Ford Fiesta and a whopping 90 per cent of them had never owned a Ford before.

In the first six days, Ford sold 10,000 Ford Fiestas (meaning they made millions...).

Ford didn't stop there. The success drove Ford (pun completely intended!) to look even closer at social media. They went looking for actual feedback from consumers. They went to sites such as http://www.SyncMyRide.com (a forum site where owners of cars talk to one another), which had logged a number of complaints about the automated voice on the Ford SYNC system. This information helped Ford make improvements to the quality of the voice.

So all in all, Ford used forums, Flickr, YouTube and blogs to implement an incredibly successful social media marketing campaign.

Clorox

Clorox took social media and tweaked it to create incredible revenue and optimal awareness. What they did was host a Green Works Webpage in 2010. They targeted women between the ages of 25 and 34. The goal of the social media marketing campaign was to increase awareness of Green Works, products that are environmentally friendly. The tool that Clorox decided to use was Facebook, targeting users that had listed 'green' and 'clean' on their profiles.

A Nielsen follow-up study done after the campaign showed that the 'intent to purchase' the Green Works detergent went up by 7 per cent among Facebook users. The follow-up study also showed that there was a whopping 12 per cent increase in brand awareness. (These are pretty big figures for such big brands with massive awareness already.)

Budweiser

During the football World Cup in South Africa in 2010, Budweiser launched one of the most successful Facebook campaigns to date. Their campaign was called 'Bud United: Show Your True Colors'.

All the campaign did was make it so that followers could paint their faces on their Facebook profile with their favourite team's colours. This endeavour generated an incredible level of engagement with followers, with more than 2.5 million people opting to paint their faces.

Almost 1 million people 'liked' the Bud United Page by the end of the campaign. This is one of the most classic examples of how a company can generate engagement with their target audience using social media and get the users to create your ads and content for you.

So what about the little guy?

I know, you're sitting there thinking that the big boys can do social media marketing successfully for sure. After all they have the manpower and the money to back their efforts. So let's take a look at a few small companies and how they used social media marketing the right way. Also remember, in general, social media marketing is a free exercise.

Gonuts with Donuts

Gonuts with Donuts is a small company based in Sri Lanka that successfully created an advertising campaign on Facebook. This was so successful they now have more than 10,000 followers (most companies barely crack a few hundred) to whom they post updates on Facebook on a regular basis but they have increased their sales volume so much that they have been able to open up several additional stores.

Triumvirate Environmental

Triumvirate Environmental is in business to help clients make sure that the work environment is as safe as possible. They make sure that their clients are compliant with all safety standards. Furthermore they help clients create solutions for disposing of hazardous waste, as well as assisting with other environmental programmes.

They started doing online marketing in 2006 using Google AdWords. At first their marketing was lacklustre but once they started focusing on inbound social media marketing to support their lead generation techniques things started taking off.

The result? Over $1 million in revenue that they directly attributed to social media marketing by using search engine optimization, blogging and the business social network LinkedIn. Today they use a combination of social media tools to increase revenue and brand awareness that includes blogging, Facebook, Twitter, LinkedIn and other online marketing tools. Not bad for free!

AJ Bombers

AJ Bombers is an even smaller company, located in Wisconsin and employing 20 people. What's impressive about their social media marketing endeavour is that they are a pioneer in the industry.

Joe Sorge, the owner of AJ Bombers, will be the first to admit that the key to social media marketing is to first have a great product. Sorge believes that is what he has. Simply put, the best burger in town.

The first part of their social media marketing started with Twitter. They have an incredible 4,000+ followers. Bombers used Twitter to not only let people know about the new restaurant but also to track what people were saying about it and adjusting as they went.

They also started to utilize Foursquare (which allows users to log in and tag places that they have visited) and they combined that with clever promotional events. In this game AJ Bombers partnered with another local company that sold boats. It ended up becoming a fun and interactive game for social visitors that generated more customers coming into both AJ Bombers and the other retailer.

What it all means

Social media marketing offers an avenue for small businesses to compete with the 'big dogs' and, when properly used, can give your company extra business on a large or small scale. Remember though that you aren't always going to see a huge return on your social media marketing efforts at first. Word-of-mouth marketing can take some time, and takes effort on your part like anything else.

Here are a few traits that all successful social media marketing campaigns run by small businesses have in common:

- They all commit weekly resources that are used to create content and engage customers in social media.
- They all use a method that's able to provide insight into how social media marketing is affecting their business so they are able to establish what is working and what isn't.
- They all regularly use a combination of platforms such as Twitter, blogs, Facebook, LinkedIn and other tools to create content.

- They **don't** use every social platform out there; they invest their time in the platforms that their target audience uses and have the best ROI.
- They all use social media to generate traffic to events that are offline as well as online.
- They all establish very clear expectations for their customers as to the frequency and types of social media interactions that their company is willing to provide.
- They all use social media to establish their company as a thought leader in the industry. Be a pioneer!
- They all make sure to use clear calls to action and opportunities to create leads and acquire new customers through social media.
- They don't just put stuff on social media, they also pay attention to what is out there. They read what people are saying about them and their competition and use that to improve what they are doing.
- They all keep a balance between organic and paid search engine traffic.

Hopefully by now you can see a little bit of the impact that social media marketing can have on your business.

If a small burger joint in Wisconsin can use it to generate thousands and thousands of followers and into joint ventures with other local businesses then the possibilities are endless for your business as well.

Now tomorrow we are going to look at how to get started with social media marketing and I really can't wait to show it to you. Make sure you have paper and a pen to take some notes while going through the next chapter because I am going to be walking your company step by step through the process of creating a truly 'kick-****' social media marketing campaign.

Until then, have a great rest of your day!

Summary

Today we focused on some case studies, both big and small. We looked at Ford with their blogger outreach that ended in massive sales, Budweiser's campaign that ended in tons and tons of interaction and fans, and Clorox who experienced a huge jump in brand awareness simply through a Facebook like campaign.

For the little guys we saw that even a place in the wilderness of Sri Lanka can find customers and drive business through social media, and that creating games with Foursquare and combining it with different business partners can be a good way to success.

We also learned that focusing on social platforms that matter for your business like the company that focused on business-to-business relationships on LinkedIn that produced huge revenue.

Most of all, I shared with you the main things that businesses that succeed in breaking through in social media have in common, which can pretty much be summed up in this

SUNDAY

MONDAY

TUESDAY

WEDNESDAY

THURSDAY

FRIDAY

SATURDAY

statement: they are balanced, pioneering companies that focus on the bottom line in all they do, and because of this they pay attention to what is working, what isn't, and pay attention to each and every customer complaint and compliment.

Questions (answers at the back)

1. The Ford Motor Company gave Fiestas to:
a) Other companies ❑
b) Groups of random people ❑
c) Bloggers ❑
d) Your neighbour ❑

2. A key part of Ford's marketing was:
a) YouTube ❑
b) Twitter ❑
c) Flickr ❑
d) All of the above ❑

3. Budweiser asked one simple thing during its World Cup campaign:
a) Dress special ❑
b) Paint your face your team colours ❑
c) Get a temporary tattoo ❑
d) Give them money ❑

4. Social media is only for the company 'giants' out there:
a) True ❑
b) False ❑

5. Go Nuts With Donuts does at least this one thing to create buzz:
a) Special promotion posting ❑
b) Posting pictures ❑
c) Posting videos ❑
d) Coming up with clever questions ❑

6. Triumvirate Environmental probably initially found success on LinkedIn:
a) Because that social site is better then Facebook ❑
b) LinkedIn caters to businesses (which is Triumvirate Environmental's target market) ❑
c) Triumvirate Environmental got lucky ❑
d) We can't really be sure ❑

7. AJ Bombers found success on:
a) Twitter ❑
b) Foursquare ❑
c) Facebook ❑
d) A and B ❑

8. Foursquare is a good site for:
a) Multinational corporations ❑
b) People to say hi to friends ❑
c) Only businesses ❑
d) People to find local businesses and local businesses to be found ❑

9. You should:
a) Try every social site and hope you find the best ❑
b) Research to figure out which social site is best for you ❑
c) Ask your geeky friend which is the best site for you ❑
d) Guess which are the best sites for you ❑

10. You should always:
a) Commit weekly resources to social sites ❑
b) Be working to get new leads ❑
c) Interacting with your customers ❑
d) Do all of the above ❑

TUESDAY

Getting started with social media marketing

Welcome to Tuesday!

Now it is time for us to get into the real meat and potatoes of social media marketing. Let's recap what you have learned so far:

- Social media is any media platform where the users create the content with high levels of interactivity such as Facebook, Wikipedia, Flickr and YouTube.
- Social networking is only one tool of social media, not the whole enchilada.
- Social media marketing is using various social media tools to build your online reputation and create solid relationships with your target audience.
- That there is a right way and a wrong way to do social media marketing.
- Social media marketing is really just good-old-fashioned word-of-mouth marketing that we all know and love taken to a huge level because of the size of the audience.
- It is free for the most part and very powerful.
- That when a company does social media marketing the right way the ROI is incomparable.

Take a moment and get out a piece of paper and a pen. Today we are going to go through the steps to setting up your social media marketing plan and I'm going to steer as far away from 'corporate-speak' as I possibly can. Plain English will do the job fine for us here.

Creating your social media marketing plan

By the end of this exercise, you should aim to have your entire marketing plan in front of you.

Remember social media marketing can't be a separate entity from the rest of your marketing. It all needs to work together towards the same goal. Marketing plans are frequently adjusted to meet a current need so that you are looking at creating a social media aspect to your overall plan. What is the goal of your current marketing plan?

So, ask yourself these questions:

- Is my current marketing plan bringing me closer to my desired goals?
- In what ways can social media further my marketing efforts?
- What do I want to achieve with social media marketing?
- Who am I trying to reach?
- Do I know where they are on the web?

Take a few moments to answer those questions. Your answers don't have to be exact and there isn't really a right or wrong answer. Asking those five questions is really just to get you going and thinking.

You see, before you can go forward you have to have an idea of where you are now.

This is where the paper and pen are going to come in handy because we are going to walk through a ten-step process for laying the foundation of your social media marketing plan.

Ten-step process for creating a social media marketing plan

1. Determine your goals

Determining the goals of any marketing endeavour is vital to the success of those efforts so don't go past this point till you have got this nailed. If you don't know why you are doing something, you aren't going to be motivated to do it correctly and eventually (sooner rather than later) you are going to stop doing it.

It's like kicking a ball in the middle of a football pitch in a championship game and not knowing the idea was to get to the end of the field and kick the ball into the goal! You would just kick the ball for a bit, get the snot knocked out of you by the other pros, and you'd probably end up running home to your parents or going and do something else more fun.

So answer these questions:

● What do you want to get out of your social media marketing efforts? More customers/leads? If so how many?
● Do you want greater brand awareness? If so, you need to clarify exactly what this means.
● Do you want more visitors to a website?
● Why exactly are you doing social media marketing?

Here are a few possible answers to get you started:

● to generate direct sales
● offering it as a form of customer service
● reputation building
● to build customer loyalty
● company/product/service launch
● company/product/service re-launch.

The goals are really endless. The key is to determine what your goals are and to make them doable and measurable. Write them down now and let's move to the next step so that we can work through creating the foundation of your social media marketing plan.

2. Evaluate resources

This is important to determine and define. Why? Social media requires interaction, and if you are going to use social networking as one of the tools you need to know who is going to maintain that and where the content that is going to be used is coming from. This is your online reputation we are talking about: don't pass this step by saying 'I'll figure it out later'. That just won't do!

So now answer these questions to the best of your ability:

- Who is going to create the social media content? (Blogs, articles, videos, images, status updates, etc.)
- Who will maintain the social media accounts?
- Who will be the voice(s) of your business, the one responding to questions on your company's behalf?
- Do you have the in-house technical ability to be a part of online conversation? If you answer no, are you or a member of staff willing to learn or are you able to outsource?
- Can you, or someone you have on your team, write well?

Knowing if you have the right people in place is vital. Without the right people your social media marketing will fail, regardless of how incredible your plan is. If you don't currently have these key people you need to look at how you will acquire them. We will go over that later.

3. Know your audience

We are going to assume for the moment that you know who your audience is. You may have already spent the time needed to establish the demographic you are going after based on the products or services you offer. When it comes to social media marketing, understanding your audience is really what you need to do.

You need to understand where your target market is online. This isn't the same as your demographic or running an ad in the paper or putting a billboard up somewhere to catch the attention of everyone, including your market. No, social media marketing is about getting to know your market on an intimate level.

This is where a little research needs to be done. You have to determine the places they frequent online. Everyone almost always assumes that Facebook is the first place or, worse, the only place to go. Yes, Facebook is great and I would agree that it should be a part of most social media marketing plans but it is only a part.

From a social networking point of view there are hundreds if not thousands of social networks out there. Wikipedia has a partial list of some of them and who they cater to. See http://en.wikipedia.org/wiki/List_of_social_networking_websites for more details.

This is just a small sample of the social networks. Just skimming through the list you can see each social network has their own audience, and this is why Facebook can't be the only social network your business uses. Just because a sector or niche-specific social network may 'only' have members in the hundreds or thousands, it doesn't mean you should ignore it. These will be laser-targeted potential customers and clients.

Beyond the social networks, are there particular forums or online communities that your audience frequents? Where do they get the information they need to solve a problem they have? Take the time and find out because those are the places you want to be; if it helps, think about what your audience would type in a search like '[your sector] forum' or '[your niche] blog'.

Once you have established where your audience is you can figure out what type of information they want from you. You will get to know their likes and dislikes. I cannot stress enough that social media marketing is really about getting to know your market and catering to their needs. The selling comes later.

Now when you create content you aren't selling to them, not directly anyway. You are providing a service to them, engaging them, finding out their exact needs and building a relationship based on trust and respect. You are giving them a reason to buy from/work with you and not your competitor.

4. Create amazing content

Don't treat your audience as if they are not as smart as you. Once you have figured out where they are online, and you have spent time finding out what they want, take the time to create content that gives them what they want and makes them feel special and smart for finding you.

If you notice that your audience prefers videos or images and that's what really gets them excited and talking, it really wouldn't make much sense just creating a plain ol' blog post.

This isn't about reinventing the wheel. This is about making the wheel you are offering better than everyone else's out there, so check out what is working with the other wheel makers and do it better or different (in a good way).

5. Marketing effort integration

All of your social media marketing efforts need to work together. This means that they need to feed off one another. Cross-promote your social media accounts to your audience. If your audience is on a social network, there are a few blogs that they frequent and they like video, then you need to make sure you let them know that they can find more great content on your blog with integrated YouTube videos and on playlists on your YouTube channel by promoting this on your social network page.

Your social media marketing and the traditional marketing you are doing **also** need to work together. You need to be promoting your online endeavours on your brochures, advertisements, radio, etc. These marketing efforts should all be working towards the same goal and they should all be working together to support one another. This is marketing synergy at its core.

6. Create a schedule

If you are an entrepreneur starting and running your own business and your employees consist of, well, just you and your dog, creating an effective schedule is very important. It is very easy to spend more time than is actually needed on a social network. If you are using multiple social media platforms you want to make sure that you are allocating enough time in your day to use them effectively.

Getting sucked into emails and social networks are two of the biggest productivity killers that a businessperson or employee can get caught up with; honestly, from a marketing perspective, you don't need more than 20 minutes on a social network. So create a schedule: spend five minutes on Twitter before checking your email, then pop onto the social network. You will want to repeat the same thing at the end of the day before you close up shop. Twitter, email and networks.

7. The 80/20 rule

This is important. We have stressed that social media isn't really about you, it's about your audience. We have also mentioned that social media isn't really where you sell your product or service right off the bat. So when you are online using your various social media tools, keep in mind that 80 per cent of your time should be spent on activities that are not self-promoting and really no more than 20 per cent should be spent on self-promotion. Social media marketing is about helping your customers/clients.

8. Quality over quantity

This is twofold. It is far better to post content that is useful to your customer be it only once a day or a couple of times a week than to flood them with useless crud (to put it nicely). It is also better to have 1,000 loyal engaged followers than to have 10,000 followers that sign up to get something and then never interact with you again.

Quality goes a lot further than quantity. Less is most definitely more.

9. Control

It is your audience that will dictate the flow of any online conversation. The reason that you want them to do this is that you want your audience to feel as if the conversation is theirs. When someone is able to take ownership, and make something theirs, they develop an emotional connection to whatever that thing is. You want your current and potential customers to have an emotional connection to you, your company and your brand. They need to feel as though they are the most important thing to you and not their wallets.

10. Life learning

You're going to use social media to learn about your audience and you need to understand that this is an ongoing process. Who your audience is today may not be who they were 18 months ago or who they'll be in a year's time. Needs change, likes change, people grow and change. Social media is your inexpensive way to stay on top of and anticipate what your customers will need next.

You can use these changes to create and launch new products or services. Think about how compelling it is to the consumer that a new product was created just for them based on what they have said to you. Can you imagine anything more powerful than that? Nope, me neither!

Social media marketing strategies and tactics

After going through the process of laying out your social media marketing foundation and:

- defining goals
- evaluating resources
- knowing where your audience is
- determining what your audience wants/needs/likes
- creating content
- understanding how your marketing needs to integrate
  - the 80/20 rule
  - quality over quantity
- understanding who needs to control conversations
- constantly learning about your customers

you now need to lay out the strategy or tactics that you want to use to reach your audience effectively.

We aren't going to go over every possible strategy for every possible social media tool. Each one could be a book in and of itself. What we are going to cover here are the basics. These are the building blocks to an effective strategy regardless of what tool you use to implement them.

Assess your environment

A situation analysis is probably one of, if not the, most critical components of any marketing plan. You want to take some time and gather information from a variety of sources including internal sources, newspapers, magazines, trade journals and other credible resources. The information you are gathering is really the '**You Are Here**' arrow on a map. You are going to see what is going on in your business and what is going on around you.

Some things you are going to look closely at:

● Product: what are you selling?
● Price: what are you charging for your products/services?
● Promotion: what are you doing right now to talk to your customer base and motivate them to open up their wallets?
● Place: where are you selling your products?

Once you have the answers for the internal items, move to external factors:

● Competition: who are they and what are they doing? Perhaps we need to define competition: we are going to go with the definition that your competition is any company that sells a product or service that solves the same customer problem that you do. Know what your competition is doing, what is working for them and what isn't and ultimately how you can do it better.
● Consumers: who is your market, where are they, what are they doing and where are they going to get their problems solved?
● Economy: this is fairly straightforward but just for fun this includes balance of trade, Gross Domestic Product (GDP) and consumer confidence.
● Regulations and laws: this includes what the Government has passed as well as regulatory agencies such as Financial Services Authority (UK), Environment Agency (UK), the Environmental Protection Agency (USA), the Food and Drug Administration (USA) and so on.
● Technology: this includes technologies used to do business and technologies used for suggesting new products.

Don't just brush over this. You really want this to be as detailed as possible because it is going to guide the decisions you make on how you are going to use social media tools to further your marketing efforts.

Know your audience

Notice how this keeps popping up? You have to know who you are catering to. Who is most likely to buy what you are selling? What is the best place to meet them and convince them you are the answer to their problem? It is your purpose to solve what ails them. If you don't know what's bothering them, or what it is they need you are going to have a problem reaching them.

Know yourself

You need to take an honest look at what your strengths are. For example if you are terrible at writing, the whole blog thing may not be the right tool for you. That is not to say that you can't or shouldn't blog, it means you need to find someone to convey your message for you.

What resources do you have that you can commit to social media marketing, this means money and products as well as time and connections?

Set goals and objectives

Create a set of realistic objectives you want your social media marketing to accomplish. You can do this with each tool. Say you are going to use Facebook: what is your goal? Do you want 100 likes in your first 30 days? Do you want to use Facebook as a customer service vehicle?

Set realistic goals: my recommendation is the usual 30 days, 90 days and 180 days until you get the entire first year. Take baby steps: you have to crawl before you walk, walk before you run. Social media marketing done in the wrong way is difficult to undo. Take the time to do it right the first time.

Keywords

Social media marketing is all about content. Quality content drives traffic. It gets the reader's attention and motivates them to take action. What is the most important part of quality content on the web? **Keywords.**

Search engine optimization (SEO) cannot be ignored in the realm of social media marketing. SEO, in simple terms, is the art of formatting your website's pages and your website as a whole so it shows up in the first page, or ideally No. 1, in the search engine results page for a given search phrase (which we call a **keyword**).

You can get an idea of what your target audience is looking for by going to Google and doing a search for 'Google Keyword Tool', then click the link to be taken to the tool.

I use this tool almost every day. To help find out what people are searching for, Google, in their infinite wisdom, have provided us with the means to actually see into people's minds, at least at the time they were searching for something.

Type in a keyword you think your customers are looking for (or enter your website address) and the Google tool will pop out all the related keywords plus how many times that phrase was searched for in the previous month and how much competition there is for the phrase in paid advertisements. (Only use the search volume numbers as a guide and for comparison purposes between groups of keywords.)

This initial research will help you generate ideas for content to bring people to your website or blog.

A bit of horrific but relevant self-promotion. If you're serious about your social media, you also need to know the basics of SEO. I highly recommend grabbing the guide *Teach Yourself Search Engine Optimization In A Week*. I also wrote it, so you know it's good!

Topics

You are going to get your topic ideas from your keywords and the knowledge you have about your target audience.

Your topics should cover questions that consumers have, give them information, entertain them and motivate them to want to come back.

Creation of content

The content you create should be on the planned topics you have. You can also share content that other writers have written. With that being said, you **must** credit your sources. You can use Google Alerts (http://www.google.com/alerts) to keep track of trending topics.

Top tip
Set up Google Alerts to send messages to your email every time there is new content posted about your keyword.

Top tip
Use Google Alerts to notify you every time a new mention of your company name is posted online. This will enable you to take action to fix a newly discovered problem or rectify a customer's bad experience almost instantly. Think that might look impressive to your online audience?

Social platforms

Look, there is no way to use every single social media platform out there. If you had a team of people dedicated solely to your social media marketing you might be able to come close.

The good news is that you don't need to use them all. You only need to use the social platforms that your audience is using. If it isn't Facebook, then don't waste time, energy or money on Facebook. Go where your potential consumers are.

Remember the Wikipedia list of social networking websites. Go back and read through them and also go to Google, Bing or whatever search engine you use and search for something like '[niche] social network'.

Engagement

Once you get the visitors, connections, likes and followers, what are you going to do with them? How do you plan on converting them from being visitors to customers?

Analytics

It's not a bad idea to measure the success of the social media platforms you are using. Understand that you don't want to dump a platform based on the first 30 days, but you do want to know if you should tweak what you are doing to get a better following and more interaction.

What aspects of your marketing do you need to test before you actually launch? Now depending on the size of your company and what it is you actually do, you may not be able to test a marketing message before running full throttle with it. If that is the case, start small. Don't blast every social media account you're planning to use, pick one, use it for 30 days, make some tweaks and then look at adding the next.

Budget

Before you cringe, generally speaking social media marketing is free. The cost has more to do with time than money spent. If you have to hire someone to manage your social media marketing, that is something else.

This is where we again want to point out that there is no such thing as a social media marketing guru or expert. There are a number of good social media marketing consultants out there and one or two excellent ones [ahem]. There are also people who specialize in a particular social media platform. For example, the way you use Facebook is different from the way you would use LinkedIn.

You also need to understand that they aren't going to do anything you can't do. You are paying them for their time and their expertise. Sometimes it is worth it, especially if you don't have the time to do social media marketing on your own.

Contingency planning

At some point, something will go wrong. What are you going to do? You need to have a plan because in the online world once something is out there, it is out there.

Fixing a failure as quickly and seamlessly as possible, so it doesn't have a lasting impact, is vital. Here are the main things you need to have a 'Plan B' for:

- negative social media mentions
- website downtime
- product failures
- unsatisfied customers
- cover for illness or holidays.

You need to be able to pay attention to what people are saying about you, your company and your products/services.

One person I know did a search every few days on Google for the company name and only what had been said about it in the amount of time since he last checked. (Alternatively you can use the Google Alerts hot tip no. 2 that I mentioned earlier to have these new updates automatically emailed to you or to the inbox of one of your employees.)

The no-nos of social media

We can also call this the 'What Not To Do If You Want To Be Truly Successful' and in honour and homage to 'the man', David Letterman, here are your top ten social media marketing no-nos:

10 **Don't break the golden rule:** be nice. Social media is very much a 'pay it forward' type of tool. Thank people and offer a helping hand.

9 **Don't neglect your social accounts:** the last thing you want to do is create multiple social accounts and get bored with them and forget them, or worse, create only one that you never interact with. Be social and stay active to engage customers. You don't want to give a bad impression, as it takes too long to undo those. Would you open the doors of your store and then go for a walk leaving your store unmanned?

8 **Don't lie:** integrity is very important for the long-term success of your business. This is your reputation at stake here. Your avatar should be you, not someone else. Don't send private messages, tweets or updates that get people to click on a link that says something like 'click here to see how I got 10,000 FB likes'. Any links that you put in your updates should be to a blog post or article you have somewhere.

7 **No self-promoting and aggressive behaviour:** no, no and no again. Social media marketing is all about the soft sell. It is about building relationships. **Never** make your posts about selling a product or talk about how awesome your company is. Can you talk about a product or service? Yes, but make it about how that product or service can help your consumer. You don't even have to mention that it is something you offer. Look at the problem your consumers are having and offer a solution to them but don't 'hard sell', i.e. ask them to go to this link and 'buy today'.

6 **Don't create social media accounts without having the essentials in place:** you need to know who is in charge of maintaining and updating accounts, have a strategy in place **before** you start, and establish guidelines and a policy for your social media marketing.

5 **Don't apply a catch-all approach:** yes, naturally you would sell your product or service to anyone that came up and wanted it, but you can't market to everyone. Define your audience and go after those who are most likely to buy what you have to offer.

4 **Don't broadcast all the time:** people are following you for two reasons: they have a connection to your brand and you provide them with useful and engaging content. Don't inundate them with posts and Tweets. Then you become spam and no one pays attention to you.

3 **Don't remove issues immediately:** yes, you read that correctly. Don't take a negative comment or complaint down immediately on your Facebook page or wherever. Work it out, provide a solution. This shows consumers that you care and are willing to make an effort to rectify a problem. Only take it down if it can't be resolved.

2 **Don't have the personality of a wall:** your brand needs a voice, a consistent voice. You want to provide a familiar and comfortable atmosphere on your social media platforms to nurture and grow your communities. It doesn't matter if you have multiple people taking care of the social accounts; the voice needs to be the same.

1 **Don't ignore social media:** not too long ago, you weren't really in business if you didn't have a website. Now we have moved beyond that. To be competitive in this day and age you not only need that website but you need to be socially active. Consumers want to know the company they are considering spending money with. You need a social media presence to be successful.

Whew, that was a lot of information to cover in one day but I think you did just fine. In our next couple of chapters we are going to walk through getting you set up on some of the most popular social media platforms.

Summary

Tuesday was filled with creating your social media plan. This basically involved you determining why you are doing what you are doing by determining your goals and objectives to be able to track if you are achieving them or not.

Then you needed to determine *who* is doing the work of social media and *who* your audience is exactly. Then you determined *what* your quality content is, or at least you now have a good idea what makes great content.

You also know *when* you are going to have time and created a schedule to produce this great content. This process will never really end as you will constantly be learning and your audience's tastes will also be changing and evolving, so don't get complacent.

Lastly we determined *where* you are in the market. How do you compare in those categories listed to your competition?

SUNDAY

MONDAY

TUESDAY

WEDNESDAY

THURSDAY

FRIDAY

SATURDAY

This day then ended up with what to do when the you-know-what hits the fan, and the things you should never do on social media (be sure and write these next to your computer screen).

Questions (answers at the back)

1. Your different social accounts:
   a) Should each go in a slightly different direction to make sure all your bases are covered ❏
   b) Should all go in the same direction ❏
   c) Doesn't really matter which direction they are going, just need to be social ❏
   d) I pay people to think about those things ❏

2. You can have the best plan in the world:
   a) With the wrong people it can still succeed ❏
   b) With the wrong people it might do all right ❏
   c) With the wrong people it'll still be great ❏
   d) With the wrong people it will not work at all ❏

3. Knowing your audience is:
   a) Not necessary ❏
   b) Sorta necessary ❏
   c) Required ❏
   d) Not a good idea ❏

4. There are X number of social sites, where X means:
   a) 5 ❏
   b) 10 ❏
   c) 50 ❏
   d) Thousands ❏

5. What is better then having 10,000 followers that don't interact with your page?
   a) 20,000 followers that don't interact with you ❏
   b) 1,000 followers that follow your every post ❏
   c) Your dad as your only follower ❏
   d) 2,000 semi-interested people that are not your target market exactly ❏

6. You need to set what for your Facebook campaign?
   a) Goals ❏
   b) Objectives ❏
   c) Ideas ❏
   d) All of the above ❏

7. You should always have a contingency plan:
   a) True ❏
   b) False ❏
   c) It doesn't matter ❏
   d) It depends on the site ❏

8. Bad things to do include:
   a) Self-promotion ❏
   b) Aggressive behaviour ❏
   c) Not being nice and helping people out ❏
   d) All of the above ❏

9. Things to do include:
   a) Interacting with your customers ❏
   b) Being customer orientated ❏
   c) Always telling the truth ❏
   d) All of the above ❏

10. The worst thing you can do is:
a) Be a jerk ❑
b) Insult your customer's
parents ❑
c) Ignore social media ❑
d) Be bland ❑

SUNDAY

MONDAY

TUESDAY

WEDNESDAY

THURSDAY

FRIDAY

SATURDAY

WEDNESDAY

Phase one of your social media takeover

At this point you should have:

- a clear understanding of what social media is
- a better understanding of what social media marketing is
- good examples of how big and small companies have used social media marketing to improve their business in all areas
- a clear understanding of the basic principles that go into creating a social media marketing strategy
- a better understanding of how to create a social media marketing campaign
- a better understanding of what not to do in the realm of social media.

Today is a great day, because we are going to set up various social media accounts and finally get you all started. I will make sure you set these up the right way because it can affect all of your efforts from here on. (It is that important and I don't want you to knock it right out of the gate.)

Of course you can go back and fix things later, but doing it right the first time is easier than fixing it long after the fact, and if you do something wrong there is no guarantee you will find out about it anyway! (People *never* tell you why they don't buy.)

I want to make one thing clear: I cannot cover every single social media platform out there. Each could be a book all by itself so what I am going to do is break the 'Super Social 8' up into two days and teach you how to set up accounts on those platforms the right way the first time and the others that may be geared more towards your audience will most likely be similar.

Blogging

Before I dive into how to set up your blog, I want to provide you with a few statistics on why you should be blogging and give you some ideas on how to blog.

According to Mindjumpers:

● Blogs reach 80 per cent of all Internet users in the USA.
● Of all the time spent online, 23 per cent is spent on blogs (that is twice as much as time spent on gaming).

According to Marketing Charts:

● Around 60 per cent of bloggers post once a week, 10 per cent post daily.

There is a direct correlation between the frequency of blog posting and customer acquisition. Of companies that posted multiple times a week, 92 per cent acquired a customer through their blog. This is compared to bloggers that posted monthly whose customer acquisition dropped to 60 per cent and for those that posted less than monthly, their customer acquisition fell to just 43 per cent.

Blogs are considered the single most important inbound tool for marketing. They make up more than 80 per cent of the services that are used most often and are considered important or the most important tool for business. (Emphasis added by me.)

Blogs in general are free to set up and are usually part of the website you are creating or have. Writing the content of course is the tough part. If you don't want (or are not sure how to, don't have the time, etc.) to write the content, it is pretty easy to hire someone to do it for you and for a good price as well.

There are a number of great freelance sites you can turn to such as oDesk.com and eLance.com being two of the better-known ones. You can also run an ad on Craigslist (US) or Gumtree (UK) or even post an ad at your nearest college or university.

If you can afford it, find a professional consultant whose job is to create content that drives business, but if you're on a budget, I recommend hiring someone from either oDesk or eLance.

Note. Copy and paste any written content created for you into http://www.copyscape.com to make sure it hasn't been plagiarized from someone else before you post it on your blog.

Purpose of the blog

Blogs should be your company's online marketing nerve centre. They tie everything else together and are the next step to a customer making a purchase from you. If you have multiple social media accounts, then your blog should not be more than one click away from any of them.

Blog content makes a great thing to post and can get people talking. So regardless of which other social vehicles you use be sure to have a blog.

Step one: choose your blogging weapon

Now, let's get into what it takes to set up your blog the right way. We are going to start with the basics. The first thing you need to do is make sure you have a blogging platform installed on your website.

There are a number of different blog platforms out there and obviously I don't know where your website is hosted or what type of server it is sitting on, so you may need to confer with your geek-in-charge as to which blog platform is the most suitable.

One of the easiest to use (and my preferred blog system of choice) is WordPress, which can be downloaded free from http://www.wordpress.com. WordPress has made blogging a piece of cake. They have a plethora of widgets you can use and plugins you can get that give you more functionality and make optimizing the blog for the search engines a breeze. But to be fair there are other platforms such as Joomla, Drupal, Movable Type, BlogEngine.net and Expression Engine to name but a few. Do a little research at this point to find what will best suit your needs but always remember WordPress!

Step two: installing the blog on your site

Once you have picked the platform it is time to install it on your site. A lot of this will depend on the hosting service and the set-up you have running at this point. This could be as simple as running a script and then designating the directory you want the blog to be installed into. Assuming you don't have tech staff to do this for you, don't waste any of your own time trying to do this; you can hire a web developer from oDesk or eLance very cheaply to do this for you.

Step three: making the blog pretty

Design, while it might seem trivial, is something to spend some time thinking about. You should go with a design that is very similar to or the same as your business website. Fortunately there are thousands of free and low-cost customizable templates that make design pretty easy.

Typing something like 'free [blog system] themes designs templates' into a search engine should bring up all of the designs you'll need. One thing you should bear in mind is a lot of free templates and themes automatically add a text link back to the designer (or advertiser) at the bottom of each page.

My advice would be to spend a few pounds, dollars, etc. and buy a professional template or theme. For WordPress themes, I always come back to these sites as they all have plenty of choice.

- http://www.elegantthemes.com
- http://www.studiopress.com
- http://www.woothemes.com
- http://themeforest.net

Once you have the blog set up you need to think about the content. Take the time to research the keywords you should use based on your product or service and your customer base (use Google's keyword tool). You want to be sure that you and your customers are using the same language, otherwise they may never find you.

Your content also needs to be informative and engaging. This is the place for the soft sell. You don't use your blog to go 'This is my product/service, buy what I am selling now or else your hair will fall out and no one will like you.'

Instead you need to show them why they should buy from you. In the realm of types of content, there are three primary categories: newsworthy, evergreen and personal. Let's quickly go through those three, shall we?

Newsworthy content

Google released a new update in late 2011 that they termed the 'Freshness' update. The purpose of this update was to make it so that when certain queries are made, such as queries relating to major time-sensitive events, they are categorized differently and will rank better than other content written to meet traditional SEO strategies.

In other words, give Google what they want. Relevant, timely and engaging content related to high priority industry news. For example, if a new product or service is released in your industry or something is making news which you have expertise in, be sure and give the world your two cents on it and post it on your blog. You never know, one of your posts could suddenly get popular and go viral.

I remember reading a story about someone who wrote something on Michael Jackson a few hours before his death was announced. When he checked his stats the next day, he had thousands of new visitors and subscribers.

Evergreen content

This is content that you post that will forever be valuable to your readers. Say for example your business is in search engine optimization, the best tactics will change based on the new updates that major search engines make but the best practices will always be the same, so content talking about educating your customer will always be useful.

To get the most out of your evergreen content focus the content on good long tail keywords that are niche specific. These would be keywords that have consistently high search volume **and** a low number of competing pages.

Note. It is important that you focus on keywords that are specific to the niche you are working in because the search engines are getting smarter every day. If your site uses keywords with high search volumes that aren't specific to your niche just to grab traffic, you will be dinged and penalized.

Personal content

This is the content that you need to think of as you talking to your customer personally. This is where they get to 'meet' and get to know you, the proverbial 'person behind the curtain'.

This is very important content when you are thinking of social media marketing. It is also based on word-of-mouth marketing and relationship building. There is only so much that your customers need to know about you. They don't need to know what you had for dinner or if you painted your kitchen (I know it looks great but they really don't care), but they do need to know enough about you to learn to like you and also how your business came into being and the reasons why they should trust you.

Facebook

Let us start off again with a few statistics of businesses on Facebook to give you an idea about your competition.

According to Mindjumpers, practically every large charity and major university in the United States has a Facebook page, but less than 60 per cent of Fortune 500 businesses do.

Regarding wall posts on Facebook by your competitor's fans, 95 per cent are not answered by them! (What a great way to set yourself apart from everyone else: actually answer.)

According to Jeff Bullas, with regard to local businesses, 70 per cent already take advantage of Facebook (so this means your competitor down the road probably has a Facebook page). Good thing you have got me to talk you through how to run yours brilliantly!

Now for two **very important** stats about Facebook.

Facebook is the leading source of referred traffic at 26 per cent, compared to Twitter, which refers just under 4 per cent! This means if you're marketing to the general public and want to make real sales, go to Facebook (though Twitter does have its uses, which will be talked about later).

SMI has noted that 52 per cent of consumers no longer follow a brand on Facebook because the content that the brand posts has become boring and repetitive. (Don't make the same mistake.)

Now, if you are on Facebook for personal use, then you already know that it seems Facebook is always changing (err, wait, I mean 'improving') their service for users. So it should come as no surprise that they are frequently changing how businesses can set up Facebook pages.

As of right now, November 2012, this is the best way to set up your business Facebook page.

Classification

There are six different classifications you can pick from:

● artist, band or public figure
● local business or place
● entertainment
● company, organization or institution
● brand or product
● cause or community.

The purpose of this classification is ranking: the more precise your classification, the better ranking you will get when users search. You also want to make sure you use relevant information to your field.

Basic information completion

Upload your photo. Facebook will prompt you to upload two photos: a profile pic and a cover pic. Facebook issues important guidelines for those pictures. One biggie is not to use your cover picture as an advertisement. What this means is that your cover pic can't just be made up of lots of words. It needs to be mostly just an image.

The profile pic is the one that will show up every time you comment on postings and is therefore really important. So this is the one image that everyone will see with everything you do on Facebook. Your profile pic dimensions need to be 180 × 180.

Then there's the 'About' section. This is a very short blurb, so make it concise and powerful as you only have two to three sentences. This will show up on your main page so make sure that it also includes a link to your website. It also needs to give the information that makes your brand different so that your page is more appealing to followers.

Admin panel

Consider this your HQ. It is from your admin panel that you want to manage your Facebook business page. The admin panel has a few options and features that you can use to optimize your page as well as get statistical feedback on your activity, so you will see how well posts are doing, which posts generate the most engagement and what went viral.

The 'Edit Page' option is in the upper right hand corner and it also has a number of options available. The first option is 'Update Info'. This tab will let you update your basic info. You can also fill in the form for the 'About' part of the Facebook business page that a follower can click on to read all about you.

You can also use the 'Build Audience' section to quickly and easily invite all of your friends to like your page and encourage them to share your page with their friends. To do this you need to fill your page with content. Once you get content up, take some time and invite some brand advocates to like your page. There are also Facebook advertising tools that you can use.

How to fill your page with content

The lovely timeline brought about the cover photo. Use this space as the 'stop, stare, I need to be there' image. You want that image to grab the audience's attention and make them read through your page. As we stated earlier there are requirements for the image. It needs to be 851 × 315 pixels. It needs to be mostly image. You cannot use it to run an advertisement. If you do, Facebook will shut you down.

Custom tabs

Facebook makes it easy for you to create an endless number of tabs on your page, but the four tabs that everyone sees first when they land on your page are the most valuable real estate on your page and are the only four that you can truly customize to fit you. What does this mean? It means that you really need to think about what you want those four tabs to be.

I recommend using a tab for your blog, a tab for your images, a tab for your videos on YouTube (if you have an account), and a tab for them to click that has a subscription form where they can give their email address for some cool freebie you will give away.

Posts

The content on your page needs to be a very nice mix of different types of content. Images, videos, music, polls, statements and so on. Knowing what your followers want to see and click on is important, so to start do a variety and then go back and compare them over the long haul to see which performed the best.

A new little useful tip for your posts
You can click on the little star in each post in your timeline to highlight the post horizontally across your page. Highlighting a post does two things. It makes it look like you have a cover photo in your timeline and marks the post as an event in your timeline. You want to highlight the posts that announce a new product, service or event. If you are in the business of promoting others, you can use the highlight feature to promote business associates, joint venture partners or other similar associates.

Monitor your page

Much like having a killer website is only great if people visit it, the same holds true for your Facebook page. Use the tools they give you to monitor what is happening on your page so that you know how to improve upon what you are doing. Learn the Admin panel inside and out.

Also, make sure that you respond to messages and posts that followers send to you. Keep the conversations going and set yourself apart from 95 per cent of all the other businesses!

Measure your efforts

By now you will have created and shared a business Facebook page, a page that accurately represents your brand. Now you need to measure all your hard work so you see what isn't working and how you can improve the Facebook experience for your followers and your business.

Remember social media marketing is all about relationships and word-of-mouth marketing. You want people to share your Facebook page.

It is important to say right now: it is possible for you to do everything right in terms of marketing and Facebook not be a success for you. Facebook does not work for every business.

Twitter

First, some stats. Mindjumpers states:

- There are over 271 million active Twitter users. (By active, we mean users who log in once a day.)
- One third of marketers have generated leads through Twitter and 20 per cent have closed deals.
- The vast majority (92 per cent) of retweets are on content that was deemed interesting.
- Almost half of all the Twitter users rarely post anything, instead they read and retweet the content created by others.
- More than half of the Twitter users access Twitter on their mobile device (keep this in mind).

Jeff Bullas shares:

- More than half of Twitter users use it to share new stories and links and the other half simply retweet.
- Of the 100 largest companies in the world, 77 of them maintain a Twitter account. Media outlets, however, are the most active users.

The set-up for Twitter is fairly easy and unlike Facebook, which is constantly making changes that most people do not want, Twitter is basically the same and has really only made minor tweaks for users to get the most out of their account since it started.

Jump on over to https://twitter.com and click on the 'create an account' option. All you have to do is enter your name, email and password. On the next screen you are going to be able to set your username (ideally this should be close to your business name) and once you submit that, your account is now live.

Twitter tries to help you find people, companies, charities and such like that you may want to follow with the Twitter wizard. They break it up so that you are following five in each category including, celebrities, businesses, technology, sports and other categories.

Make sure that you confirm your email address by clicking on the link that Twitter has sent to your email. Once you click on that link to confirm your account you can add more information about your business.

Go to the administration tab at the top of your profile. This is usually represented by a silhouette of a person or a cog, then click 'settings' and then 'profile'. Then upload an image. There are two ways to do this: use your logo or the image of the person who is going to maintain the account. If you use a person, remember that this person is going to be the face of your Twitter presence.

Enter your real name, insert your location, include a web address and write the bio about your business. This bio needs to include who you are, what you do and what you will be talking about on Twitter.

You can also change your design by going into the 'Design' area of your Twitter account. Here you can change the look of your Twitter page. Twitter offers a number of different set themes you can use or you can add a custom background image. There are also sites you can visit that offer Twitter 'skins' if you want to use them to help make your Twitter page stand out or you can hire a designer to create a custom one for you very cheaply.

You can also tell Twitter when you want to be notified via email. It can be every time someone mentions you in a tweet, when you get a direct message or if you get a new follower.

Twitter is where you are going to give short and sweet pieces of information that make your target audience do something. Either they visit your website, come into your place of business, follow you on another social site or go to another source to get more information. The goal of Twitter is to motivate your followers to do what you want.

For example, if you are a bricks and mortar business and you want them to come in, you can tweet a Twitter-only sale.

 Super ninja tip
Google no longer indexes Twitter tweets in their search engine. Grab yourself a http://www.twylah.com account (currently free at the time of writing) and link it to your Twitter account. Each of your tweets will have a separate 'page' that is indexed by Google.

LinkedIn

If you are a company that caters to other businesses, LinkedIn is a social network that you **cannot** ignore. It is specifically for 'Business to Business' (B2B) companies.

Here is pretty much the only stat you need to know: it is the most effective social network for B2Bs with 65 per cent of companies on LinkedIn stating that they have acquired new customers through their connections on LinkedIn.

So we are going to jump right into the company set-up and we are going to operate here on the premise that you already have a personal LinkedIn account. (If you don't have one, you need one to do this and it is recommended you maintain both the company page and your personal page as well as it helps your customers feel they are talking with a real person.)

Log in to your personal LinkedIn account. On the homepage you are going to click on the 'Companies' tab across the top.

On the far right of the Companies page you will see a little link that says 'Add a Company', click on it. This will bring up a form where you will enter your company name and email. Once LinkedIn sends you a confirmation email you will click on that link to complete the building process.

Once confirmed, LinkedIn asks you one more time to log in to your personal account. This will then take you to your 'Company Overview' page. This is where you enter all the details about your company. Fortunately there is a LinkedIn page wizard that makes this a fairly painless process.

You can set up which employees (if any) will be admins on your company page. Should you choose to or be able to do this, those individuals must each have a personal LinkedIn account. You will naturally be the first administrator and the others below you. It is always a good idea to have more than one administrator just in case of an emergency, **but** make sure that the people you choose are people you can trust to represent your company.

Write your company description. This is the very first thing people will see when they come to your LinkedIn company page so **make it count!** This should be a concise explanation of who you are, what you do and why people should connect with you on LinkedIn. Remember this is a professional social network so this isn't where you are looking to make friends necessarily: you are looking to convey to other businesses why it is you they need to do business with.

Keep following the set-up wizard as it walks you through the setup-process. It is going to allow you to put in all the other places people can follow you or get more information about you.

Once all the information is complete you can start putting up status updates and building your following. Make sure to include your LinkedIn profile URL to your email signatures, website and all other online sources. This lets the people you already know, and who you are already connected with on other sites, to follow you on LinkedIn.

The best way to start getting leads is to go to the groups that are specific to your niche. Become active and post relevant questions and good info from your blog. Then, after a while of doing that, if you find a good opening or area that isn't covered yet, create your own group.

Summary

On this wonderful day we learned how to set up four different essential social accounts.

First, we set up your blog, which will become your nerve centre. Then, your Facebook account, where most of your customers probably are. After this your Twitter account; this is where you can drive traffic from. Finally we went through signing up for LinkedIn, the essential place to find B2B partners and other services you may need.

We went through the three forms of content that you should have on your blog: news-related posts (to show you keep up with your niche), evergreen content (solid principles that your readers will always find useful) and personal posts (that show your love for all things *Doctor Who*).

I also mentioned some things to get yourself noticed on these services, for instance the fact that 95 per cent of page posts by customers on business pages never get answered! If you can't run all these things yourself, in particular your blog, then I recommended looking into outsourcing to oDesk, eLance, or getting a consultant.

SUNDAY

MONDAY

TUESDAY

WEDNESDAY

THURSDAY

FRIDAY

SATURDAY

I told you about the ways to not get yourself in trouble on Facebook and get you the most business on LinkedIn. On Facebook be sure and don't put a call to action in your cover photo and on LinkedIn be sure to finish your profile completely and if possible get former customers to leave reviews or feedback.

Questions (answers at the back)

1. Blogs are important because:
a) They are the nerve centre for everything else ❑
b) They are the next step on the purchase trail ❑
c) They provide good content to post to other mediums ❑
d) All of the above ❑

2. I recommend XXXX for content creation for your blog?
a) A personal consultant ❑
b) oDesk ❑
c) eLance ❑
d) Any of the above ❑

3. Which of these is not a form of content discussed?
a) Newsworthy ❑
b) Unique ❑
c) Evergreen ❑
d) Personal ❑

4. What percentage of business Facebook wall posts never get answered?
a) 10 per cent ❑
b) 30 per cent ❑
c) 65 per cent ❑
d) 95 per cent ❑

5. Posts should be:
a) All of one kind (picture, video, or statement) ❑
b) Diversified all the time ❑
c) Diversified but with the type that tests the best as a slightly higher percentage ❑
d) All one type per day ❑

6. It is always important to monitor what is going on with the Facebook page.
a) True ❑
b) False ❑

7. LinkedIn is best for B2B business, almost making it a requirement.
a) True ❑
b) False ❑

8. What percentage of companies that serve businesses on LinkedIn report making a sale simply through LinkedIn?
a) 35 per cent ❑
b) 65 per cent ❑
c) 15 per cent ❑
d) 96 per cent ❑

9. What is the most important part of the company page?
a) The profile picture ❑
b) The description ❑
c) Your posts ❑
d) All these and more are important because those who are searching for want a complete picture ❑

10. The best place to start getting contacts on LinkedIn is:
a) Facebook ❑
b) Chat rooms ❑
c) The other niche specific groups in LinkedIn ❑
d) Friends ❑

THURSDAY

Phase two of your social media takeover

Welcome to Thursday (yay, it's almost Friday!), where we are going to jump into the next four major social media marketing platforms. Can you believe that the week is almost over?

All right that is enough lolly-gagging, let's snap to it, soldier!

At this point, you should be familar with the following:

- what social media is
- what social media marketing is
- examples of businesses big and small that have used social media marketing to improve all aspects of their business
- the foundation of social media marketing and what it takes to create a social media marketing plan
- how to create a social media marketing campaign
- the things you should not do in social media
- how to set up the first four of the big eight social media platforms: blogging, Facebook, Twitter, LinkedIn.

Today we're going to cover YouTube, G+, Pinterest and StumbleUpon. Now, you're going to notice that I will be covering a couple of these four a little differently than yesterday. The reason is that G+ and Pinterest are fairly new additions, not only to social media, but also to businesses to use for their marketing purposes.

YouTube

YouTube is an absolute must as part of your social media strategy. YouTube is now the world's second largest search engine (displacing Yahoo Search in 2011) and is, depending on who you believe, either the third or fourth most popular website on the entire Internet.

YouTube serves **4 billion** hours of videos every month and during 2011 had a **trillion** views (equating to 140 views for every single person on earth). People love watching videos and you need to figure out ways to exploit this incredible platform for your company or business.

YouTube has a Get Started page that walks you through the set-up process. You will want to think about the username you enter because it will become the name of your YouTube channel. There are a few different ways that you can come up with your username.

The obvious first choice is to use your company name. That's great for companies that are already known. If you are a new start-up company with a strong brandable name, try to get it as your username or alternatively you can try to use your most desired keyword for the username.

Why would you do this? Google gives a little 'weight' to a webpage or URL when a keyword is in the domain name or somewhere in the URL (and if you are an SEO expert reading this and howling I'm talking rubbish after Google's Penguin and Panda updates, sorry, you're wrong).

When creating your YouTube username keep in mind that you can't have any spaces or special characters. You can however use upper and lower case letters.

Once you get all of that completed, YouTube is going to ask you to sign in with a Google account because Google owns YouTube. If you don't already have a Google account they are painless to set up and YouTube will offer you a link to set one up if you don't have one. I highly recommend you set up a Google account just for your business. You'll be using it for your G+ account anyway!

Don't tie it to your personal account. In the world of business, keeping your business and personal activities separate is very important. Make sure you follow the steps to confirm your account. This is usually done with a confirmation text or email.

By now, you are a pro on setting up social media accounts. Setting up your YouTube account is very similar to the Facebook and Twitter accounts you already have. You are going to click the 'edit' button next to your profile section of your channel. Make sure that you fill out every field that applies to your business. Keep in mind that the information that you put in here will help people find you. Tell them what they can expect from your YouTube channel.

If you are a bricks and mortar business be sure to put in local information about your business.

Ignore the fields that ask for interest, about me, books and movies and the like if they don't apply to your business.

Customize

Above your channel are several buttons, one of which says settings. Click on that to create the right title for your company channel and make sure to add tags to help people find your channel. Click on the 'show advanced options' link to really customize the colour of your channel and upload a background image.

Note. Once again, if you don't have the graphical skills or staff to do this, there are tons of freelance designers/artists who can do this for you cheaply.

If you use the modules, you can create different items that show up on your profile such as Friends, Recent Activity and Subscribers. Again, just as in Facebook when you are thinking about those tabs, think about what you want people to see right away on your profile.

Add videos

The whole point of having a YouTube channel is to upload videos that help your brand. Let's say you don't currently have any videos of your own yet. You can look for other industry videos that are relevant to what you do and mark them as a favourite by clicking the 'add to' from the drop down menu under favourites.

Once you have a few, you can go to your Videos and Playlist setting and show your favourite videos as featured videos until you have created your own.

Promote your channel

Just as with all other social media platforms, you are not the only user. YouTube has millions upon millions of channels. Your channel needs to stand out in order to be found and seen. Add the YouTube icon to your website, take some time to browse other related channels and comment on their videos.

Using social media tools to promote your business is only one aspect of social media marketing: you will also need to promote the various other social media accounts you are using.

Major marketing trick alert. Where you can, embed your YouTube videos in your blogpost, Facebook pages and especially your G+ page (discussed next). This is all tracked by Google, and they will give it a higher rank in YouTube (and ultimately Google's search index itself) the more you can share it and the more it is then shared after that.

Google+

According to MediaPost, the Google search engine is used by 85 per cent of the global Internet users on a monthly basis. Using that domination on the Internet in late 2011, Google launched Google+ (G+), their new addition to the social media landscape. Unsurprisingly, by September 2012 G+ had more than 400 million registered users with 100 million active monthly users.

Even though only 25 per cent of G+ users are deemed active, I personally believe that G+ is the most under-appreciated social media platform out there at the moment and should be given top priority in your social media marketing strategy, regardless of whether you market to businesses or consumers (yes, even above Facebook).

Why? Two reasons:

● Google and G+ are 'open' systems and networks. It's relatively easy to syndicate your content from G+ to other places, including Facebook. It's extremely difficult to syndicate your content out of Facebook and Twitter.

● While it's true Facebook is the world's largest social network, G+ directly ties into the world's largest search engine at Google HQ (**1.72 trillion** searches a year).

First you will need to have set up a personal G+ profile. Once you have a personal account you can begin setting up your business account.

Simply visit the 'Create a Page' on G+ and follow the guided steps to get set up. You will need to pick from one of five categories:

Local Business or Place: this is any business or place that has a local address that customers can visit. If you pick this category Google will ask for your country and your phone number and if Google can locate you they will use the information they find tied to your phone number to populate your G+ profile. If not, you can add it all in yourself.

Product or Brand: this could be cars, electronics, clothing and financial services to name but a few. With this option you simply enter your website and page name and pick the category that best fits your product or service.

Institution, Company or Organization: this category includes pages for non-profit organizations, companies and institutions. For this option you would list your page name and website and just as you would with product or brand, pick a category that most closely matches the type of company.

Arts, Entertainment or Sports: if you are creating a page about a movie, book or sports team this is the category you would pick. Here again you will need to enter your page name and website as well as choose the category that most closely represents what you fit into.

Other: if by chance you don't feel that your company really fits into any of the above categories this is the option you would choose. This will allow you to enter in your page name and website without having to narrow it down further.

All of the above categories require that you state whether your page's content is appropriate for users that are 18 years

SUNDAY MONDAY TUESDAY WEDNESDAY THURSDAY FRIDAY SATURDAY

old and above or 21 years old and above and note if the content will specifically be alcohol related.

Customize

Do you notice a theme yet? It is important that you take the time to make your page on any social media platform noticeable because you are going to be competing against millions of others and you need to stand out.

Make sure that your profile includes a photo, your logo or the person that is the face of your business, or any other image that is relevant to what you do. Include your tagline. Once your customization is done, G+ will ask you to share your page through your personal G+ account. You can skip this step until you are completely done with your profile and have put content up.

Edit

This is where you are going to go through every possible item about your business and fill in the blanks for G+. We mean from the name of your company to the description of your company to your hours of operation.

Include your website URL and all contact info such as phone, email, Skype, any other messenger service you use and so on. You can also include the links to your other social media profiles.

Pinterest

On a personal level, this is a favourite! From a business perspective, if you can use Pinterest and use it correctly, you can beat every competitor you have because very few businesses are using Pinterest or taking advantage of the user base there yet.

So let's start with some interesting stats.

MediaPost states that 83 per cent of Pinterest users are female. In the United States the most popular categories are birthdays, fashion, desserts and clothes. Here is the really interesting information from MediaPost: 22 per cent of the 'pins' come from New York, 15 per cent come from Los Angeles and 10 per cent come from Minneapolis, which beats San Francisco with 8 per cent, even though Pinterest is based just down the road in Palo Alto.

Pooky Shares says that in the UK the most popular categories among users are blogging resources, venture capital, SEO/marketing, web analytics and crafts. Though Pinterest has barely been around for a year they tie with Twitter when it comes to the amount of traffic they refer to websites coming in at just under 4 per cent.

Not only that, but Pinterest drives more traffic than YouTube, Reddit, LinkedIn and G+ combined and is becoming a leading driver of traffic to retailers. But it's not only retailers who can take advantage of Pinterest's incredible growth and engagement; service businesses can also leverage Pinterest.

One example is Mr Rooter, an American plumbing franchise who are using Pinterest to create top-of-mind awareness for their company by publishing funny pictures of their action figures in different locations around the world as well as creating a DIY board showing people how to fix simple plumbing problems around the home.

Now let's discuss the really interesting part about Pinterest and why you need to include it in your marketing plan. It is an image-based social network that grew an incredible 4,000 per cent during 2011 with more than 4 million users, hitting 10 million monthly unique visitors faster than any other standalone website in Internet history.

Not only that, Pinterest users only rival LinkedIn users for buying power!

So not only does Pinterest keep all of those users engaged, they also **buy!** The average Pinterest user spends an hour or more per month on the site. So Pinterest still has a lot to grow but when it does, if it continues to keep its users engaged, it will be massive for your business even if you're selling B2B.

Let's get set up

Originally you needed to be invited to join Pinterest, now you can simply sign up. You can create an account with your business Facebook account or your business Twitter account. After signing up you can create your username. I recommend that you use the same username here that you have on Twitter or Facebook because you want to promote brand consistency. Follow topics that are pertinent to your business and complete the process by following your Twitter and Facebook users.

Build your boards

The beauty of Pinterest is that as soon as you 'pin' something to your board it directs people to the URL that is associated with the image. So if you are a business that has products to sell, create boards around those products. But don't let your products be the only thing you pin about because that is going to turn your followers off.

Get creative

Looking at a bunch of boards all about products is boring. Create boards based around what your target audience is interested in. So let's say you have a clothing line, or fashion is your niche, you can create boards based on colours, styles, attitudes and accessories.

Interact

It is social, so it isn't just about your own boards. Take a look at what other people are pinning and comment on the images. You could even create a board dedicated to things that complement what you offer. Kind of a pay it forward approach, which can go a long way in attracting new customers and building relationships with other companies.

Google Analytics

Google Analytics will help you keep track of how many of your pins are sending traffic to your website. This will help you determine what pins your followers are responding to so that you can tweak your boards and create new ones based on engagement.

Just log into your Google Account and then go to http://www.google.com/analytics to get yourself a free account.

StumbleUpon

This is a bookmarking social media tool. So unlike everything we have talked about so far, you're not going to create an account and build a profile page and invite all your connections to come and follow or like you.

StumbleUpon is an excellent tool to have in your social media marketing plan because it isn't based on your network. Instead it will generate a larger number of random hits because StumbleUpon is open to a broader audience (over 25 million registered users as of November 2012 according to their homepage).

So now let's get you ready to take advantage of this service.

The set-up is really simple and self-explanatory. All you need to do is go to http://www.stumbleupon.com, follow the guidelines StumbleUpon has for small businesses and in a few minutes you will be up and running.

Next, you will want to allow discovery of your webpage. The beauty of StumbleUpon is users can select the type of content they're interested in, so by categorizing your content correctly you will get targeted visitors to your pages. When someone visits a page on your website, via StumbleUpon, a small banner will be floating at the top of the browser window where the visitor can then 'thumbs up' or 'thumbs down' your content depending on whether they like it or not.

The more times you get a 'thumbs up' the more your content will be shown to other people who have also mentioned they are interested in that type of content in their user profile. This gives your content the ability to go viral very quickly providing it's excellent.

You don't have to just rely on StumbleUpon users to 'thumbs up' your content. Each webpage you promote with StumbleUpon gets a unique shortened URL which you can send to other followers and subscribers on other social media platforms where you can reach out to them and get them to 'thumbs up' your content using the floating banner at the top.

Note. Make sure you are creating unique content for your web page. The better the content, the more visitors and 'thumbs ups' you are going to get. StumbleUpon also makes a point to highlight original work. This means that content that you simply copied and pasted from another source is not original or unique.

Summary

Thursday was all about signing up with four other social media spots, including YouTube, the giant of video that will drive lots of relevant traffic to your site. As well as that, getting a Google+ account is also pretty necessary as it has a lot to do with SEO.

We also covered Pinterest, which is also a great place to reach women specifically (though more and more men are using it) visually, and the social tool StumbleUpon, which is great at broadening your base.

Be sure to put your keywords in your YouTube channel name if you can. Don't tie yourself to your personal account unless you want to make another personal account afterward. Be sure and keep things separate here (particularly with G+ and YouTube pretty much auto-connecting now): be aware this can happen to you.

Some further tips: promoting your videos and all of your blog posts on G+ will almost guarantee they will get indexed faster. Be sure to customize every page you get your hands on, just remember to keep a common

SUNDAY
MONDAY
TUESDAY
WEDNESDAY
THURSDAY
FRIDAY
SATURDAY

feel and logo through out. Every page should not be completely different.

Pinterest is great because you are probably already making images for Facebook, so why not post your images here as well? Remember to interact and post images from others as well as comment, and target your images at your general market and age.

StumbleUpon is a great tool to use to get traffic to your various properties, but don't just recommend your stuff. To use this right keep it open whenever you surf the web and be sure and highlight cool posts wherever you find them. This way, your posts of your content will never get flagged as spam.

Questions (answers at the back)

1. YouTube is all about:
   a) Audio files ☐
   b) Videos ☐
   c) Music ☐
   d) All of the above to a greater and lesser extent ☐

2. YouTube likes it when you post their videos around your various other platforms (even their competitors as long as they get a link back).
   a) True ☐
   b) False ☐

3. Google+ is mostly populated by:
   a) Males ☐
   b) Females ☐
   c) Both ☐
   d) Unknown ☐

4. This is probably because:
   a) It makes business sense to be here ☐
   b) Men just are cool like that (oops did I give away the answer to the question...?) ☐
   c) They are experimenting ☐
   d) All of the above (though possibly not B) ☐

5. Pinterest is unique in that:
   a) It is all about images ☐
   b) It keeps its users engaged ☐
   c) Almost 25 per cent of its users are from NY ☐
   d) All of the above ☐

6. Pinterest is populated by mostly:
   a) Men ☐
   b) Women ☐
   c) Both ☐
   d) Unknown ☐

7. The best way to get followers is to:
   a) Interact ☐
   b) Interact a lot ☐
   c) Interact more than others ☐
   d) Interact only with people you like ☐

8. StumbleUpon is:
   a) A way to get your website in front of a broader audience ☐
   b) A rock you can trip on ☐
   c) A service which can drive lots of targeted traffic ☐
   d) Both A and C ☐

9. Who should you get to 'thumbs up' your content on StumbleUpon?:
   a) Anybody on StumbleUpon – it really doesn't matter ☐
   b) SU users who are interested in your type of content ☐
   c) Your subscribers and followers on your other social media accounts ☐
   d) Both B and C ☐

10. StumbleUpon could be the only source of traffic you need:
    a) True ☐
    b) False ☐

FRIDAY

Phase three: quality content creation

All right after today we only have one more day until you are ready to really get going on social media marketing. How time flies! Today we are talking in depth about content.

Content is the key to any marketing success and amazingly your greatest source of content topic ideas is your target audience. All you need to do is pay attention to what they are looking for and asking about and then deliver the content that meets their needs.

This is usually the part of marketing where we hear the biggest sigh, because writing is one of people's least favourite things to do. The good news is that you always have a few options when getting quality content created for your social media platforms.

Before we dive into your content creation options, let's do a very quick recap of what we have gone over to date.

- You know what social media is.
- You know what social media marketing is.
- We have gone over examples of how big and small businesses have used social media marketing successfully.
- You know what needs to go into a successful social media marketing campaign.
- You know the basic foundation that you need to have to build a social media marketing campaign.
- You know what not to do.
- You know the 'big eight' in the world of social media marketing and how to set up your accounts.

Content curation

The latest buzz in the marketing world when we are talking about creating good content is content curation. Unfortunately many businesses (big and small) don't understand what content curation is **or** how to use it to help with branding.

To help make this as easy as possible, let's define what content curation actually is.

Content curation is when a publisher collects the best content related to a very specific niche and targeted to a particular audience then embellishes that content through the addition of personal expertise and opinions. This embellished content provides increased value to that particular audience who reads it once it is published.

You may be sitting there wondering how content curation is different from any other form of content copying. The difference is that this content is:

- editorially selected
- provides added value
- embellished.

It is more than just regurgitating content that is already out there. The key is to retell the story with your personal slant to it. You must focus on the human element and always increase the value of what you are sharing in your content curation.

With that being said, let's take a look at how, based on a few of the social media platforms we have talked about, you can use content curation to your advantage.

Pinterest

The success of Pinterest in such a short amount of time is evidence that content curation works and that it is one of the hottest activities online right now. You should already have your account set up and we have already talked about creating boards.

Use Pinterest to tell the story of your brand to your followers. Don't just upload your own images; repin other user's pins so that your audience has a more cinematic experience with your brand. There is an old saying that a picture is worth a thousand words. Find those images that show your followers who your company is and what makes you stand out. Stick to these three principles:

1 **Authenticity:** you can't tell a story with images if you don't first have the story in words. Take the time to create your story. What brought your company into being?
2 **Consistency:** remember the human element (i.e. everything must be in order and make sense with your story) and the key difference between content curation and typical content aggregation (this is usually where a computer or a person who doesn't care just copies a bunch of slightly related material and puts it up hoping people find it). Make sure the images you use have a personal tie to your brand, your company's story and your personality.
3 **Fresh and pinnable content:** generally speaking, most brand engagement that takes place on Pinterest is tied to the company website. To encourage users to pin your content, add a Pinterest button to your website and a 'Pin It' button so that it is super easy for people to pin your content.

An online magazine

There are a few free content curation tools on the market that make it fairly easy to create your own online magazine that focuses on your niche or a topic of your choice. If you opt to do this, make sure that the content you are using is content that your audience is interested in. Remember they need to find value in the content or it isn't going to be read.

You can use paper.li, storify.com or scoop.it to make it simple to editorially pick content for your mag. Make sure that your content tells a story and gives your reader an 'experience'. Think about it like this. Disney created those attractions where you get to sit and watch a movie or a play and they make it 4D so that most of your your senses are engaged: sight, touch, sound, and smell. At the end of the day this is content curation as well.

While your content can't be scratch and sniff, it can be written well enough to make your reader feel like they are part of it.

Blog curation

One of the best examples of how to effectively use content curation on your blog is to take a look at what The Daily Beast (http://www.thedailybeast.com) does. They take some of the best content on the web and put it on their blog and allow writers to give their 'two cents' on the content. So it isn't that they are just keeping a log of comments at the end of the blog post, but writers take the content and interject their own thoughts and feelings into the piece.

You can also curate the content on your blog and then include individual posts throughout the day about that content. Each post that is added that day will provide additional commentary on the original piece, or you can give your readers an expert review/analysis of the content to add that extra value.

There are tools you can use that are free such as SocialMention (http://socialmention.com) or Google Alerts (http://google.com/alerts).

Email marketing curation

Creating an email newsletter is an easy and effective way to curate content and share useful information with your list. Here you can use content that you have already created for other reasons or you can use content that others have created.

Again, there are a number of really great tools that you can use to make the process easier. There is a tool that XYDO (http://xydocuration.com) offers that will help curate content for your email marketing and it gives the click-through rate a boost.

Top-quality content

Never compromise on quality. Often small businesses take shortcuts on marketing because they feel that once they have the flow going saving a bit of money or a couple of hours' worth of work won't affect profitability over the long haul. OK, the first time it may not, but the second and third time it is going to cost you customers.

How many times have you, or someone you know, said, 'Well so and so didn't use to do things this way' or 'I remember when I really enjoyed it here but now it just feels so blah'.

These are the feelings you generate when you deliver sub-par content and it will cost you customers. The content you put out should always be the very best you can do. When curating content is done, make sure that the original content is valid and that it matches your business and your brand. You may find it costs as much time to do that right as it does to come up with original content itself. Either way it is worth it.

Original content

I almost hate to even have to talk about why it is important to have original content, but just as social media has done wonders for connecting people everywhere it has a downside as well: content is copied and pasted and claimed as being the work of the person 'borrowing' it.

Nothing is more likely to cause me to immediately click off and ignore a website forever than when that website or company tries to use the work of someone else and claim it as their own.

Every second of every minute you have spent creating a killer social media marketing plan (or any marketing plan) will go down the drain the moment you start posting content that is duplicated from others. The search engines don't like it and will punish you severely for it and your customers won't like it either. The search engines will consider your site spam and your customers will consider you a fake.

It doesn't take much to write original content. Chances are pretty good that the business you are starting or running is a business that you are passionate about. Something made you start it, what was it?

Why is it an area you went into? Tell your customers why you started your business. Tell them why you are passionate about your service or your product. Tell them why they, the customer, matter to you.

You don't have to write a book a day. For most of the social media platforms we have talked about you only need a few sentences at a time to get a conversation going and have your followers respond.

If you really don't want to write the content yourself and you don't have a writer on staff, hire a freelance writer. You can find them on Craigslist, oDesk, eLance and a dozen other freelance websites. When you hire a writer there are a few things you want to look for and pay attention to:

Experience: they don't have to be professional writers for *The Times* or *The Washington Post*, but you do want to know they have written the type of content you are looking for before.

Native speakers: I am a firm believer in the fact that if you can't speak the language you can't write it convincingly, especially British and American English. Your writer needs to be able to speak to your audience convincingly to sell your brand.

Social media experience: we are talking about social media here, so I want to focus on looking for someone that understands how social media works because the content is a little different from basic web content. This content has to be monitored and responded to, and it **must** engage the reader.

It is up to you if you sign a contract with the writer or work through a service like the ones I mention above. You will want to proof the content and run it through copyscape.com because remember, in the end, it is your name and your company that is on that writing.

Another pet peeve of mine is reading poorly written content. It insults your readers and it tells them that you really don't care about them because if you can't take the time to write informative content that is written in the proper form, why would you care about an issue they may have with your product or service?

 Top tip
To quickly double-check spellings and grammar before posting to your website, blog or social media account, copy and paste the content into Microsoft Word and hit F7 and Shift-F7.

Summary

Friday is here, and it was all about delivering great content to your subscribers via your blog, and Facebook posts, etc.

I described the latest fad (which is pretty cool and useful) called content curation. This is where you take other great content and inject a lot of yourself into it and embellish it a lot to make it almost a totally new piece of valuable content for your audience; this could be explaining a survey or simply explaining a really cool news item in your niche.

Pinterest shows us how content creation can work for images and videos. Definitely spend a bunch of time browsing through this place and thinking how you could do the same.

Tools for content curation include socialmention.com and Google alerts. Use them well and use them often! There are many uses for these two tools.

Nothing, and I mean nothing, really beats awesome quality original content that only you can create with your unique personality. Show your passion and zeal and let me tell you the search engines and people will find

SUNDAY
MONDAY
TUESDAY
WEDNESDAY
THURSDAY
FRIDAY
SATURDAY

you. It may take some time, but they will find you.

If you have to hire outside writers, be sure and follow the guidelines and be sure to check if it is fun, interesting and relevant before you post it, and never post something that you copy from someone else without acknowledging them as the original author.

Questions (answers at the back)

1. Content curation is:
a) Copy and pasting content and having people comment on it ❏
b) Editorially chosen, well embellished material that fits in with your brand where you acknowledge the original author ❏
c) Content that has been gone through with a comb ❏
d) What museums do ❏

2. The website that shows that content curation can work well is:
a) Pinterest ❏
b) Craigslist ❏
c) oDesk ❏
d) Facebook ❏

3. Another way to curate content and add value to it is:
a) Create a website based on it ❏
b) Make every page of your website about it ❏
c) Create an online magazine ❏
d) Phone a friend and tell them about it ❏

4. To see blog curation done well, go to:
a) The Globe Weekly ❏
b) The Star ❏
c) The tabloids ❏
d) The Daily Beast ❏

5. Email marketing curation is another nice way that customers would like to get content:
a) True ❏
b) False ❏

6. Your content should always be:
a) Just enough to get by ❏
b) Incredibly top notch all the time ❏
c) Hit and miss ❏
d) So-so (You are working on it, you can say...) ❏

7. A key to quality content is:
a) Knowledge ❏
b) Work ❏
c) Passion ❏
d) Intelligence ❏

8. Make sure if you hire writers that they have:
a) Skills in your market's first language ❏
b) Experience in writing about similar topics as your business ❏
c) Experience in social media ❏
d) All of the above ❏

9. A way to check content for duplication is:
a) Copyscape ❏
b) Spam Buster Plus ❏
c) Google ❏
d) Yahoo ❏

10. No matter what you do, do this:
a) Try to trick your audience into buying ❏
b) Create a good user experience ❏
c) Enjoy yourself whether the audience enjoys it or not ❏
d) Use others content and put your name on it ❏

SATURDAY

Managing, metrics and scaling up

Today I am going to just jump right into what you need to know and we will do a recap of the week at the end. There are quite a few things to cover and as we all know, time is precious at the weekend.

It is important to both monitor and measure your social media marketing efforts, but as with creating the marketing campaign, you also need to create a plan for measuring and monitoring.

SUNDAY

MONDAY

TUESDAY

WEDNESDAY

THURSDAY

FRIDAY

SATURDAY

Define your objective

In other words, why are you monitoring your efforts? There needs to be a very clear goal as to why you are putting in this extra effort.

Why will you monitor?

Here are a few possible objectives:

- I will monitor my social media marketing because I want to be alerted immediately when people are talking about me (negatively or positively).
- I will monitor because I want to be able to respond to my customers' questions/concerns quickly.
- I want to set up a system of information exchange with a support team so issues are handled seamlessly.
- I will monitor so I can join conversations quickly when people are talking about [keyword] so that I can enhance my credibility.

Where will you monitor?

Remember that we talked about social media being a two-way street? It is all about conversation. The heart of social media is to build relationships with your customers. But it is impossible to be on every social platform all the time or all at the same time... or is it?

There are fabulous tools like HootSuite or HubSpot that let you pull in all of your social networks and monitor and respond from one single dashboard. This allows you to see what is being said on your accounts at the same time and you can write a quick post and with a few clicks post new comments to one, two or all of your social networks at the same time.

Don't overuse this though because it shows up on your updates that you are using a service and some people don't like that because it looks like you just want to save time and not really spend time with them as a person (yes, it is silly but very real).

What will you monitor?

Monitoring is keyword based which means doing keyword research and choosing the right keywords is important.

There are the obvious words to monitor such as your name, the name of your company, your brand, your products and the names of other key players in your organization.

Prioritize your monitoring

There are just so many social media platforms on the web that you really don't need to monitor all of them. Decide what sources are most important to you and your customers and monitor those platforms. If you have a team, you can also monitor the platforms we will call fringe platforms (the ones where they may talk about you but not really where your target hangs out). A way to do this is just to use Google Alerts as we talked about earlier for picking up new content with your company name or about individuals in your organization.

Plan your monitoring

OK, so you are monitoring what people are saying about you, your company and your products. We all hope that it is all good that is being said, but what happens when there is a problem? How will you handle it effectively and in a timely manner? Remember that we said you don't always have to remove negative comments: they can offer the chance for you to show your customers your willingness to work things out. If you can't fix the issue, then remove the comments.

Sometimes you can't remove it though i.e. in the case of some of the local feedback. In this case, try to overwhelm the negative comments by emailing your list of customers and asking for positive reviews on the website that has a negative review.

Likewise, when people are saying good things about you, how do you show your appreciation?

Think about blogger feedback, customer advocacy programmes and possible joint ventures to improve branding for both partners. You need to think about all of the possible scenarios that social media marketing will open up to you and have a plan for handling them all appropriately.

Involvement of others

Let's face it, social media is a bigger, badder beast than anything else we have ever seen. Therein is the challenge. You may need a team to help you address the 'faster than the speed of light' tweet that just came out. How you handle this really depends on whether it is on you or if you have a team.

Frankly, I recommend pulling in at least one freelancer to help you stay on top of what is going on if you are a one-man/woman show. You really don't want to leave tweets, posts, updates, comments or feedback sitting there until next week. It is always best to respond within 24 hours.

Listen to your target audience

Hopefully in the course of your monitoring efforts you have come across one place that seems to be the place where you can get the most information about your industry or your target audience. Don't just create an account and start jumping into the conversation talking about your product.

Listen to what is going on, listen to what is being said, pay attention to the problem that is being talked about. Once you figure out the dialogue, the jargon they are using, the interaction among members, slowly start to get involved. Offer advice on how to solve a problem that you see people discussing. You need to establish yourself as someone who knows what they are talking about before you start pushing your products.

Inbound vs. outbound conversations

Outbound conversation refers to you proactively getting involved in conversations that are taking place out in the market place that focus on your area of expertise. Inbound refers to the conversations that people are having specifically with you.

When you are a part of a large discussion you don't want to put links to your website or your product demo. However, if someone approaches you directly it is acceptable to provide them with a demo or a link to your website. It is important to know the difference and pay attention to the rules of engagement for each type.

Relationship building

Once you have identified a few spheres of influence, it is time to look for ways to build relationships with those spheres. In any conversation that is taking place it is fairly easy to figure out who is driving the conversation.

Do not, however, just look at these thought leaders as nothing more than connections. You need to get to know them, understand where they are coming from and understand who they are before you make a pitch to them. One-night stands don't last for a reason. In the professional world you want to build relationships with those who have influence, that are going to last and that are mutually beneficial to both of you.

Tools of the trade

You need to select monitoring tools that fit/work with the social media platforms you are using. Make a list of what you need the monitoring tool to do and do the research to find the one that is going to work the way you need it to.

Taking it to the next level

Once you find what social media platforms work for you, it is time to take a look at how to expand. What can you do to pick it up a notch so that your social media presence is really on fire? That is really going to depend on the platforms you are using. I am going to list a few different platforms and provide you with three ways to ramp them up.

Blogs

Update your blog frequently! I recommend two to three times a week though other sources may tell you once a week. Just make sure it is more than once a month.

Post your blog post URL to your social profiles multiple times; use a tool like buffer.com that will post your link multiple times as it is fairly easy to have a post get buried by the stream.

Include social share icons at the top and bottom of your page. Why? Because some people like to share as soon as they land on your page while others share once they are done reading. Always make the share buttons easy to find and always encourage their use by mentioning them and even have pointing arrows at them if you can.

Facebook

Offer unique and free products available only to your Facebook followers. After all, who doesn't love free stuff, and you want to remind them that there is a reason to continue to follow you on Facebook.

Create a consistent visual brand on your page. You can customize your profile pic, your cover pic and the icons associated with the different apps on your page. Use them to reinforce who you are.

Encourage your fans to make sure they see your updates. Seems silly to even point it out, because if they aren't seeing your posts you may think this is a waste of time. However, due to the fact that Facebook is ever changing, just because someone liked your page in the past does not mean they are seeing every update you have. They need to follow these steps to make sure they see all of your posts (http://alwaysupward. com/blog/fb-fans-arent-seeing-your-posts-and-how-to-fix-it/).

Twitter

Make sure you have a username they will remember. Now it must meet Twitter character limits and be available, but you want a name that they will remember that represents your brand.

Split test your bio: routinely change your bio on Twitter and keep track of the number of new subscribers that you get with each bio. It can and will change!

Follow users that follow experts in your industry: do this to find new followers as well as to give your perceived authority a boost because what will happen is many of those people you start following will follow you back. Don't just follow though; also involve these leaders in your conversations and specifically tag them in some posts.

Google+

Take advantage of the enhanced video and image galleries: it is Google after all, and they do have the coolest media features out there so use them to your fullest advantage!

Post on a regular basis even if you are the only one doing it. G+ will eventually explode due to the reasons I mentioned before. Don't stop or slow down just because you are the only one doing it. This is one place where being the pioneer in your industry will pay off.

Host G+ Hangouts on air with YouTube; give your company's YouTube channel a nice boost by creating a G+ hangout with your followers and customers. Keep in mind that right now videos are ranking really well and take advantage of that.

LinkedIn

Make sure you pay close attention to the SEO keyword when you are working on your company profile. You want your profile to be available to those who are looking for companies or individuals with your expertise.

Join the LinkedIn groups that are pertinent to your niche. After all, how can you be an industry expert if you aren't engaged in groups that focus on what you do and interact with the people you want to connect with.

Start your own group if you can't find a group on LinkedIn that addresses your niche or your service/product.

Pinterest

Go after the micro-demographics. It is true that overall Pinterest is primarily populated by young to middle-aged females but you can look for subgroups within that demographic to appeal to. Like mothers who work from home and have small children or the twenty-somethings who are ready to get married for the first time.

Create themed boards based on industry trends. The board topics need to be narrow and monitoring industry trends offers you a great number of ideas to work with.

Take advantage of all three Pinterest linking channels: each pin offers you three chances to link the pin back to your website.

Summary

The last day of this week. Bittersweet. But today, we learned how to monitor and measure your social media program.

Be sure to define your reason for monitoring and what you are looking for. Then define where you are looking and use hootsuite. com or Hub Spot to really be able to see what is being said to you from everywhere you are involved from one screen.

Be sure to monitor at least your keywords, such as your name, the name of your company, your brand, your products and the names of other key players in your organization. Be sure and spend some time thinking on this section, as you might think of more.

After choosing where you will watch all the time, plan exactly what you will do when something bad happens. Will you personally get involved? Or do you have someone else that has a way with words that can do better?

Most of all, this day I hope you learn to really listen. Don't just sell all the time, but watch the conversations and the tones of them and the questions being said and how they are

SUNDAY
MONDAY
TUESDAY
WEDNESDAY
THURSDAY
FRIDAY
SATURDAY

answered, and so on. This way, when you start broadcasting and getting involved you will already have a good idea as to what is effective where you are.

Bookmark and highlight the things you learned in the 'taking it to the next level' section today. Get all your accounts up and running, start to get fans and content moving, then come back to revisit these now that you have experience: they will make so much more sense to you.

Questions (answers at the back)

1. First, you need to:
   a) Get started monitoring ☐
   b) Monitor for everything ☐
   c) Check all of the social platforms at once ☐
   d) Define what you are monitoring for ☐

2. Monitoring is:
   a) Hard ☐
   b) Easy ☐
   c) Keyword based ☐
   d) Needs to be focused ☐

3. If you can't remove bad feedback what do you do?
   a) Give up and go home ☐
   b) Find the person who made the comment and beg them to remove it ☐
   c) Learn from it and move on ☐
   d) Overwhelm it by emailing your happy list of customers ☐

4. It is probably not good:
   a) To go it alone ☐
   b) To try to do everything yourself ☐
   c) To not have a team ☐
   d) All of the above ☐

5. Hootsuite:
   a) Helps with searching Google ☐
   b) Keeps track of all your social accounts ☐
   c) Responds to all your accounts ☐
   d) Both B and C ☐

6. When dealing with other leaders in your industry:
   a) You should ask to partner with them first thing ☐
   b) Learn as much about them as possible before approaching them ☐
   c) Keep sending them messages until they respond ☐
   d) Just friend them and wait for them to contact you ☐

7. You should blog:
   a) As much as possible ☐
   b) Once a month ☐
   c) Four times a month ☐
   d) At least two or three times a week ideally ☐

8. You need to treat your Facebook followers:
   a) The same as everyone else ☐
   b) Specially: you should give them special sales/services to make it worth following you there ☐
   c) Worse than the rest ☐
   d) Indifferently: you need to just post stuff through Hootsuite not directly interact with them. ☐

9. LinkedIn profiles should be keyword-rich so it is easier for your potential clients to find you.
   a) True ☐
   b) False ☐

10. On Pinterest you should going for:

a) The masses   ❏
b) The individual   ❏
c) Men   ❏
d) Micro-markets of the female gender   ❏

WEEK 4

**Public Relations
In A Week**

Introduction

'If a boy meets a girl and impresses upon her how wonderful he is... that's Advertising.'

'If, instead, he tells her how lovely she looks, how much she means to him and how much he cares for her... that's Sales Promotion.'

'But if the girl seeks him out because she has heard from others what a splendid fellow he is... that's Public Relations!'

I remember going to a PR conference in the UK once where one of the speakers flashed up this 'definition' of PR on the screen. We all laughed, but, despite our different backgrounds, we could all identify with his theme.

Public relations is the practice of conveying messages to the public with the intention of changing the public's actions by influencing their opinions. By targeting different audiences with different messages to achieve an overall goal, PR practitioners can achieve widespread opinion and behavioural change.

Communications is seen as being a key element in business, with PR experts increasingly called on to advise senior management on appropriate communications strategies, *before* decisions are made, rather than being called on to defend them *after* they have been made.

But PR is not just for self-conscious organizations. If you are looking for a job or an in-house promotion; or if you are trying to publicize a fundraiser for your local charity; if you're trying to advance a cause, or you want others to appreciate your point of view, you need your voice to be heard.

Similarly, politicians of all parties work with PR experts not only to promote their point of view but, at the most basic level, to help them get re-elected!

Even royal families around the world employ PR experts to massage their image for the general public, as do film and pop stars, sports personalities, broadcasters – and, for that matter, anyone in the public eye.

Nowadays there is a veritable plethora of communication channels available, ranging from traditional newspapers and magazines to online outlets including ezines, social networking sites and blogs. Some of these are good in some situations, but hopeless in others.

Throughout this week we will therefore be concentrating on how we can effect the flow of information and how we can achieve the desired mindset change in our target audiences.

SUNDAY

Who needs PR?

PR – or public relations – is all about getting people to talk about your business in a positive way. Increasingly, companies throughout the world are building links with their various target groups so that they are regarded in a better light by their customers, suppliers and industry regulators.

To a certain degree, PR follows the same principles for small companies as for big organizations – it's just a matter of scale. Even the smallest business can use publicity to broaden its customer base and improve the sales climate for its products.

Significantly, too, many in-house communications departments have matured to a point where they are being asked to drive through significant internal cultural change programmes, in place of – or certainly hand-in-hand with – the human resources or marketing departments.

When it comes down to it, PR is all about communication. It means talking to your stakeholders, whether they are your suppliers, customers... or even your own staff.

Today we will look at the nature of PR, and especially:

- the key role played by communication, including language
- how changing perceptions is the bread-and-butter business of PR
- the importance of the who, what, why and how.

Looking after a company's public image

Public relations is all about human relations – the psychology of interrelating with your different audiences – and a critical aspect of growing any business. Everything you say and do is part of your PR campaign. It is the image you project every day to everyone you meet. It is about you and your company becoming a force in the public eye on a regular basis.

Overall, PR is just one part of the overall marketing mix. It is likely you will also be undertaking other activities such as maintaining a website, getting testimonials and product feedback, sending out newsletters, direct email campaigns, possibly even advertising, and so on.

But, unlike advertising, editorial is usually free and regarded as independent, and therefore more likely to be credible. And many companies have learned that a bit of free editorial is worth many times that amount of space in advertising.

As well as raising awareness of your brand, PR can also be used to educate your target audiences about your position within your particular industry, ultimately (you hope) generating more enquiries and sales leads, as well as traffic to your website and/or shop.

PR can cover a host of activities, such as:

- press releases
- appearances in news stories
- company profiles
- opinion articles
- quotes in features
- product reviews
- case studies
- blog posts
- social media postings
- audio and video clips such as podcasts and video casts
- advertorials
- competitions.

PR is not difficult – it's just about common sense (except, as they say, common sense is anything but common!). However, it is time-consuming and you do need to prepare yourself first.

TIP PR is, to put it simply, all about communicating your ideas and values to your target audiences.

Communication

What do we actually mean by communication?

There doesn't appear to be one definition accepted by everybody. It is one of those grand-sounding words which can mean everything and nothing at one and the same time. All businesses need to communicate with their employees if they want the best out of them; with suppliers if they want the right raw materials at the best price; with shareholders if they want to keep them on their side; with customers if they want to

SUNDAY

MONDAY

TUESDAY

WEDNESDAY

THURSDAY

FRIDAY

SATURDAY

make any profit at all, and with the community at large, since no one – let alone any company – can act totally unaffected by those who surround them.

TIP *Without exception, communication lies at the heart of every successful – and unsuccessful – business.*

Successful communication applies as much to manufacturing industries as it does to service sector or public sector organizations. Everyone is involved in one way or another, but the problem is that few people are taught to communicate in a manner that is suitable for business.

In social communication – especially now in this Internet age – we can afford to be sloppy in what we say since, in general, both parties know one another and understand that things left unsaid can be taken as read. However, in a business environment, communication has to be clear, precise and unambiguous and, if you want to avoid misunderstandings at some later date, it needs to be formal in nature and planned carefully.

SUNDAY

MONDAY

TUESDAY

WEDNESDAY

THURSDAY

FRIDAY

SATURDAY

A two-way process

Communication – whether it involves organizations, individuals or groups of individuals – requires a minimum of two parties. Although one party may be the initial sender of a message and the other the initial receiver, both sides need to take on both roles if successful communication is to occur. This is because feedback – even if only a nod of the head – is essential if the sender is to get confirmation that a transaction has been completed.

Types of communication

The ideas communicated can be **verbal** or **graphical** – verbal encompasses any message that is spoken, written or emailed, for instance, while graphical refers to a message that can be encapsulated as a visual image. (After all, we are always being told that a picture can paint a thousand words!)

Although these **direct channels** are essential elements of communication, there are a number of other **indirect channels** that many businesses ignore, but which can be a major source of poor communication if handled improperly. Think of the importance of body language, for instance. We are all very quick to make instant judgements of people by the way they look or the body signals they give off.

Someone who is unable to keep eye contact and is always looking away from you is likely to be giving off indirect signals that he or she is untrustworthy or certainly not someone you can rely upon, even if the real reason is shyness.

Barriers to communication

Communication can also be prevented or minimized by interference that stops a message from getting through. Extraneous noise, be it someone playing a trumpet in a neighbouring apartment, or someone's ghetto blaster turned up too high, can often divert the receiver's attention from the real message getting through.

However, interference in the form of **preconceptions** on the part of the receiver can also play a major role in a lack of comprehension. If your customers don't trust you as a company because of something they may have heard about you, then it may not matter what you say to them because everything you do say will be treated with cynicism or simply not believed.

Barriers can exist in many different forms, but the effect is the same: core messages are either hindered or stopped altogether from getting through.

The key role of language

Ever since humans set foot on this earth, language has been at the heart of communication. Even babies, who have not yet learned to talk, can still communicate. When they are hungry or unwell or uncomfortable they cry and their carer soon understands that they want feeding or changing, or whatever else they need. It might take the worried parent a while to work out what the problem is, but there is still a communication there, of sorts.

Early humans also expressed their feelings and experiences without using words. Using facial expressions and their hands, they could communicate using body language – something we are still good at today, often subconsciously.

As we developed language skills, people used words to convey what they were feeling. With alphabets, writing gave yet another powerful boost to convey thoughts, ideas and feelings.

Nonetheless, most of us don't have to think very long to come up with names of people we know who are anything but good communicators. There are several reasons for this and some may not always be correctable.

In many parts of the world, most notably in the Middle East and South-East Asia, there is a plethora of foreign expatriate workers who do not communicate using their mother tongue, and of necessity this leads to the use of inappropriate tenses, declensions and conjugations, not to mention the strong regional accents or differences in the use of language on a regional basis. (It is said, for instance, that Mao Zedong could not be understood by many of his audience in Beijing when he declared the new People's Republic of China in front of the Forbidden City, as his Hunan accent was difficult for northern Chinese to understand!)

Yet, despite these apparent drawbacks, it is amazing how well people can communicate with one another even when there is a lack of a common language.

Changing perceptions

PR practitioners work with facts, perception and truth every day. It's what we do for a living. As practitioners, we talk almost casually about changing perceptions – but what does that really mean?

Perception is the process by which humans collect information and a basis for how humans see things. When we talk about changing perceptions, what we actually mean are two things:

1 changing individuals' ways of perceiving
2 changing their understanding and opinions.

This is important to remember because it is easy to ignore one part or the other. PR has two functions – education and persuasion. **Education** seeks to change the way someone perceives an event and **persuasion** seeks to change how the individual interprets facts that have been perceived.

One can have knowledge of a subject and a separate opinion about it that may or may not relate to that knowledge. Knowledge leads to understanding. Opinion is judgement, or a formed conclusion.

There are two basic states of understanding – good or poor. But we can identify *three* possible types of opinion – good, bad or neutral. If the individual is on our side and knows us well, good PR can reinforce his or her understanding and opinion. If the individual knows us well and can't stand us, we try to rebut the person's negative comments about us. If the individual doesn't know us well, but thinks highly of us, we educate that person about us and reinforce the good opinion – and so on.

The who, what, why and how

All organizations need to communicate with a number of **different audiences**, and sometimes what they say to one will not necessarily be the same as what they wish to say to another. Likewise, what feedback they solicit from one may not be what they solicit or receive from another. External audiences, for instance, may be given a slightly glossier picture of the fortunes of a company than those within the organization. There will almost certainly be those, too, who will need to be 'in the know' with regard to any bad news or commercially sensitive information, and so getting to know your audiences has to be a key consideration in any PR campaign.

There is a very fine dividing line between showing something in a good light and giving misleading information.

Just as important as identifying the key audiences that you wish to reach and communicate with is knowing what it is you want to communicate and why you are trying to say it in the first place.

If that sounds like simply stating the obvious, then consider how many organizations tend to 'open their mouths before putting their brains into gear'. This week we will be looking at some of the things you may wish to be communicating with your audiences since communications can only really be viewed in a holistic way; otherwise one could argue that the whole exercise has been a waste of time.

Finally, knowing what it is you want to communicate is only half the story. So over the coming week we will also be concentrating on how the flow of information can be effected.

Summary

Today we have seen that the art of public relations is all about the skills of persuasion and of either changing or reinforcing mindsets in order to achieve a particular outcome.

Quite apart from all the other skills needed in carrying out our PR work, the core of good PR comes down to communicating our messages in the most appropriate and accessible ways to our target audiences.

This communication does not just incorporate the verbal messages we give out. The way we behave and conduct ourselves will play a major role in the fortunes of our business.

The way we give out our messages, together with the way we target who are the recipients of these messages, will also play a major role in how well our business performs.

In short, it is no exaggeration to claim that the role that PR plays can be a decisive factor in whether our business is ultimately successful or not!

SUNDAY

MONDAY

TUESDAY

WEDNESDAY

THURSDAY

FRIDAY

SATURDAY

Questions (answers at the back)

1. Company communications should be primarily focused on talking to...
   a) Your customers ❏
   b) Your suppliers ❏
   c) Your staff ❏
   d) Anyone who has something to do with your company ❏

2. Internal cultural change programmes should be led by...
   a) The PR department ❏
   b) The HR department ❏
   c) The marketing department ❏
   d) All three together ❏

3. The PR function is primarily to do with...
   a) Maintaining a relationship with the media ❏
   b) Sending out newsletters, press releases and direct mail ❏
   c) Being responsible for the company website ❏
   d) All of the above ❏

4. When comparing coverage of your brand or products...
   a) Editorial coverage is far superior in value to advertising ❏
   b) Editorial coverage carries more credibility than advertising ❏
   c) Editorial coverage offers better value than advertising and is also far more credible ❏
   d) None of the above ❏

5. Which of the following is *not* true?
   a) Communication requires a minimum of two parties ❏
   b) Someone who will not look you in the eye is likely to be untrustworthy ❏
   c) Good communication can be affected by body language ❏
   d) Communication can be verbal or graphical ❏

6. When we talk about changing people's perceptions, what we really mean is...
   a) Changing the way they gather facts ❏
   b) Changing their opinions ❏
   c) Changing their understanding ❏
   d) All of the above ❏

7. In PR terms, it is normally appropriate for external audiences...
   a) To be given only good news about a company ❏
   b) To be told the bad news along with the good to gain credibility ❏
   c) To be given exactly the same information as told to staff ❏
   d) To be given a glossier interpretation of the facts than is given to employees ❏

8. PR is only useful...
a) To large organizations or companies who want to increase market share ❏
b) To small companies who want to broaden their customer base ❏
c) For changing public perception of a company, not of its products ❏
d) None of the above ❏

9. Which of these statements is true?
a) Good communication is not possible between two people who do not have a common language ❏
b) Emailed communications are dangerous because they can be ambiguous ❏
c) SMS should never be used for important communications ❏
d) None of the above ❏

10. If we want to change perceptions, we need to...
a) Change the way people learn about new facts ❏
b) Change people's opinions ❏
c) Educate someone so he/she knows something he/she didn't know before ❏
d) All of the above ❏

SUNDAY

MONDAY

TUESDAY

WEDNESDAY

THURSDAY

FRIDAY

SATURDAY

MONDAY

External audiences

We have seen that PR is intimately wrapped up with the way you communicate with your stakeholders: your key publics and your target groups – the people who will receive your communications.

Consider for a moment this list of products and services together with their primary stakeholders:

- hospitals: patients
- stores: customers
- schools: students
- radio: listeners
- airlines: passengers.

In this list, you will see that the target group or public that a hospital has to focus its communications on are its patients. In the same way, stores need to communicate with their customers, schools with their students (and parents!) and so on.

Understanding what drives stakeholders' desires and needs is an important skill in PR, which is all about winning the support of the public by addressing their wants, interests and needs rather than your own. In essence, it is all about psychology.

Today we will be looking at:

- how to promote your company's products and services to the outside world
- how to create a positive image of your company as a whole
- extending PR beyond customers and clients to, for instance, suppliers, financial analysts and government.

First things first

When planning an external PR strategy, your first job is to identify all your audiences before you can even begin to think about what it is you wish to get across to them. Not all of those intended recipients will want the same information, or even require it in the same format. So, to begin with, you need to work out in very simple terms...

- what you are trying to say
- why you want to say it in the first place
- to whom you wish to talk.

How are you going to get your message across?

Many people are so anxious to get talking that they often don't think through what it is that the potential recipient might be interested in finding out! Yet the secret of good communications – and ultimately of PR – is to put yourself in the mindset of your recipients and to think through what it is that you want to say to them that will be of interest to them. That is no easy task.

In addition to the content of your communication, PR is also the result of what you do, as well as what you say, and what others then say about you. For instance, if you were to go for a job interview, the first and most important impression is the one you give on entering the room. Before you even open your mouth to say hello, you will be judged on how you look, your dress, your manner, your attitude and how you speak. Body language is a crucial aspect of the way you will be judged; and a job interview is just as much about successful PR as it is about improving the attitude of potential customers or suppliers.

Over the past two or three decades, the way we do business has been turned on its head. Increasing competition – especially from overseas – and a rise in customer expectations means that today's company cannot ignore the need to communicate well with its customers or it will simply fall victim to those competitors – perhaps on the other side of the world – who communicate better. Why, after all, should a prospective customer bother with you if your main competitors are only too happy to communicate with them and you're not?

These communications could be at the simplest level. Think about when you go to the supermarket, for instance. Often there are new products such as shampoos and detergents on display. Perhaps there is also a salesperson describing the advantages of these new products. He or she might even be giving samples of the product to the shoppers or offering a discount.

PR is working here to help launch or introduce new products and encourage people to buy them by:

● creating an awareness about their existence
● differentiating them from similar products in the market.

In a similar manner, companies can remind consumers about existing products, such as a particular brand of coffee or a type of paint, by:

● organizing special events
● putting on displays at exhibitions
● putting together a window display in a shop
● holding media events
● distributing pamphlets and brochures.

So today's organization needs to concentrate on marketing communications as well as on providing customer service and after-care in a way that will retain those customers in the long term. Poor service, a lack of understanding of customer needs and arrogance on the part of the organization are the main reasons that customers become ex-customers, rather than price alone.

A grey area

Of course there is a grey area in which it is difficult to differentiate between 'pure' public relations and marketing communications. But why worry about such distinctions? PR is all about changing and improving attitudes and that means that any communications from a company will have an effect on its reputation, regardless of what you call it.

Measuring opinion

Measuring opinion is a crucial part of building an appropriate or successful PR plan. Not only is communication a two-way process but a company that gets genuine feedback from its customers and target groups will be better equipped to know what messages it needs to put across as well as how to impart them.

Very often companies assume they know what their customers are thinking. However, they tend to see the situation from their own point of view and could be blinded to some of the problems that others experience simply because they come from a different mindset.

For this reason, consumer surveys and questionnaires are widely used to garner the views of prospective customers because they are cheap and easy to organize and can give useful information on demographics of the different marketplaces. The trouble is that they tend not to be very accurate because they usually deal in generalities and they take little account of people's perceptions.

TIP

In some parts of the world (most notably in Asia), there is a culture of not wishing to offend, and so many people will proffer the answers they feel are 'wanted' by the surveyor rather than say what they genuinely feel.

Nonetheless, surveys are useful for identifying trends and for getting a 'broad-brush' picture in order to identify areas for more in-depth and specific research, which can then be undertaken in a more specialized and focused way.

Often, the next stage is to set up focus groups which can provide subjective and objective information as well as allow customers to get involved in the decision-making process. Here the composition of the groups is of paramount importance and typically eight to ten participants will be an optimum number. A relaxed environment is essential to encourage open discussion and a facilitator who is experienced in chairing such meetings is necessary to keep the group focused.

The resultant reports and data can prove extremely useful in honing the communication plan and promotional activities, not to mention the possibility of changing the actual product if something major crops up!

Promotional PR

Promoting your goods and services can include a wide variety of activities in gaining the attention of your prospects. Advertising, media relations, events, direct mail, and even the packaging of the goods themselves, say a lot about your company and its products. All play an important part of the communications and marketing mix, building your brand and gaining you market share, as well as letting people know what you as a company stand for.

Promotional activities in the main are all about tempting your prospects by creating a feeling of excitement about your products or services, or a feeling of belonging to a tribe which

SUNDAY
MONDAY
TUESDAY
WEDNESDAY
THURSDAY
FRIDAY
SATURDAY

is associated with your company. There is always a strong temptation when communicating the positives to overplay the benefits that a prospect will get, but exaggeration is something that has a terrible habit of coming back to haunt you at a later date.

The dangers of hype

This is something that advertising professionals must always weigh in the balance. For instance, I remember going to a promotional day in Saudi Arabia for a major 4 × 4 car manufacturer. Hundreds of prospective customers were given the opportunity to test-drive the new model on a desert terrain obstacle course. The banners around the course loudly proclaimed such messages as 'There is no such thing as Cannot!'. How those self-same marketers must have cringed when one of their test cars failed in its attempt to drive up a steep hill and had to be eased down the slope for over ten minutes by an army of helpers pushing and pulling the car in an attempt to keep it on the track.

Customers are becoming ever more discerning because of their greater ability to choose more widely. Most customers only want to get good service and be told the truth about delivery, quality, terms and conditions, and so on. So check all your small print. It may be *legally* right but is it losing you sales because of its attitude?

Case study: poor service = poor PR

A friend of mine recently flew on a major European airline from her home in Beijing to Germany. Unfortunately, she forgot to present her frequent flyer club card at check in and subsequently tried to 'reclaim' her frequent flyer points. Despite being told by ground staff at the German airport that she could do this online, she made three attempts to do so once she had returned to Beijing. She was told that she would have to send in the original boarding passes and purchase receipts to their head office, despite the fact that she was able to quote the eTicket number of the flight, as well as the seat details.

Her response was that, since she could quote the eTicket and flight details to the likes of KLM and Qatar Airways, both of whom could check such details against her current frequent flyer membership, then why couldn't this airline, which is a member of IATA and uses the same ticketing arrangements. The airline, however, was adamant that their rules insisted on them seeing the original ticket stubs. Perhaps this was a hark-back to pre-Internet days; but the result is that my friend swears she will never travel with that airline again.

Multiply that a number of times by others who must have had the same experience and the likelihood is that many people will in future try to fly any other airline rather than this one – simply because of an outdated and illogical 'rule'.

Suppliers

The majority of businesses have to get their raw materials from an outside supplier. In the past, traditional communications with suppliers have been on the basis of beating them down to the lowest possible supply price, but this does not make for good long-term business relationships. The brief of most purchasing departments is to source supplies at the lowest possible price, and certainly in the public sector it is normal to go for the lowest tender, commensurate with delivery.

Suppliers, naturally, understand this mindset. However, put yourself in their shoes and things begin to look a bit different. It is in every organization's interests to have good relations with its suppliers, and this depends more than anything else on well-planned two-way communications, which can play a major role in improving business performance. Yet suppliers, as one of the stakeholder groups in a company, are often still treated in a less than friendly manner despite the company's dependency on their goodwill.

Owners and shareholders

Regardless of how well a business is doing, it has to keep its owners and shareholders properly informed about the current state of the organization. Owners invariably start many of the communication processes by asking endless questions of the board, to which they want answers.

Shareholders tend to be either institutional or private and, although both need to be kept informed, it is necessary to communicate effectively with brokers, analysts and the financial press as well, especially – but not necessarily only – in the case of larger companies.

'Ordinary' shareholders tend to be influenced by the financial press and larger companies often have a shareholder relationship manager whose sole job is to communicate with financial journalists, city analysts and major shareholders. The manager's role is to establish and keep communication channels open so that they will communicate their findings to a larger audience and hopefully in a manner which will be informed and fair rather than speculative.

The financial performance of a company, however, can only be one aspect of a company's communications agenda and therefore it cannot be isolated from the rest of the communications and PR functions of an organization. Financial PR needs to tie in with the messages being put out by the corporate affairs and PR departments, where these functions are split up – as is the case in many larger companies.

Corporate affairs

We all work in a world dominated by regulations that have been imposed by some governmental or professional body. We may not like it, but most of these regulations are the rule of law and every business needs to comply with them. Many impose considerable costs on a business and it makes sense, therefore, for organizations to monitor them and to try to influence the policymakers before their ideas become law.

Larger companies can employ lobbyists on their behalf both to monitor and to put forward their views to the bureaucrats. Smaller businesses can use their collective membership of bodies such as chambers of commerce or professional institutes to represent them.

Community relations

The perceptions of the people who live and work in the vicinity of your business can play an important role when you are attempting, for instance, to get planning permission for expansion or when trying to recruit the right local staff.

Many large organizations have programmes for establishing good community relations, which could, for example, include:

- sponsoring local cricket matches, concerts or art exhibitions
- maintaining the flower beds in the centres of traffic roundabouts
- taking disadvantaged kids for a weekend away.

At a time when all businesses are watching the pennies, a little bit of local largesse can go an extremely long way in helping get your local messages across.

Many larger firms actively encourage their employees' involvement in the community in some way. Some organizations second their staff to work in the locality on special community projects. Others actively support voluntary work or provide facilities for events. In doing so, companies make an effective bridge between themselves and the local community and improve the perception of themselves in the process.

Case study: PR and charitable activities

One of the major dairy products companies in the Middle East puts charitable functions at the very heart of the way it operates, with personal support often given by the CEO himself. The company regularly supports people with disabilities, special needs schools, the training of young people, and other charities too numerous to list here.

Of course, these charitable activities often lend themselves to useful photo opportunities with resultant media releases – something that this company has not been slow to pick up on. However, the essence of the scheme is at the core of its corporate ethos and it certainly doesn't do it any harm at all to be thought of as a thoroughly decent company.

These schemes work if they catch the public imagination. And they can be great fun too. The essence, though, is for the company to be seen to be putting something back into the community and being magnanimous about it.

Before embarking on a community relations programme, it is essential to...

- think through your parameters
- calculate how much time as well as money you want to devote to it
- appoint a member of staff as the main point of contact for all outside communications
- be realistic and try to choose a programme which has good photo opportunities
- make sure you tell the world at large about it – locally, regionally and nationally, if not internationally.

Summary

Today we have seen that the ultimate objective of PR is to develop and build a sustainable corporate image and reputation for the business. This involves building a positive working environment with all those who can play a major role in improving the overall image of a firm among those with whom it deals. In the areas of quality and performance especially, expectations need to be communicated with all those involved in providing the service to the end client.

Although PR should have a separate and defined role of its own, it must also work in tandem with the marketing department if it is to have any hope of creating a favourable business climate for the company, as well as a reactive strategy to be able to deal efficiently with crisis situations.

Comprehensive PR strategies should educate, inform, explain and persuade. So knowing who it is you want to persuade or educate is an essential part of the PR mix. And once you know whom you want to talk to, the next thing to consider is the best ways of reaching them. And, as we will be finding out tomorrow, there are very many different communications channels available to reach your targets.

SUNDAY

MONDAY

TUESDAY

WEDNESDAY

THURSDAY

FRIDAY

SATURDAY

Questions (answers at the back)

1. When planning a PR strategy, which of these is the most important parameter to consider?
   a) What you want to say ☐
   b) To whom you wish to say it ☐
   c) Why you want to say it ☐
   d) All of the above ☐

2. When you go for a job interview, which of these is the most important aspect upon which you will be judged?
   a) How you dress ☐
   b) How you speak ☐
   c) What you say ☐
   d) Your mannerisms ☐

3. If you draw yourself a communications map...
   a) It is impossible to miss any of your target audiences ☐
   b) The relationships between your messages follow on from the relationships between target groups ☐
   c) The relationships between target groups follow on from the relationships between your messages ☐
   d) You need to highlight the different paths to reaching your target audiences ☐

4. Compared with 50 years ago...
   a) There is a greater need for companies to communicate with their customers ☐
   b) There is less of a need for companies to communicate with their customers ☐
   c) Increasing globalization means companies must always communicate with potential customers overseas ☐
   d) Customers now purchase more from a sense of need than they ever did before ☐

5. Which of these statements is false? PR can be used to help launch new products by...
   a) Differentiating them from other similar products ☐
   b) Placing advertisements strategically around a supermarket ☐
   c) Organizing special events ☐
   d) Distributing pamphlets and brochures ☐

6. The most common reason given by customers who desert a brand is that the company... ☐
   a) Offers poor service ☐
   b) Doesn't communicate with its customers ☐
   c) Is arrogant and doesn't listen to the needs of its customers ☐
   d) Prices its products too highly ☐

7. Most companies...
a) Know exactly what their customers want ❏
b) Have no idea what their customers really want ❏
c) Have a good idea what their customers want ❏
d) Use surveys to better understand how to sell their products to their customers ❏

8. Surveys are...
a) Useful for identifying trends in public perception ❏
b) Useful for accurately painting a picture of what a customer wants ❏
c) Not very useful since they take little account of people's perceptions ❏
d) A waste of time in some parts of the world because people say what is expected of them rather than what they actually feel ❏

9. Advertisers operate differently from PR practitioners since...
a) They need to worry more about the accuracy of what they say ❏
b) They tend to over-promote a product or service ❏
c) They can dictate what is and isn't said about their product ❏
d) They need to concentrate more on humour and approachability in getting their messages across. ❏

10. A company can always improve its relationship with its suppliers by...
a) Communicating better ❏
b) Insisting on the lowest possible price commensurate with delivery ❏
c) Comparing a supplier's costs with those of its competitors ❏
d) Seeing any problems from their point of view ❏

TUESDAY

Dealing with the media

It's a truism that one of the quickest and easiest routes to reach your target audiences is through journalists writing for magazines and newspapers, or broadcasting via TV or radio. For the past few years, there have also been the added major outlets provided by the Internet and social media – something we will be taking a look at tomorrow.

Good media relations can be critical for any business and play a significant role in the fortunes of a company. Handled correctly, your relationship with journalists can be advantageous for both sides – a win-win situation.

The secret is in striking a balance. Businesses should understand the importance of having good relationships with journalists. They can be a highly effective mouthpiece for communicating with your audiences, and it's in every company's interests to nurture a good relationship with them.

It's important to understand that a journalist has a job to do – that is, filling airtime if she's a broadcaster, or filling column inches if she's a print journalist. When you give a journalist a good story, you are actually doing her a favour. However, if she writes something about your organization that is correct but you don't like it, then, frankly, that's a fact of life and something you have to learn to live with.

Today, then, we will look at:

- the tricky balancing act a PR practitioner must perform working between company/client and the media
- building up relationships with journalists and reporters
- the importance of being aware of how the media – a newsroom, for example – works.

The PR as intermediary

The company

The media

It is the PR practitioner's role to act as intermediary between the people inside the organization and the journalists out in media-land. Almost all companies deal in the jargon of their trade, and it is up to the PR person to put all this into plain language that everyone can understand when presenting it to the outside world.

Identifying the right journalists to speak to for any story is as crucial as identifying your audiences in the first place. But journalists need good stories, so don't waste their time by giving them stories that are substandard or of not particular interest to them. They won't thank you for them and, worse still, you could badly damage your credibility with them in the future when you might most need them.

A reporter's need to talk to PR practitioners is dictated by events and circumstance. There are reporters who never need to deal with PR practitioners, although they may use a PR product, such as a press release. But reporters who avoid PR people shield themselves from potentially useful information resources, while PR practitioners who ignore the media limit their usefulness, and if they abuse editorial access they can even do the organization harm.

News media limitations

If you think about it, a newsroom is nothing more than an information factory. Raw material – the stories – come in at one end, they are refined and repackaged and are then sent out again. In most cases, news is time critical, but, apart from this, it is a straightforward process of repackaging stories to suit a particular audience.

Whether print or electronic, workers in this factory – the editors and reporters – process and publish content with an eye on consumer interest and/or accuracy and fairness to gain and keep readers, listeners or viewers. They define the news, and the order and presentation of stories. They essentially act as gatekeepers and filters of information at both fact gathering and editing levels, deciding at the end of the day what their readers and viewers will be told.

A typical newsroom is buried in information, but often this information might not be appropriate for the publication or broadcast station. Other information could be too costly to vet for accuracy so it will also end up in the waste bin.

Journalists in reality often have a difficult balancing act to play to satisfy their stakeholders:

- A reporter writing short stories for a business page from press releases and agency copy has a totally different job from that of an investigative reporter trying to prove that someone in authority has acted improperly.
- Everything in a news factory is geared to delivery of a product on time.
- One reporter might understand a complex explanation of a product or political situation better than another and accordingly treat the story in a totally different way.
- One reporter might be willing to spend extra time on a story or even report a story in which an editor has no interest.
- Some reporters are better visual, text and personal presenters than others.
- Reporters, too, are only human; and inevitably a reporter's beliefs about issues, persons and news can limit the type of stories he or she does.

SUNDAY

MONDAY

TUESDAY

WEDNESDAY

THURSDAY

FRIDAY

SATURDAY

Getting messages out

If you wish your company news to be dissipated through traditional media outlets, it is essential to understand how and why the media operate in the way they do and the limitations to which any journalist has to work.

If your company's stories are not compelling, they will get lost in the information flow. It is also important to realize that if you get into the news, someone else doesn't. This competition for a reporter's attention creates a role for someone who knows the media and can deal effectively with them, such as you – the PR practitioner!

The corollary of this is that if your organization has compelling news, it may be published whether you like it or not. This is an even bigger reason to use practitioners who understand media operations and what can and cannot be expected to be achieved in mitigating negative news. Of course, if the news is positive, that same practitioner should best be able to advise on how to get maximum benefit from it.

Essentially, the PR expert should be gathering facts, setting up interviews, providing graphics and photos, gaining access for reporters to key people and assisting the reporter before and after news is published. This is a time-consuming process, but the results it can achieve make it well worthwhile.

The PR practitioner's role faces both ways – using knowledge of the news-gathering process to help his company tell a story and knowledge of his company to help the reporter relate the story to his target audiences. He is an intermediary who tries to satisfy both sides, although this is not always possible, and many is the time that PR people feel like piggy-in-the-middle, satisfying neither the media's appetite for facts nor their bosses' wish to protect themselves and their companies from criticism.

PR men and women ultimately have loyalty to the organization that pays them and, as a result, they can be irritating barriers to reporters when they are not permitted to speak for the organization.

Reporters understand this dual role and appreciate knowledgeable practitioners who steer them in the right direction and save them time when reporting a story. However, a PR practitioner may want a reporter to focus on a story or facts the reporter considers irrelevant or ignore facts the journalist feels he or she needs. This, by its very nature, can create tension between the two.

If you, as a PR practitioner, want to gain the trust of a journalist, then it is beholden upon you to:

- deliver information and interviews the reporter needs
- provide clear and accurate facts to the reporter, whether good or bad
- be available when a reporter calls and handle his or her request quickly and accurately.

At the same time, you must always allow for the fact that ultimately your first priority must always be to your company rather than to the journalist.

Equally, a reporter gains credibility with a PR person by reporting fairly and accurately. If a PR person finds a reporter inaccurate, dilatory about interviews and elusive, the practitioner will go elsewhere to get a message out.

TIP *Dealing with reporters is like dealing with customers. You talk to some frequently and others only once. And, like customers, it is important for PR practitioners to treat reporters well. Most reporters are trustworthy professionals trying to do their jobs.*

Because a reporter may deal with a PR practitioner only once or infrequently, it is up to you to know and become well known to reporters and not vice versa. Practitioners who avoid journalists or make no attempt to cultivate reporters consign themselves to low credibility with news media and lack of access when they need it.

However, it is no good thinking you can cultivate links with journalists by taking them out to dinner or even to an event such as horseracing if you are not able to talk meaningfully about your company. It may be very nice for the journalist to be taken out to dinner, but if she has nothing in the way of new information to show for her time spent, she will consider the whole exercise a waste of time.

It's not just about wining and dining!

This was the scenario faced day after day by PR executives in a certain defence company in the Middle East, which is probably best left incognito. They were given the unenviable instruction to cultivate relationships with local journalists, but at the same time they were not allowed to say anything whatsoever about the company, while the directors also had a policy of 'no comment' to any press enquiry. What did those directors sitting in their 'ivory towers', think they were hoping to achieve?

Limiting PR

In an era when some companies feel they have too much information written about them, they may limit their PR people to talking about issues that benefit the company only, such as marketing communications to boost awareness of products, services and brands. However, companies have more issues than marketing, and some reporters may want to explore them.

This is especially true with high-profile individuals and companies. When PR people become barriers to legitimate stories, they lose credibility with reporters who see individuals and companies as part of the larger environment and fair game for different kinds of stories. Reporters cannot be forced to focus only on a company's narrow, self-interested issues, and companies that subsume PR under marketing communications are, consciously or not, narrowing the issues a PR professional deals with and increasing their risks when issues arise that are out of the PR person's knowledge base.

Despite this, companies often place PR, or its equivalent, under a Chief Marketing Officer (CMO) whose focus is to build awareness and sales. This can work only if the CMO has as an expansive view of the company and its relationships to its stakeholders as the CEO. Unfortunately, that is rarely the case.

CEOs expect CMOs to build consumer loyalty, increase market share, and justify expenditures for marketing communications. CEOs want to know that money spent on marketing is actually resulting in profitable sales. The CMO, under pressure to show bottom-line results, is not going to spend much time on issues such as recruitment and retention, diversity, shareholder unhappiness, impacts of legislation, community pressure and a host of other stakeholder concerns that a typical PR department handles.

Thus, it is likely that a marketing communications focus will be forced to shift over time as other issues arise. The traditional structure is to have marketing-focused PR at the division or brand level and a corporate-focused department reporting directly to the CEO. This is generally regarded to be the best approach.

Truth, fact and perception

Reporters reach large numbers of individuals and directly influence opinions about reputations, products, services, issues or individuals. That's why they are so important, and are worth cultivating. If reporters get it wrong, others suffer the consequences. But reporters are, after all, only human. Like all of us, they perceive the world from their own perspective. Ideally, we would all like to deal with reporters who have open minds, as we can then try to educate them to our point of view.

For example, a reporter who knows little about a particular market sector might not necessarily know what to ask a CEO about his or her business. The PR practitioner can help the reporter grasp details of that sector in order to conduct a meaningful interview. The practitioner will, of course, try to guide the reporter to relevant facts that place the company or client in the best light, and the reporter understands this. When a reporter knows a subject in depth, the PR practitioner can equally provide the supplementary facts that the journalist needs to write a story accurately.

Of course, PR practitioners may suggest to a reporter that one fact is more important than another, but the reporter may not judge it that way. As a result, fact ranking is inherently biased. However, that isn't necessarily harmful because reporters and editors tangle with fact and perception constantly. They are – or should be – masters in separating the two.

It is only when a reporter is manifestly wrong and out of control that a PR practitioner should even consider appealing to an editor over the reporter's head. This rarely happens because most journalists are taught to respect truth, fact and perception.

Changing opinion

What a journalist does with the facts he or she has gathered is also critical. Some news organizations believe a reporter's job is to state facts accurately and keep opinions to themselves. The BBC World Service radio station, for instance, keeps a clear dividing line between reporting facts in its news bulletins and commenting on those facts in its current affairs programming. BBC World News TV, on the other hand, regularly has comment mixed in with the straight reporting of news. Media get reputations based on how their reporters approach the issue of opinion and it is important for the PR person to understand this.

TIP *Practitioners should be informed about reporters they deal with and avoid situations where there is high risk. Learning about reporters comes from researching stories under their bylines and from experience with them.*

Of course, a journalist may have a hidden agenda, saying he is reporting such-and-such a story and then change course after an interview starts. Most journalists are trustworthy, but the PR practitioner should always be on her guard. With sensitive topics, it is essential to prepare the interviewee thoroughly for tough questions. This is why media training is important and why you should always insist that, at a minimum, your interviewee talks through the likely questions the journalist may throw at him. Clients who want to undertake interviews 'off the cuff' on tough topics are simply asking for trouble!

Trust is an essential component of PR–journalist interaction. If the PR practitioner is unknown to the reporter, there is no trust to begin with. If a PR practitioner says to a reporter 'I will get back to you', but never does, he or she will lose trust. If the PR practitioner is caught lying, or at least 'fabricating the truth', then trust could be lost for ever. If the practitioner faithfully returns calls, answers questions and plays straight with a reporter, a journalist will begin to trust him or her.

The same is true for journalists. An unknown journalist is trusted less than a known one. The journalist who 'will get back to you' but never does is not trusted and the journalist who burns sources by breaking his or her word to them loses them for ever. Truth, fact and perception live through interaction between reporters and PR practitioners.

There is never a time when a practitioner achieves a state of full trustworthiness, and there is never a time when an independent journalist is completely under control. Perception is relative to the story being pursued and to the credibility of both the reporter and practitioner.

Maintaining a spirit of accuracy is the best way to build credibility with reporters who value accuracy. Maintaining a spirit of service towards reporters and their needs enhances a practitioner's credibility because a reporter has to get a job done. Working with a deadline mentality supports reporters who live by deadlines.

Summary

Journalists can recognize a good story in seconds, so be sure to be able to tell yours simply and succinctly. Don't waste the journalist's time by rambling on about something he or she is unlikely to be interested in!

Understand who your audience is. Before you approach any media outlet, research it.

Build up relationships. By building relationships with reporters it means they are more likely to take your call when you've got an important story to tell. But treat everything as being 'on the record', no matter how close you are to the journalist.

Get your pitch right. Be upfront with the journalist about what you want. Wrap up your approach within 15 seconds and remember to ask if the journalist is on a deadline and if he or she would prefer you to call back later.

And remember: CEOs love coverage. A full-page story in a magazine or newspaper is something tangible you can show to your boss!

SUNDAY

MONDAY

TUESDAY

WEDNESDAY

THURSDAY

FRIDAY

SATURDAY

Questions (answers at the back)

1. PR practitioners need to keep up good relations with journalists so that...
   a) They aren't too nosey about your business ❑
   b) They can be an effective mouthpiece for your organization ❑
   c) They can be persuaded to retract pieces that are critical of your business ❑
   d) You can talk in confidence about your business without fear of being quoted ❑

2. When sending in some news to a journalist, which of these statements are not true?
   a) It is the journalist's job to write about it in a jargon-free way ❑
   b) It is the PR practitioner's job to explain it in jargon-free terms ❑
   c) Jargon has no place in news for general consumption ❑
   d) Jargon helps give a story more authority by setting the right tone ❑

3. Reporters only deal with PR people...
   a) When they want clarification on a news release they have received ❑
   b) In order to widen their information sources ❑
   c) When they want to speak to a CEO or other board member ❑
   d) When they are short of story ideas ❑

4. When journalists write up stories for their readers...
   a) It is up to the journalists themselves to decide what stories are suitable for their readership ❑
   b) A newspaper editor has final say over what goes into the paper ❑
   c) Journalists tend not to use stories that would cost them too much in time or resources to cover ❑
   d) The PR person should suggest story angles that a journalist can use ❑

5. When journalists write up stories from your press releases...
   a) It is incumbent upon them to contact you if there is something they do not understand ❑
   b) They will spend enough time on the story to get all the facts as they understand it ❑
   c) Their own beliefs and experience are likely to impact the way they cover the story ❑
   d) They are likely to hand over their material to another department if the subject matter is more suited to it ❑

6. When a journalist decides he or she wants to write something about your company, it is up to you, the PR practitioner, to...
a) Gather as much background information for the journalist as you can ❏
b) Provide graphics or photographs to accompany the story ❏
c) Give him or her access to key people and places which the journalist might not otherwise be able to find ❏
d) All of the above ❏

7. As a PR person...
a) You should always put the company's interests ahead of the journalist's ❏
b) You should always help the journalist get his/her story ❏
c) It is your responsibility to explain to the company management why it is necessary to help the journalist ❏
d) It is your responsibility to steer the journalist to cover the story in a certain way ❏

8. If a reporter misrepresents a company in his story, you as the PR practitioner should...
a) Demand a retraction at the next available opportunity ❏
b) Point out to the journalist the error of his or her ways and suggest a follow-up story to put the record straight ❏
c) Swallow your pride and put it down to experience ❏
d) Never deal with the reporter again ❏

9. If your boss is to be interviewed about a sensitive subject by a journalist...
a) She should always first have been media-trained ❏
b) She should rehearse answers to predictable questions in advance ❏
c) She should ask for a list of the questions before the interview ❏
d) She should simply decline to be interviewed if she is afraid of what the journalist might ask her ❏

10. When approaching a journalist with a story...
a) Always research the type of articles that journal covers before picking up the phone or sending the email ❏
b) Research when the next edition of the journal is going to press ❏
c) Never talk off the record when briefing the journalist ❏
d) All of the above ❏

WEDNESDAY

Social media

The world is changing, and with it a media revolution is taking place that is changing the 'normally accepted' ways of doing so many things.

According to media tycoon Rupert Murdoch, quoted in *Wired Magazine* way back in July 2006, 'to find something comparable, you have to go back 500 years to the printing press – the birth of mass media... Technology is shifting power away from editors, the publishers, the establishment, the media elite. Now it's the people who are taking control.'

Fifty years ago the 'media' consisted of newspapers and magazines, broadcast TV and radio and very little else. Now you can also add in cable TV, podcasts, social networks, satellite TV, the Internet, mobile Internet, text messaging, blogs and a whole lot else besides.

And in another 20 years? Who knows what?

One of the biggest challenges of this new order faced by PR professionals is the 'community' aspect of online communications. What is PR, after all, but the intention to communicate, build relationships and influence people? So new PR tools, media channels and a change of culture require nothing less than a completely new approach to this centuries-old art.

In Week 3 'Social Media Marketing' we looked in detail at social media. Today, then, we will go over:

- how new media has revolutionized the business of PR and yet how fundamentally it has remained the same
- how to use blogging to develop your company's profile
- how to use social networking media such as Twitter and Facebook to generate interest and 'buzz' about your company and its products.

Plus ça change...

These are exciting times for PR professionals as what is happening now has never happened before. Online PR in particular is a completely new environment in which we need to relearn how to communicate – or our businesses will simply die. It is not an added extra, to be considered as a possibility when planning our PR strategies; it requires a completely new approach to our whole way of planning a PR campaign.

And yet... in some ways everything is exactly the same as ever it was – building relationships in order to influence. It could even be argued that online PR is actually a much purer form of what PR should have been and what it used to be before it got diverted and grew into so many other areas. Online PR actually puts things back where they should be. Online puts the 'public' back into 'public relations'!

Already, well over half of all online PR is no longer done by agencies. The PR 'leaders' of old are now way behind the mainstream players online. Digital PR offers huge new opportunities, but it is also seen by some old diehards as a threat. Depending on which PR magazine you read, it is claimed that around a half of all PR clients are dissatisfied with their agency's online PR offerings.

The biggest problem (or opportunity, depending on your point of view) is that the online world continues to change so fast. Probably the best way to get digital-savvy is to play around and get involved with the different platforms.

It is essential to integrate online PR with traditional forms of PR. One does not replace the other, but they must be used in partnership to get long-term overall success.

This new world order was aptly summed up by Sir Tim Berners-Lee – the 'father' of the Internet – who said:

'The idea of the Web as interaction between people is really what the Web is all about. That was what it was designed to be, as a collaborative space where people can interact.'

The numbers quoted by research agencies regarding Web statistics are truly awesome, and they seem to increase exponentially the moment a particular statistic is released. For instance:

- there are estimated to be in the region of 2.8 billion people online (source: www.Internetworldstats.com)
- Google handles over 40,000 search queries every second, or about 1.2 trillion searches per year (source: www.internetlivestats.com)
- A new blog is created somewhere in the world every half a second (source: www.wpvirtuoso.com)
- Wikipedia has 4.6 million articles in English, together with articles in over 270 other languages (source: www.wikipedia.com)
- Over 6 billion hours of video are watched on YouTube every month (source: www.youtube.com)
- Twitter normally takes in over 500 million Tweets every day, or 5,700 Tweets per second (source: blog.twitter.com)
- There are over 54 million Facebook pages and over 1.3 trillion monthly Facebook visits (source: www.statisticbrain.com).

The effects of this were neatly summed up by Kathleen Schneider, an Executive Director of Dell Europe's marketing division when she told a conference that on any given day there were some 40,000 meaningful conversations about Dell products online. You can imagine the difficulty they must have in mapping these conversations!

Individuals have now got a disproportionate level of influence. A blogger in his or her bedroom can get a global readership – and this totally changes the perspective of the PR professional. On the positive side, there are a huge number of online forums, so this is a really good opportunity from a brand point of view for a company to listen to what people have to say about their brand or products.

Yet, despite the statistics, many company executives continue to act like King Canute and ignore this potential online opportunity. They still believe that a story appearing in print is worth much more to their business than a story appearing online. In part, this is a psychological reaction to placing more value on something physical – something you can actually hold in your hands. But consider this statement by Steve Fowler, Group Editor of *WhatCar?* magazine:

> *'I get 900,000+ visitors a week to whatcar.com and 127,000 readers a month to the magazine. But people still think that the magazine is much more valuable to be in.'*

Consider, too, the statistics of readership of the *Guardian* newspaper in July 2011:

- print publication: approximately 250,000 copies
- *the Guardian* online: up to 39 million unique readers per month
- *the Guardian* online is the fifth most popular newspaper site in the world.

And add to this what Emily Bell, Editor of *Guardian Unlimited*, says – 'One-third of our traffic on *Guardian Unlimited* comes from stories more than a month old' – and you will see that the power of online coverage is not just in the sheer numbers of readers, but in the fact that your story stays in the public domain for a much longer time… in theory, for ever!

Now consider the following research about how journalists work, put together in a study by Middleberg/SNCR:

- 98% of journalists go online daily
  - **92% for article research**
  - **81% to do searching**
  - **76% to find new sources and experts**
  - **73% to find press releases**
- 56% of journalists also use blogs regularly
  - **33% to uncover breaking news or scandals.**

What has become clear is that this revolution is not just about technology. It's a cultural shift. Advertising doesn't work as it once did and people are a lot more marketing-savvy than they used to be. Everything is becoming socialized. Consumers no longer accept being 'talked at' – they also want to 'talk with you'. All of this is good news for the PR profession because (in theory) this is what PR is all about!

Simply put, some things just haven't changed: channels and media may change but the need for good PR remains constant.

Some things, though, have changed:

- It has never been cheaper or easier to produce content.
- Clients can bypass the media and communicate directly with their audiences.
- Audiences can easily communicate with each other on a large scale.
- The news cycle lasts longer – online news sources act like a permanent archive.

So it appears that PR models need to adapt to keep up with what is going on in the real world; and although it throws up new problems, the new technology can also help the overworked PR professional.

At the same time, as the numbers of influencers are both multiplying and changing, more effective messaging is required to reach this new body of people; and as the speed that messages spread through networks gets faster and faster, PR people need to adapt and develop their crisis procedures to handle much larger threats than ever before.

New opportunities

Although there are plenty of negatives that PR people need to adapt to with the new media era, there are also numerous new opportunities in online PR. For a start, you can now...

- **LISTEN** to your publics in ways which were previously not possible
- **IDENTIFY** influencers/issues related to your brand, organization and industry
- **ENGAGE** with multiple stakeholders in relevant and exciting ways
- **MEASURE** your outputs, and the resultant outcomes of your online efforts.

Interaction with media

The most obvious element of online PR is the way you can now interact with the media and the ease with which you can now find coverage of your organization. Remember that both negative as well as positive coverage has a much longer lifespan online than in traditional print.

News online is regularly refreshed, and because it is also searched for rather than simply viewed like a newspaper, it becomes much more relevant to the reader, who may even forward the article to a friend or colleague.

This means it is also now important for the PR professional to monitor online in order to keep up to speed with new developments in real time. The benefits cannot be overstated. At the very least, it acts as an early-warning system for potential crises. But it is also a global and highly cost-effective focus group that can give you excellent feedback on what the public really does think about your products and services.

With the advent of new media, too, there have appeared numerous niche publications that service a very precise (and often tightly focused) vertical market, giving you an excellent entrée to specific target groups that you might have found difficult to reach before. Normally, these are professionally managed sites that may even have a journalistic or editorial team, together with several contributors who are trade focused and could even be focused on location, interest topic or gender.

However, when informing new media about your company's news, the traditional elements of news releases (which we will be looking at in detail tomorrow) are as important as they ever were. All must contain a headline, core facts, possibly the inclusion of approved quotes, a 'Notes for Editors' section at the end and, of course, contact details. In addition, though, we now have the added benefits of being able to include navigation, hyperlinks in the body of the copy, links to previous coverage as well as links to other 'backgrounders' and FAQs (frequently asked questions).

Add to that an armoury of multimedia content, including video, audio and images, and your humble news release can take on a completely new and more exciting persona of its own.

Blogging

A recent newcomer to the Internet world of reporting has been the blogger – or 'web-logger' (a term originating in 1997, with the word 'blog' following two years later). Written in a conversational tone, blogs are now written by millions of people about many millions of subjects.

In some ways, blogs are just like conventional websites, except that... they are not! For a start, their content is frequently updated, they are written by the blogger him- or herself, and often contain multimedia. Two-thirds of bloggers are male, while half are in the 18–34 age group.

According to the blog search engine Technorati:

● 82% of bloggers post reviews on products and brands
● 42% talk about brands they love

- 63% post about company information and gossip
- 79% blog about their experiences with customer care.

For the PR professional, therefore, blogs are not only important sources of information about a company's products and services, but are also a perfect platform for giving out information as well.

In the 'blogosphere', they say there are three types of bloggers:

1 **thinkers** ...who create thoughts that weren't there before and who usually write long posts
2 **linkers** ...who act as filters for their readers so they return for more, and who tend to have short posts
3 **stinkers** ...who don't have much of an interest in what they're blogging about (they do it simply because it's fashionable) and who usually have very little to say.

The process for putting up a blog is not at all difficult, but it is not something that should be rushed into without any thought. Some companies start off with an internal blog that any staff member can contribute to. This is the ideal way to explore possibilities and to develop a corporate writing style.

You could get your new army of bloggers – together with other staff who are interested – to comment on the blogs, effectively expanding your site and developing your blogging culture.

Here are a few useful ground rules when establishing a company blogging site:

- When developing a corporate blogging policy, it is essential that your people understand what can and what cannot be posted. Obviously, due to the nature of a particular business, some things cannot be discussed, including commercially confidential information.
- You will need to remind employees that everything they write on the Web is in theory available for ever. Some companies tend to add a disclaimer to their blog sites stating that the bloggers' thoughts are not necessarily those of the company.
- When inviting comments from readers, it is a good idea to let people know that you retain the right to moderate any comments, and that you will not allow offensive comments

to be published, but that you will not alter the contents of comments if they are included.

Don't be afraid to make some mistakes at the beginning. Everyone does, and it is an ideal way to learn. You will need to establish the strategy of your corporate blog and define an editorial policy. You want, after all, to engage with your readers, so you will need to create compelling content and post regularly to get them coming back for more. You will use keywords to ensure your blog is picked up by the search engines, and, of course, you will have a link to your blog from your company website's homepage.

Case study: Marriott Hotels

If you would like to see an excellent example of corporate blogging, then look no further than that of Marriott Hotels' Chairman and CEO, Bill Marriott (www.blogs. marriott.com). A self-styled 'Neanderthal' when it comes to blogging, Marriott posts on average a little more often than once a week. He doesn't use computers himself, but instead dictates to a member of his global communications team who goes away and transcribes his thoughts into a blog. She also reviews any comments received and then prints them out for him to read. If there are any he feels he wants to respond to, he tells her what he wants to say and she responds on his behalf.

On some occasions, fewer than ten people leave comments to his blog. However, on 20 September 2008 Bill Marriott posted about a bomb blast outside the Marriott hotel in Islamabad. He received 233 comments, overwhelming in their condolences and support. His three posts that week received 7,300 visits – about 200 per cent above its average weekly count.

This single occasion shows how useful the hotel company's blog turned out to be. It was an established blog that gave the company the means to reach out to customers and employees with an authentic expression of grief.

Marriott's Senior Director of Public Relations, John Wolf, said that the 'Senseless tragedy' post, together with the subsequent reaction, was a perfect example of everything they had hoped to accomplish when they first launched Bill Marriott's blog:

> *'The personal nature of Bill Marriott's blog has given the company much more than a face to a name. It has, as brand experts say, helped us make an 'emotional connection' with our customers and other constituents. And it has shaped what people think about us.'*

This was further reinforced by a comment from Marriott's Head of Communications, Kathleen Matthews:

> *'Marriott has made more than $5 million in bookings from people who clicked through to the reservation page from Marriott's blog.'*

By encouraging comments to be posted (whether or not you choose first to moderate them), you can get instant feedback and measure the success of your blog.

There are plenty of free blog platforms you can use for your blogs. Perhaps the two most used are WordPress (www.wordpress.org) and Google's Blogger (www.blogger.com). Many are open source and allow you to fully customize the look and feel of the blog – which is important for branding purposes – as well as allowing you to add functional plugins.

Some bloggers can be very influential, especially in vertical markets. If you want to contact a blogger about his or her column, the rules of engagement are somewhat different from the way you might treat journalists, simply because the majority of bloggers are not journalists.

For a start, you should thoroughly read the blog before you make contact, and never send a press release unless you have prior approval. Many a company has found itself pilloried for trying to send press releases to bloggers.

Twitter

If social media is all about community, then Twitter is community gone wild. Many people miss the point of Twitter altogether, yet there must be something there if it now has over 175 million users, attracts 55 million monthly visitors and ranks as the third largest social network.

Many have criticized Twitter as encouraging an egocentric view of the world among the younger generation. On the other hand, it is Twitter that has been widely held to be the driving force for much of the social upheaval that has been seen across North Africa and the Middle East in recent times.

Today breaking news is often reported first by individuals on the scene who are equipped with nothing more than a mobile phone and a connection to a social media site, such as Twitter. For example, on 15 January 2009, when a US Airways aircraft went down into the Hudson River, it was a passenger on the first ferry to reach the stranded plane that disseminated the first photographs and reporting of the incident. This is also true of natural disasters and ongoing events such as the clashes in the Middle East.

Twitter appeals mostly to consumers who want to feel up to date and in the know, and as a means of gathering information about new products and services or other brand initiatives that would be of interest to them. It can also be used as a quasi-PR tool in its own right – as can be seen from the myriad of Tweets posted by entertainers and other celebrities who promote themselves and their movies using this micro-blogging site. We can now read the kind of news we earlier used to find in the tabloids, direct from the Twitter feeds of celebrities who are apparently ready to 'kiss and tell'.

Facebook

Of all the social media websites, Facebook has to be the outstanding success story. It is the clear leader of the social networking pack, accounting for 55 per cent of all visits to social sites. In the online advertising market, it accounts for over 20 billion ad exposures in a single month, and this figure is growing all the time.

For this reason, it can certainly prove to be an inexpensive and highly effective tool in the PR armoury when used correctly. However, as ever, it is important to integrate it strategically with your overall PR plan.

The first issue to resolve is to identify your target audience. There is absolutely no point in getting hundreds of Facebook 'friends' who have no interest in your offerings. Facebook only permits a maximum of 5,000 'friends' so you need to create an efficient invitation strategy. Facebook also puts limitations on the number of invitations that can be sent out, so it is better to send out only around ten friend invitations per day.

If this seems a paltry amount, then consider how it will work. You begin by adding the people you know in the industry. You need to be able to identify the leaders of the pack, those who tend to serve as the mentors of the community; and then you need to converse with them and, if you have the opportunity, to incentivize them.

Here are a few useful pointers when seeking to exploit the Facebook phenomenon:

- You can use groups to find Facebookers with the same interests as your company's and those who belong in the same target audience. Monitor conversations closely to find out what's of interest to your audience, as well as any new group members who fit with your target audience.
- You can also use your Facebook friends' recommendations. Facebook recommends friends based on your current friends list and these recommendations are usually pretty accurate on relevance.
- Find out what is being said about your company and its products. You will need to do extensive research on the conversations taking place and the existing communities before taking part in them – this is time-consuming work.
- Once you have found them, you need to keep in touch with your new 'friends'. Make regular appropriate comments,

and keep an eye on your friends' status updates, as great communication opportunities may be hidden there. Keep your profile up to date with accurate information and talk as if you are part of the group, not as a typical advertiser. Always link to your website and do not forget to put your contact information to encourage a dialogue.

Case study: Hennessy Cognac

By listening to mentions of its brand online, Hennessy Cognac discovered fans of their brand on a social networking site in the US for African Americans: BlackPlanet.com.

Analysis of these conversations, coupled with further marketing research, revealed their interests, preferences and how they interacted with the brand. Based on this data, Hennessy created a tour called Hennessy Artistry. They sponsored and set up partnerships with well-known African American musicians and held events and concerts in major cities across the US, always making content from these events available to post and share online.

At the start of 2010 Hennessy held a major celebrity-filled party in Chicago for their first new product in 50 years: Hennessy Black. Some 25 million people heard about this event through a number of different news websites and over 200 blogs and websites posted video interviews with some of the celebrities.

If you were to do a Google search now for Hennessy Black, you might be surprised at the number of blog entries, image entries and mentions of this one drink!

Listening to online conversations is a vital first step, allowing you to use the information garnered to allocate your resources wisely. You'll know where to start, whom to talk to, what content they respond to and what social sites you should be concentrating on. When you know the lie of the land, it's much easier to plot your roadmap.

SUNDAY
MONDAY
TUESDAY
WEDNESDAY
THURSDAY
FRIDAY
SATURDAY

Research and strategize

When considering your PR campaign using online tools, it is essential to establish clear objectives. You need to know what others are saying about you and your products. What news articles have been written about you? What have consumers and social media users said about you online? Where do these discussions take place? In blogs? forums? Twitter? Or everywhere?

Who are the people talking about you? Are they 'on your side'? Or are they castigating you for any reason? What does Google say about you? How do you feature in its search engine?

Now define your objectives. What are the stories you want to put across to online outlets? How are you going to build meaningful relationships with the online communities? What are the best platforms to reach them? Twitter? Blogs? YouTube? Facebook?

And how do you get your content to be visible in Google?

Summary

The fundamentals of online PR are in many ways just like regular PR. Some things will never change: a company is still judged on its products and services; its innovation; its workplace practices; its corporate governance; its leadership and its performance. We still operate with the intention to communicate, build relationships and exert influence. It is just that the toolbox has changed somewhat.

So what you need to do is:

- understand how your networked audiences work
- map your online environment to gain intelligence before planning your campaign
- be flexible with your tailored communications since no single approach is suitable for everybody
- be meaningful with your messages – avoid the spin, as you will be spotted a mile off
- be altruistic – because it will serve you in the long run
- be flexible so that you can react instantly to the feedback you receive
- never be afraid to experiment – the rules are still being written!

SUNDAY
MONDAY
TUESDAY
WEDNESDAY
THURSDAY
FRIDAY
SATURDAY

Questions (answers at the back)

1. Which of these statements is blatantly untrue?
   a) New media have raised the importance of journalists to a greater degree than ever before ❏
   b) Social media could eventually make professional journalism an obsolete profession because in the future ordinary people will report the facts ❏
   c) PR is losing out as the power of social networking grows exponentially ❏
   d) All of the above ❏

2. PR agencies need to catch up with Internet technologies...
   a) To seize new opportunities for their clients ❏
   b) To protect themselves from the threat of social networkers ❏
   c) To replace traditional ways of handling PR ❏
   d) To try to stop gossip and rumour ❏

3. When dealing with social networking over the Internet, PR professionals should...
   a) Try to get to know as many bloggers as possible in order to influence what they write ❏
   b) Send out press releases and other promotional material to as many bloggers as possible ❏
   c) Send out press releases and other promotional material to bloggers writing about the company's specific market sector ❏
   d) None of the above ❏

4. The number of online readers is higher than the number of readers of printed material; therefore...
   a) More PR value is to be gained by getting editorial in printed magazines ❏
   b) More PR value is to be gained by getting editorial in online forums than in magazines ❏
   c) Journalists place more weight on a story appearing in a printed journal than in an online site ❏
   d) Advertising online is more valuable than in printed journals ❏

5. Which of the following statements is not true?
a) It is cheaper and easier to produce online content than printed material ❏
b) Companies prefer to bypass the media and communicate directly with their customers ❏
c) Customers can easily communicate with one another, bypassing the company in the process ❏
d) In theory, online news lasts for ever ❏

6. PR people need to monitor mentions of a company online in order to...
a) Get an early warning of possible problems with its products or brands ❏
b) Find company mentions in printed media that they might have missed ❏
c) Get feedback on its products or brands ❏
d) All of the above ❏

7. Blogs are important sources of information for PR professionals because...
a) Many contain reviews on products and brands ❏
b) You can discover what is wrong with your customer care solutions ❏
c) You can find out what your competition is up to ❏
d) All of the above ❏

8. When posting up a company blog you should remember that...
a) Everything written is in theory available online for ever ❏
b) The bloggers' comments don't reflect the company's official line ❏
c) Offensive posts should be tempered down to make them more acceptable ❏
d) The inclusion of keywords allows your blog to be indexed by search engines ❏

9. Facebook is an ideal site for PR practitioners to use because...
a) It allows you to send out your company's details to as many as 5,000 people at a time ❏
b) It gives you the wherewithal to network with people who have common interests ❏
c) It gives you lists of people interested in your chosen market sector or interest group ❏
d) It is available in so many languages ❏

10. Twitter is a useful social networking platform because...
a) It is the preferred networking tool of the younger generation ❏
b) It is often first with up-to-date news ❏
c) Celebrities regularly use Twitter to 'kiss and tell' ❏
d) All of the above ❏

THURSDAY

Practical pointers for powerful press releases

Journalists the world over are sent a myriad of press releases every day. Some are well written, succinct and to the point. The majority, however, are not.

The unfortunate truth is that probably 99 per cent of press releases are thrown in the bin – and most of them are written by PR agencies! Journalists and editors take about five to ten seconds to decide whether or not to use a release. Those that are used and ultimately lead to a story tend to have certain qualities in common.

There are a number of reasons why so many releases fail to make the grade. Imagine that you are a busy journalist and you have a pile of releases sitting in the inbox of your email (for it's a fact that the majority of press releases these days are emailed to journalists rather than sent as hard copy, as was the norm until recently). The first one you read is florid in style, has typing errors and is laid out badly. The second one is short, to the point, and easy to read. Which would you prefer?

Today, then, we will learn about:

- what makes a release newsworthy – and specifically the 'five Ws'
- how to write a succinct and effective news release
- other kinds of PR product such as feature stories and media alerts
- how to enrich a release through pictures.

SUNDAY

monday

TUESDAY

WEDNESDAY

THURSDAY

FRIDAY

SATURDAY

What is news?

Nowadays there is an enormous number of media categories to which you can target your news, including (but not limited to):

- the national press
- the regional press
- free newspapers ('freesheets')
- consumer magazines
- trade and technical publications
- broadcast media (radio/TV)
- the Internet.

Each sector has its own specific requirements, and the editorial material that you send out needs to be carefully targeted to match its specific needs. A story that is of interest to a local paper in Cardiff, for instance, will more than likely be binned if it is sent to a national newspaper or TV station.

One of the first things you as a PR practitioner need to ask yourself is what actually constitutes news, since it can have so many different interpretations. In general, journalists tend to stick to a simple formula when considering whether a release will turn into a story. They ask themselves what are known colloquially as the 'five Ws' when reviewing your story:

- Who?
- What?
- Where?
- When?
- Why?

In addition, journalists will throw in an 'H' for good measure:

- How?

TIP

There's also one more question journalists will ask themselves, one that is regularly ignored by PR people desperate to get their clients into the media spotlight: **Why should anyone care?**

If you want your story to make it into the news, it is important to hit all the right buttons with the media, in order to better your chances of seeing your story in the press.

What makes a story newsworthy?

Journalists have to find stories that are of interest to their audiences. They continually ask themselves what, if they were reading a publication or listening to a radio show, would jump out and appeal to them. So if you can put yourselves in the shoes of the journalist to whom you are targeting your release, once you can answer that question you've got the subject for your press release.

Typically, the following items regularly find their way into the media via news releases:

- new products
- improvements to products
- new contracts
- staff changes
- quarterly and annual figures
- achievements

- responses to a crisis
- special events
- charitable donations
- awards won
- promotions
- research findings
- human interest stories.

As producers of TV soap operas know only too well, disagreement or friction between two parties invariably leads to an interesting story. The simplest example is politics. Political arguments and posturing get a lot of press precisely because there is disagreement, conflict and unrest.

The unusual and unexpected also make interesting news, as do stories with universal appeal – such as the lifestyles of entertainers and celebrities. An appreciation of the components that go into what makes a story newsworthy will help you become successful in getting your key messages to your chosen audiences.

TIP *Before you do anything else, start with the 'Who cares?' test, and be strictly honest with yourself. Remember those 99 per cent of releases that end up in the bin. The media couldn't really care less about you or your business. What they are after is a good story.*

Journalists the world over are continually looking for good stories to fill their newspaper, magazine, radio or TV shows. All of them are under pressure from their editors to find stories that are of interest to their readers/listeners/viewers. So you can help them by meeting the aspirations of their audience. If you can show them how to do that, you're virtually guaranteed some coverage. Here are a few pointers:

- Different items, and the angle with which the stories are written, appeal to different segments of the press and public, so choose the media outlet (and the department within that outlet) carefully and make sure the release matches their needs.

- There is no such thing as a one-size-fits-all press release, and you have to be selective in what you send to whom. Are you sending a segment-specific story to general consumer media, for instance? If so, you are wasting your time (and, worse, the editors' time). As with most marketing, good news releases are a matter of being creative and thinking 'outside the box'.
- Find a special angle for your story. Does it have local appeal? Is there something unique about it? Can you combine two items such as a product announcement with a human-interest story to expand its appeal? You may have to write multiple specialized releases instead of one generic piece, but if you get more coverage, isn't it worth it?

What is the purpose of the release?

Many people the world over issue releases without a clear goal in mind, believing that it is important to appear in the media simply for the sake of being in the media. However, knowing what you are trying to achieve gives your writing focus and helps in the selection of distribution channels. It also means you have a far better way of tracking the overall effectiveness of your release.

Some of the most common reasons for sending out a release are:

- to increase or maintain awareness of your brand and products
- to establish credibility or authority within a particular market segment
- image building
- to become recognized as a source of expertise
- to help in the promotion of sales
- to drive traffic to a special event or to your website
- to change buyer/industry behaviour
- to expand your market share
- to comply with company regulations
- to increase the share price of your company.

How to write a press release

Start with a catchy, informative title. The **headline** is the most important part of your press release. It is the first thing the journalists see and if it doesn't grab their attention, they will read no further. It should be bold and interesting and, most importantly, it needs to stand out from all the other press releases with which it is in competition. If you read the headlines in your target publications, you will get a good feel for what works.

> **TIP** *The reason that newspapers and magazines use bold, attention-grabbing headlines is that this is what draws in their readers. Exactly the same strategy should be used to grab the attention of the journalists you are trying to reach.*

After the headline you should add a **dateline** at the beginning of your first paragraph. This comprises the city where your company or story is based – 'Glasgow' or 'Istanbul' – together with the date your release is being issued. This information is invaluable for journalists when they review the many releases they receive, as they may wish to 'park' your news until a later date, or to consign it to a particular section of their publication.

Next, you need to write **a solid, hard-hitting release** in a purely journalistic style (remember to answer the 'five Ws' the journalist will want to ask), keeping the language in the third person and completely free of hyperbole. Very importantly, make it perfectly clear *why* the reporter should cover your story.

The most important information should be at the top of your release, the next most important information in the second paragraph and so on down, so that if someone stops reading after the first or the second or the third paragraph, they still know what the entire story is about. (The person who reads further down only has more *detailed* information about the actual story being told.)

Refrain from verbosity, keeping out unnecessary adjectives and try to keep the release to one or two pages maximum whenever possible. If there is really a lot more information you have to tell journalists, consider adding a general invitation to contact you – 'For more information, contact ...'

Indeed, at the end of your release you should always give accurate **contact information**. Any journalist worth their salt is likely to need further information from you, if they are not simply going to copy-and-paste your release. So put a contact name, phone number(s) and email address.

Making your copy flow

One of the most common faults in news release writing is the use of sloppy language. This is particularly prevalent among those new to press release writing. Often they have picked up catchy phrases and are trying to emulate someone else's style. Perhaps they want to sound sophisticated or formal; are simply unsure of the key points they need to put across; may have padded out the release because they don't have enough information themselves, or they might not have critically read through their final offering.

And, dare one say it, in this SMS-centric new world, many aspiring PR hopefuls are quite simply illiterate!

When you read through your copy, mentally eliminate words and phrases. If the piece reads well without that extra language, delete the surplus. It will make the final version easier to read and assimilate.

If you're writing about one of many products, concentrate solely on the product in question. It may be tempting to 'tell all' but, if it doesn't support the theme, resist the temptation. You can always put in extra information in a 'Notes for Editors' section at the end – but only if it really adds to the overall story.

Remember, too, that strong nouns and verbs work better than adjectives and adverbs. A few extra words in a sentence might not seem like much of a big deal, but when most of the sentences or paragraphs have 'a little extra', it slows the pace of your writing and buries your message. Don't make readers work to find out what you want to tell them! If you really need to add subjective information, such as opinions or grand claims, credit these to an executive in a quote, rather than stating them as fact – this adds to your credibility among those of a less trusting disposition.

News or feature?

The **news style** follows the conventional newspaper approach, summarizing, as we've already said, the story's 'who, what, why, when, where and how'.

A **feature story** press release, on the other hand, resembles a magazine article and is written in a more entertaining manner. The feature often sets the tone and background before introducing the main topic.

This type of release is sometimes more appropriate for specialist magazines that might have a small readership and hence a small budget; in which case, you could be doing the editor a favour by producing a ready-made package for him/her.

The regional press also has an increasing need for professionally written features which can be used with the minimum of reworking by their own journalists. Editors appreciate items which save time and money yet still offer a valuable contribution to their publication. Editorial budgets are under constant pressure, and free material is especially welcomed by the under-resourced free weekly regionals.

If your company people have expertise in a specific subject, encourage them to write an article targeted to the audience. Perhaps an editor would be interested in featuring a regular column from your company/client. Multiply that up, though, with the prevalence of online vertical market blogs and websites and suddenly it becomes a valuable piece of marketing that can project your organization into the limelight.

Feature articles, which are usually planned months in advance and are often focused on a particular event or time of year, should have a particular theme, either directly or indirectly connected with the company's services, and generally should avoid using the company name more than once or twice. Don't cram them full of promotional copy – it has to be of genuine *editorial* interest.

Another effective way of achieving coverage is to aim for inclusion in special feature supplements that your particular target media may run. Most publications publish feature lists well in advance, so it's worth obtaining copies of relevant lists at the beginning of the year to help you identify and plan material for the future, thus increasing the chances of achieving good coverage ahead of the competition. Your advertising department may already have this information to hand in order to plan its media buying.

The media alert

As well as straight news or feature releases, there is also a type of release called a **media alert**. Essentially, this is a memo from you to TV, radio and newspaper assignment editors, city desk editors and others who decide whether a particular news event is worth covering, to alert them about news conferences, charity events, publicity stunts and other events.

The point of the media alert is, in just a few seconds, to tell a journalist about the event, how to cover it and why it's important. Most publicists are pretty good on the first two points – almost all media alerts do a decent job of telling what the event is, where it will be held and what time it starts. It's the third aspect – the 'why' – that makes the real difference, though. And that's what you have to put most effort into.

Executive appointment release

Most businesses send out a brief release and headshot when someone new is hired or a major promotion is made. That may well get them into the 'People on the Move' column in the business section; but apart from being simply an ego trip for the employee, there's not an awful lot of merit to such a story.

Instead of announcing that someone has been hired or promoted, explain why the move is significant to the company – and perhaps the market – as a whole; and then offer someone for interview, too – assuming, that is, that they are media trained and comfortable giving interviews to the press.

A picture is worth a thousand words

If you're pitching stories about your company to the media, then including visual aids gives your release far greater impact. A good photo could even be enough to move your article from the back of a magazine to the front. Photos can be the deciding factor when you're pitching a story idea. An editor who knows that you can provide photos, or that their own photographer can take photos of something interesting, might be encouraged to say 'yes' to a story idea which might otherwise have found its way into the junk bin.

 TIP *If a photographer from a newspaper or magazine does take photos at your company, you should never try to dictate or even 'suggest' what photo they should use with the article. The pictures are the property of the media outlet, which maintains full control over their use.*

Here are a few ground rules when providing and submitting photographic material:

- Put yourself in the position of the picture editor. What will his/her readers be interested in looking at? Certainly not pictures of two people signing a contract – these will go straight in the bin! So plan your pictures well in advance and write for your photographer a list of each shot you want to end up with, including details of the backgrounds and props required.
- Organize all the necessary props and backgrounds well in advance. Try to get the photographer to take a variety of shots so you have a range of different photos on the same subject for your photo library. This avoids having to send out the same old picture every time.

- Take care that the background will not merge with the subject when reproduced as a black-and-white picture. The colours may appear to be contrasting but could end up as one blur in a black-and-white photograph.
- Make sure that the picture you send can be easily cropped to fit all combinations of shapes on the page, such as landscape, portrait or square areas.
- With the ever-improving quality of digital photography and cheap scanners, most editors now prefer to receive digital pictures, provided that the quality is good enough. Newspapers typically need a resolution not less than 200dpi (typically generated by a 3 or 4-megapixel camera), while magazines will require much better – 300dpi / 6 megapixel being the minimum acceptable quality.
- Provide a photo caption explaining the 'who, where, when, why and what' of the picture.
- Always submit photos with routine news announcements, if you want to have any hope of gaining coverage.
- In general, graphs and charts can tend to be a turn-off for ordinary consumer outlets, but speciality media, of course, may well welcome pie charts, bar charts and other graphics if they can help their readers to understand complicated issues such as budgets. Sometimes, though, it is best to offer to supply information to media outlets so they can create their own graphics to accompany the article they're writing about.

Before sending out your release

Larger organizations invariably have a series of executives who have to review the release copy before it is sent out to the media. Ideally, the number of reviewers should not be too long (in order to maintain timeliness), and you should establish a process that indicates who has already reviewed the copy (such as dated initials).

If you're a small business owner, it is always a good idea to have someone else proofread your copy. Mistakes can easily slip in and it is very difficult to notice your own mistakes when you expect to see on the page something you meant to write.

SUNDAY

monday

TUESDAY

WEDNESDAY

THURSDAY

FRIDAY

SATURDAY

Where should you distribute your release?

There are over 12,500 publications and newspapers and some 800 broadcast media in the UK alone. When you add to that the many thousands of other media outlets around the world, you will realize that trying to establish which ones are relevant to you can be a somewhat laborious task.

Since an updated media contact list is essential, many companies send out their releases to a distribution service which takes on the responsibility of keeping such a list available for this purpose. Others purchase updated directories, which can be an expensive option if you do not send out that many releases. One of the easiest ways is to get onto the Internet and do a search of the media yourself, though this can be quite time-consuming.

While you're contacting conventional media outlets, don't forget to send information to Internet newsgroups, electronic newsletters and Web-based mailing lists that accept this type of news. Set up a newsroom on your own website so reporters can access your entire library of releases which you have sent out in the past. Apart from anything else, this makes their research work much easier for them.

This newsroom idea for your website can actually be used for a number of other purposes. For a start, why not prepare a brief biography of your company with a list of 'hot topics' the CEO or a manager could discuss? Journalists are always looking for new experts to interview, but invariably they go for the tried-and-trusted 'experts' for lack of time; so if you make it this easy for them, they will thank you!

Summary

Today we have seen that, to make any impact on journalists who, in the main, are inundated with news releases from all quarters, your release needs to answer the main six questions of 'who, what, where, why, when and how' within the first three paragraphs.

Your writing should be succinct – every word has to earn its place in your release. Ideally, you should make one major point in the opening sentence using not more than 25 words.

Keep paragraphs, particularly the first, to no more than about 40 words; and write in everyday speech, explaining anything the readers may not understand. Always be accurate when you quote someone, especially in headlines, and do not let your opinions get in the way of the story itself. The idea is to allow the readers to make up their minds from the facts as presented.

And, finally, if the story you send out could be libellous, send it to a lawyer first. The lawyer may be expensive, but could well cost less than the alternative!

SUNDAY

monday

TUESDAY

WEDNESDAY

THURSDAY

FRIDAY

SATURDAY

Questions (answers at the back)

1. Many press releases get thrown away by journalists because...
   a) Most of them are written by PR agencies ❏
   b) They are un-newsworthy ❏
   c) They are full of typos and grammatical errors ❏
   d) Journalists have better access to stories than PR people ❏

2. Press releases can be used to publicize...
   a) New products ❏
   b) Human-interest stories ❏
   c) Special events ❏
   d) All of the above ❏

3. Which of the following statements is true?
   a) You need to make a journalist care about your business in order to even bother writing about it ❏
   b) You can help a journalist by giving him/her a story that will interest his/her readers ❏
   c) When sending out a press release, you should issue it to as many different sector-specific journalists as you can ❏
   d) Radio producers like to receive recorded press releases sent as mp3 files ❏

4. The main reason for sending out a release is...
   a) To appear in as many media outlets as possible ❏
   b) To gauge public opinion of what your company is up to ❏
   c) To increase or maintain awareness of your brand and products ❏
   d) To comply with company regulations ❏

5. When thinking about the contents of your release, the most important part is...
   a) The 'Notes for Editors' section at the end ❏
   b) The contact number which a journalist can use to get in touch with you ❏
   c) The headline ❏
   d) The first paragraph ❏

6. When writing a release, which of the following is true?
   a) You should remove all adjectives and adverbs to make the text flow better ❏
   b) If your release is a little on the long side you should make the typeface slightly smaller to fit it all into two pages ❏
   c) You should always include an email address and phone number for further information ❏
   d) You should type it in Times New Roman font, with double spacing and ragged left aligned right ❏

7. When deciding what goes into a release, which of the following is true?
a) Modifier words add excitement to your overall writing style ❑
b) Opinions should be put in quotes and attributed to someone in authority ❑
c) Adding quotes gives credibility to your story ❑
d) The present tense is often better at generating attention than using the past tense ❑

8. Feature press releases are often sent to journalists because...
a) They can be written in a more entertaining manner by the PR officer ❑
b) They can save the media outlet time and money ❑
c) They have more credibility coming from a company in that sector ❑
d) They are cheaper than paying for 'advertorials' ❑

9. Media alerts are useful for telling journalists...
a) About a new service or product your company is issuing ❑
b) Why they should cover a particular event ❑
c) That you will be attending a national exhibition ❑
d) About your annual profit forecast ❑

10. When considering sending out an executive appointment release, you should...
a) List all recent senior management promotions ❑
b) Offer up the appointee for interview ❑
c) Attach a head-and-shoulders picture of the appointee ❑
d) Explain why the appointment is significant for the company ❑

FRIDAY

Marketing communications

Business success depends on your customers, and since the advent of the Internet and other technologies, never have real customer communications been more important.

'Enlightened' companies of yesteryear were good at basic customer care solutions such as training their receptionists to be polite and helpful, but most customers today never set eyes on the receptionist, let alone talk on the phone to anyone there. In this new Internet world, today's organization needs to concentrate on marketing communications as well as providing customer service and aftercare in a way that will retain those customers in the long term.

Marketing communications cover many different areas, from deciding who prospective customers are in the first place – as well as their needs and desires – to letting them know what products are available. The PR professional plays a crucial part in this communications effort.

Today, then, we will be looking at the two main platforms that a PR professional uses in communicating messages:

- the company website newsroom
- events, from trade exhibitions to conferences and seminars.

Measuring opinion

As is common with many PR activities, measuring opinion is a crucial part of building an appropriate and successful communications plan. A company that gets genuine feedback from its customers and target groups will be better equipped to know how to impart its own messages that it wants to get across. As we saw on Thursday, the advent of the Internet has made the process of surveying customers and prospects much easier and cheaper than it ever was.

Such surveys can be used for identifying trends and for getting a 'broad-brush' picture in order to identify areas for more in-depth and specific research, which can then be undertaken in a more specialized and focused way. The trouble is, however, that these surveys tend to deal in generalities.

Promoting your goods and services can include a wide variety of activities for gaining the attention of your prospects, and these can say a lot about your company and its products. In the main, they are – or should be – all about tempting your prospects by creating a feeling of excitement.

However, it's a sad fact that in today's technologically driven world, the PR community is doing pretty badly when it comes to putting together a useful online media resource.

Because so many journalists say that the information found on a corporate website has an impact on their decision to include that company in a story, having the right information on your website can make an enormous difference to whether you are getting media coverage. Companies and organizations which provide the right information can maximize their relationships with journalists, resulting in better coverage and increased efficiency of resources.

So just what kind of information do journalists want? Typically, the top three items your website newsroom should provide are:

1 **press releases** – including both current and archived releases (make sure you have an easy search option!)
2 **24-hour contact information** – including a specific contact person by name, title and phone number and how to reach them

3 **corporate information** – including a company profile, statistics and executive biographies.

The last should comprise information that will help journalists gain an insight into the company and its management. You should think about including some basic facts and figures: number of employees, annual sales, and any information that places your company in context.

Events as part of a PR communication strategy

Every business gets involved with events in one way or another, whether it is a major corporate exhibition or something staged at a local hall to promote a local product or interest group, and usually it is the PR department which will be charged with putting it on and making it a success.

Events come in all shapes and sizes, from trade exhibitions to focused seminars and conferences, but they all need clear objectives if they are to be measured a success.

You don't necessarily need a large budget to stage a successful event, but nothing can substitute for meticulous planning with a good team of people, and you will benefit from someone who has a great deal of lateral vision when planning for contingencies.

It is a sad fact of life that very many people set off in a forlorn attempt at organizing something without either having thought through thoroughly what it is they actually hope to achieve, or allowing enough time to do it.

It is also a truism that company management very often do not appreciate the time and effort needed to organize a successful event, while it is almost routine to find exhibitors who leave everything to the last minute and then expect everyone else to drop whatever they are doing simply to rescue them from the mess of their own making.

A successful organizer should be able to think laterally and pull together a disparate series of events, while being able to think things through logically, quickly and clearly, especially at times of great pressure. If he or she can keep a sense of perspective and a sense of humour, that is all for the better!

The type of event

So, having got over the initial euphoria of being asked to stage an event, the first thing you have to do is sit down for a moment and define what it is you are actually hoping to achieve. Only once you have done that can you even hope to make the correct decisions as to the type of event that will be most appropriate. Ask yourself:

- Is the objective to impart information, or to act as an incentive?
- Will you be launching or raising the profile of a product, handing out awards, reinforcing relationships with customers, exhorting others to do better, or something else?
- Who will be your audience? Will it be held purely within the confines of your organization, or will it be open to the world at large?

Under the headline of 'Events' you can also include the likes of gala dinners, award ceremonies and activity days – such as golf, motor racing, horse racing and general team building. Whatever it is, it needs to be planned in the same manner as conferences and exhibitions, and suitable checklists need to be created so that nothing is forgotten.

In business, it is often necessary to attempt to change the way people think and how they regard your company. That, of course, is one of the most basic remits of PR. A well-planned and executed conference can enthuse a sales force, persuade employees to change their working practices or launch a new or unfamiliar product to a specialist audience. Above all, it can enable people to come together and communicate with one another more effectively.

Choosing the best venue

Having decided upon the type of event you wish to put on, one of the most important decisions that any events organizer has to make is the choice of venue, for this one factor can literally make or break the smooth running and success of any 'do', be it a conference, exhibition or seminar. Unfortunately, many venues that market themselves for events are in reality quite unsuitable. First impressions count, and if you are let down by the location, inadequate local services or poor service from the event location itself, then your event can quite literally be ruined.

I NEED YOU TO BE MORE SPECIFIC. SHOULD THE EXHIBITION STAND BE <u>ROYAL BLUE</u> OR <u>NAVY BLUE</u>?

Start by drawing up a list of those all-important questions:

- How long will the event be?
- How many delegates are likely to be attending?
- How far will they have to travel?
- What budget is allowed?
- Will anyone need overnight accommodation?

Having decided the price band, check out the travel times and suitability of various locations. It simply is no good selecting a superb location if it is difficult to find or access is poor. Of course, it is absolutely essential for the organizer to pay a visit to each possible venue, preferably incognito and also when another meeting is going on. That way you are much more likely to be able to weigh up the look and feel of the place and judge its suitability. Inspections are important because you can never tell from a brochure or website what the downsides could be.

You should always check out the following:

- the attitude of the staff
- the quality of accommodation
- the condition of the furnishings
- the formality of the venue or room
- the ease of moving from one area to another – such as from the room or hall to the coffee area
- the adequacy of the room's ventilation
- the availability of small meeting rooms if delegates need to be split up into small groups
- the rules regarding the positioning of banners and posters
- whether the venue will be shared with other organizations
- the provision of telephones and the availability of Wi-Fi.

Make sure you speak to the person responsible for handling corporate events; don't be satisfied with just speaking to the sales manager. You need to know exactly what you can expect to get, and you should not hold back on any questions for fear of offending anyone.

Preparation and rehearsal

In preparing for an event, some kind of time planner is invaluable in order to graphically interpret timelines and dependencies. Many organizers make use of computer software such as Microsoft Project, which prepares Gantt charts and dependencies.

It cannot be overstressed how important it is to plan for all eventualities – as far as you are able. Without adequate planning, the opportunities for confusion, oversight and mistakes are considerable.

Rehearsals, of course, are an absolute necessity. Don't allow anyone involved with the show to skip the main rehearsals, especially the final rehearsal – and that includes everyone right up to the Chief Executive!

Check that the lighting is adequate for the speaker to be able to read his/her notes and that the lectern is the right height for him/her. Time each element of the show, in case adjustments need to be made while the event is actually taking place.

Remember, too, that by taking part in a public event you are (probably) opening up your company to public scrutiny. If the stand or venue looks shoddy, then what does that say about your organization? If staff members are ill informed or rude, then what confidence will your potential customers have in the company in general? On the other hand, if the stand is smart, and your staff are polite, approachable and knowledgeable, then the image of your company will be positive for all to see and remember.

Letting people know

Ultimately, though, it doesn't matter how good an event you have arranged – if no one knows about it, you are wasting your time. Yet regularly exhibitors and conference organizers fail in this most basic task of letting anyone know they are taking part in an exhibition, or staging a must-attend conference.

We have already seen that there are a number of ways of letting people know about an event – not least through the use of news releases and media alerts (see Thursday). Your promotional activities should concentrate on attracting visitors to your event. You might choose to attract as many as possible or identify your most likely prospects in advance and do everything in your promotional power to attract them to your show. Neither method is right or wrong; rather, it depends on the reasons for holding the event in the first place.

Pre-show promotion should generate more visitors than you would normally have got, had you just sat back and hoped for the best. It should also generate press coverage, which may influence some to pay you a visit; others who cannot attend for whatever reason will still have been introduced to your products and services.

As we have already seen, journalists need good stories. You, on the other hand, need publicity. So what better than making sure you create a win-win situation by following these tips to maximize your press coverage:

- Write one press release for each product or service you wish to promote.
- If you are launching a new product or service, make sure this is clearly highlighted at the top of your release.
- Give relevant figures to back up your story, especially product prices and the value of new contracts. This gives the resulting story more colour and depth and it saves journalists having to ferret out the information themselves.
- Include colour photographs if they help the story along.
- Send in your story in plenty of time. It is simply no good sending something in two days before the event and hoping that it will get space. Journalists plan well in advance, and so should you!
- If you are taking space at someone else's event, then find out if they have a press office or PR representative and, if they do, then keep them fully informed of any product launches or other news you might have. You might even find there is an official show preview that is mailed to potential visitors to raise their interest. If you can get a story about your company into one of these publications, then the chances are that you will get more interest during the actual event itself.
- At all times you should concentrate on selling the benefits of your product or service, not just its features. It is said that most people buy primarily to assuage their feelings of fear or greed. If a customer is considering buying a product or service, she is not necessarily interested in the physical attributes of the product, but in what benefits will accrue to her if she does make the purchase.

It is all too easy for someone who is close to a product or story to gloss over information that is crucial to someone else's appreciation of it. One excellent exercise is to add the phrase 'which means that' in order to link a feature with the benefits it brings. You could even end your publicity with a one-liner such as 'Following this event, delegates will be able to...' and list a few positive key factors to which the delegate can relate.

Dealing with the media

If you want to maximize the coverage of your event in the media, then you will want to follow a few simple rules:

- As we have already seen, seek coverage only for newsworthy events.
- Distribute a clear, concise media advisory.
- Make the event easily accessible to the media.
- Have a professional, friendly media check-in.
- Provide a useful press kit.
- Give journalists their own clear space at the event.
- In order to increase the likelihood that the media will cover your press conference you could send out both a 'media advisory', followed a few days later by a press release.

If you expect live television coverage of your event, bear in mind that parking can be tricky for microwave or satellite trucks, whose crews need to run cables to the camera platform and send a signal back to their station. Consult the venue manager to find out where television stations have parked their trucks in the past. In order to encourage and prepare for television coverage, include on your media advisory the phrase, 'Please advise if you are planning live coverage.'

Have a table specifically for media people to check in so that your PR staff know exactly who attended. Offer journalists a press kit and a copy of any other materials you want them to have, then escort them to a designated media area where they can work comfortably during the event. Nowadays it is normal for reporters to have their own laptop computers, so ensure there are enough power sockets for them. Snacks and drinks are also well appreciated, though not obligatory.

All the while, try to offer optimum conditions to reporters since this will increase the chances of media coverage for your event, while enabling the reporters to focus on your key messages rather than be distracted by the difficulties of covering it.

If things go wrong...

Live events are the classic time for 'Murphy's Law' to rear its ugly head: if anything can go wrong, now is the time that it will happen.

TIP *Think through your worst-case scenarios. Perhaps your guest speaker fails to show up, the lights fuse, the set falls apart or the air conditioning breaks down.*

Of course, it is impossible to plan for every possible disaster scenario, but worrying unduly is not the same as making plans for what you would do should things go wrong. Every event organizer needs the ability to think ahead, quickly troubleshoot any problem and come up with a fix. It may not be an elegant fix, but if it gets you out of a hole, then no one is going to complain. It is at times like these that you will be very glad you timed every element of the event during rehearsals.

The way in which you react to a crisis is also very important. Think of yourself as the proverbial duck – serenely gliding through the water, while paddling furiously underneath the surface. If you remain cool, calm and collected, you will have a pacifying effect on everyone else. If others see you as being totally in control it will improve the chances of the event not turning into a disaster.

Summary

Inevitably, PR professionals need to concentrate a great deal not only on showing off the company in a good light, but also on helping to promote its products and services.

You can promote your goods and services in a number of ways to gain the attention of your prospects by creating a feeling of excitement. Normally, it will be the PR department which is the main body looking after a corporate website. Very many journalists use the information on corporate websites, so it is important that they are kept up to date with the latest news and information. Companies that provide this information can maximize their relationships with journalists, resulting in better coverage.

Most PR departments, too, get involved with – or even plan – corporate events, be they exhibitions, seminars, conferences or other types of show. For all of these it is essential to plan thoroughly, leaving nothing to chance.

You can measure the success of an event in many ways, but by focusing on the objectives throughout your planning stages, you can ensure the basic foundations from which a successful event can be achieved.

SUNDAY
monday
TUESDAY
WEDNESDAY
THURSDAY
FRIDAY
SATURDAY

Questions (answers at the back)

1. Corporate websites which contain a 'newsroom' for media to access should include...
   a) Press releases – both current and archived ❏
   b) 24-hour contact information ❏
   c) A company profile ❏
   d) All of the above ❏

2. The most important thing you need to decide before staging any event is...
   a) Where you will stage it ❏
   b) How much budget you have ❏
   c) What you want to achieve ❏
   d) Whom you will invite ❏

3. The most important consideration when choosing a location for an event is...
   a) What it looks like ❏
   b) How far it is from your company headquarters ❏
   c) How well it looks after its guests ❏
   d) How good a menu it can offer ❏

4. When going to check out a venue for a conference, you should get all the relevant facts directly from...
   a) The sales manager ❏
   b) The receptionist ❏
   c) The head chef ❏
   d) The corporate events organizer ❏

5. When rehearsing a conference, which of the following are essential prerequisites?
   a) Timing the CEO's speech ❏
   b) Checking lighting and sound equipment ❏
   c) Keeping anyone out who has no need to be there ❏
   d) All of the above ❏

6. A good sign that your pre-show publicity has worked is...
   a) You get more visitors to your show than you would normally have expected ❏
   b) Your show gets front-page billing on the show daily newspaper ❏
   c) Your CEO is pleased with the turnout for his/her speech ❏
   d) None of the above ❏

7. When sending out information about your participation at a major conference, you should...
   a) Send it out three months ahead of the event to give journalists plenty of time to plan their coverage of your company ❏
   b) Send it out one month ahead of the event together with a couple of photographs of your CEO ❏
   c) Send it out one week ahead of the event together with an invitation to visit your stand ❏
   d) Send out a series of releases, spaced one week apart, and incorporate ongoing stories and photographs to keep the journalists' interest up ❏

442

8. When putting together a release about your new product, you should...
   a) Concentrate on selling the benefits it offers users ❏
   b) Concentrate on highlighting its features ❏
   c) Appeal to customers' greed and fears ❏
   d) None of the above ❏

9. When media attend one of your events, your most important consideration is...
   a) Having a specific area for reporters to check in ❏
   b) Offering your invited media a press kit about the event ❏
   c) Providing them with tea or coffee ❏
   d) Providing a designated working area with power sockets and Internet access ❏

10. If things go badly wrong at an event you have organized, you should...
    a) Learn a valuable lesson ❏
    b) Try to think laterally and come up with a solution ❏
    c) Remain cool, calm and collected ❏
    d) All of the above ❏

SATURDAY

Internal PR

For a number of years, downsizing of companies has been a worldwide phenomenon, as technology obviates the need to have the large workforces that were so necessary in the past.

When structures were split horizontally between departments and vertically between the various layers of management, many people were stopped from communicating outside their own specific departments. They were not able to see the overall picture of what the company was trying to achieve. In addition, many of the people who make up a company have little or no contact with the company's customers and are therefore limited in what they can contribute to improve the business.

The struggle for competitive edge, however, now means that the staff are much more important than they ever used to be, for without their empathy, flexibility, creativity and intuitive thinking, there is little to differentiate one business from another. For this reason, the need for internal communications has never been more important to a company's prospects.

Today, then, we will look at:

- how effective internal PR is vital for the wellbeing of the staff as well as the company more generally
- using employee surveys to launch successful two-way communication within a company
- the different conduits for staff communication.

A neglected audience

We have already seen that any communication process starts with the identification of the publics to be addressed, together with an analysis of what key messages need to be got across to them. Every organization has a large number of target audiences, all different from one another, and a clear understanding of fixed objectives is essential in the identification of the various publics involved.

However, in every organization there is always one target audience that is both close to the company while also often neglected: the employees. This is most often shown up when a message reaches the staff via the outside world, rather than being directly delivered to them in the first instance.

There are a number of reasons why organizations need to be concerned about internal communications. Not least is the fact that there is a legal requirement across much of Europe for organizations to communicate with their workforce. Legal requirements aside, however, organizations that put employee communications on the back burner are simply asking for trouble, especially in this age of mass communications and social networking.

It is far too simplistic to think that staff are merely interested in their salary, career progression, improvement of professional skills and the availability of information. There are plenty of other less obvious, sometimes intangible, interests, not least the sense of being part of a team, the role and participation in the development of the business and so on.

Given these elements, both material and non-material, it can be seen that employee satisfaction is an important objective for any organization and needs to be properly addressed, not least through a comprehensive communications programme. It could even be argued that the effort expended on employee communications should be at least of equal importance to the amount of effort exerted on external relations.

As such, internal relations are very much a part of the communications mix and therefore part of the basic responsibilities of a PR practitioner, who should be highly conscious that the quality of internal relations is a critical element of each organizational system. Indeed, one could go further by saying the quality of internal relations directly influences all external relations in terms of effectiveness of the relationship itself, while enabling a company to accomplish its goals in the most effective ways, in less time and with lower costs.

TIP

The PR practitioner's role nowadays seems more and more intricately woven in with that of the human resources (HR) department, concentrating on the delivery of company messages to the workforce.

The science of internal or employee communications is probably bound more by the principles of psychology than any other PR discipline, since it is essential to tap into people's innermost feelings and use them in a positive way to help the communication process across the company. That means understanding that immediate reactions to problems often disguise deeper feelings, which need to be unlocked.

Delivering the goods depends on a director's ability to harness the ideas and creativity of his/her staff, who need to be fired up and encouraged to behave in a way that supports the long-term ambitions of the organization. Employees all have needs and aspirations that need to be met if the directors and senior management want to get the best out of them. Good communications up and down the workforce are therefore an essential part of the management of a company.

Involving the workforce

In principle, the best way to communicate with the workforce is to make the bulk of general information available to everybody in the organization, with exclusions being as few as possible. This is where the communications department and HR need to work in close harmony for effective internal exchanges to take place.

Employees need to feel that they, too, can help set the agenda, allowing them to bring up problems that they face or anticipate and encouraging them to be discussed openly. Problems, especially, faced by those at the sharp end of the business need to be addressed quickly if customers are not to become aware of internal trouble within the organization.

The reality in many companies does not make comfortable reading. Some of the best news stories an organization has to tell about itself are well-known to everyone except its employees. This can happen for many reasons, but invariably the organization can become so focused on getting its message out to the world at large that management just assumes everyone working for the company already knows what is going on, as if by a process of osmosis; or they simply fail to dedicate the time and energy to keep their own people in the loop. This can invariably lead to poor morale, increased turnover of staff, and a bad image problem for the company.

Yet it is one of the greatest truisms of all time that a company's best ambassadors tend to be those self-same staff whom management are routinely ignoring in their day-to-day working lives. Since most people assume that anyone who works for a salary is only in it for the money, someone who sings the praises of their employer's products has a very high level of credibility to any audience, be they friends, relatives or complete strangers.

TIP *Motivating your employees to speak out positively on behalf of their employer could not be easier. Simply tell them what the company is doing, what their role is, why it is important, and solicit their comments and suggestions. This internal communication is an essential element of PR.*

In internal communications, more than in any other PR discipline, honesty is definitely the best policy. People will often accept bad news if they are well informed and given the reasons why something has happened. But if you are caught hiding some of the key facts, you lose credibility, and it will be very hard to regain the employees' trust after that.

SUNDAY

monday

TUESDAY

WEDNESDAY

THURSDAY

FRIDAY

SATURDAY

Surprisingly, many HR departments communicate too little and they're only too happy to hand everything over to the PR or communications department. HR people tend to regard themselves as the technicians handling pay schemes, leave entitlement and such like, whereas PR people are seen as the spin doctors whose main function is to put the message across, however unpalatable it might be.

But getting staff on side with the company they work for is one of the easiest aspects of the PR function. You could, for instance:

- conduct monthly or quarterly meetings where all employees are given an update on the organization's goals and progress
- hold regular meetings offering recognition to staff for their contributions

- solicit suggestions for improvements in the workplace
- give employees a first look at new products or services and the plans to promote them
- produce a monthly employee newsletter and/or create an intranet site that discusses company news and highlights employee initiatives
- select a charitable cause that is related to the company's mission and provides employees with an incentive to volunteer, and then publicize their efforts.

One of the key principles of effective internal communication is not just to tell your people what is going on, but also to explain why something is happening in the way it is. If your people don't understand the problem that you are attempting to solve, they won't feel any ownership of the solution you are proposing, and as a result not be proactive in its implementation. When employees are informed about what their organization is doing and recognized for their role in its success, they will become some of your best ambassadors.

In order to develop a strategy of actively encouraging two-way employee communication, senior management need to create an environment in which this type of interaction will thrive. This invariably means ensuring that there is commitment to full internal communications all the way through the organization and that all employees are empowered to an appropriate degree in implementing company policy.

The employee survey

An employee survey is an excellent way of gauging where to start this process while at the same time signalling to the workforce that their opinion is actually wanted and will be listened to. Nowadays it can easily be carried out using an intranet with answers emailed to a central processing department, or even using an external survey website that promises to keep your employees' answers confidential. You could, of course, still use paper-based forms, though this takes up more time and resources and offers little in the way of benefits over easily set-up online surveys.

SUNDAY
monday
TUESDAY
WEDNESDAY
THURSDAY
FRIDAY
SATURDAY

TIP *Anonymity is essential in the employee survey, and everyone must be convinced that what they say won't be held against them in the future. For this reason, many companies prefer to use outside survey firms that can guarantee anonymity and impartiality.*

Remember, though, that if you invite comment and criticism you will be expected to address the real issues which can no longer be simply swept under the carpet. Only undertake a survey if there is real commitment from the highest levels of the company. And just because a company has gone to the lengths of having a written policy of employee empowerment and of full internal communication, it will be a total waste of time if those at the top of the hierarchical tree don't live by that policy themselves. It simply is not good enough to have a 'don't do as I do – do as I say' policy, for all respect and support from your employees will disappear in an instant.

First, in order to gather some demographic information – to put the data into some kind of meaningful sequence – you need to ask your staff to complete some basic questions, such as their level within the organization, their location, length of service and age – for it is a well-known fact that such basics can play an important part in the way people feel about a company.

Next, you should ask them to indicate on a scale of one to five their level of agreement to a number of statements you make – for example:

- I enjoy working for this company.
- I understand the company's goals and priorities.
- The company has a good reputation.
- I am confident in the future of the company.
- Senior management does a good job of managing the company overall.
- My function is well managed.
- I feel loyal to the company.

Surveys completed online can have their data sorted and databased very quickly and easily with the plethora of online tools available (many of them free), and can give an instant snapshot of the mood of the company. Importantly, this data also gives a good indication of where you can now concentrate your efforts for further research.

 As well as producing a great deal of useful information, a survey can have a very positive effect on staff morale.

Don't forget to give feedback on the analysis of the results – ensuring, of course, that confidentiality is maintained, or your next survey will not yield much of any use.

Strategizing your internal communications

A communications strategy needs to encompass many things, if it is to be successful. For a start, it needs to reflect a company-wide culture in which values are of more importance than mere words written in the company mission statement (which in practice few employees ever bother reading, let alone remembering!). Most importantly, messages across the company need to be consistent if they are to be trusted and people are to understand and play their full role in any changes that will affect both themselves and the company.

So in putting together your communications plan, you need to make it sufficiently detailed to define what methods and conduits are to be used throughout the organization, while ensuring that it is the strategy that defines the media, rather than the media dictating what strategy is to be implemented. This often means that there will be no substitute on occasion for real face-to-face communications between management and staff.

In all communities – be they companies, schools, or any other type of gathering – there is invariably an informal communications network in place, regardless of what management sets out to do. It's called the gossip network and it's fed by rumour. An internal communications strategy therefore needs to be able to work with this or counteract it effectively, and the best method of doing this is to ensure that staff are empowered to give feedback and positive suggestions and that their feedback is actually acted upon in some way.

Questions and comments from the workforce should be actively encouraged and, wherever possible, this information should be freely disseminated so that employee trust is built up over a period of time.

Sometimes it may be necessary for totally different messages to be given out to internal staff than to external audiences – such as when a company is going through difficult times when it needs its own people to understand what is going on, but which, for obvious reasons, it doesn't want leaked to the outside world. However, in normal circumstances steps need to be taken to ensure that internal messages don't conflict with external messages in order to risk credibility with either audience.

Naturally, there are times when confidentiality demands that delicate information cannot be released early. However, in that case employees should always be told at the same time as an official announcement. Lack of information is the number-one breeding ground for rumour, and once started it is very difficult to counteract. Staff will want the facts, and want them straight.

This is one of the main reasons why internal communications are best driven by the PR department as a whole, rather than delegating it to others such as HR, who of course will still need to have a major input to the plan.

During times of crisis, the support of staff becomes especially valuable, as their friends and relatives seek their account of events, and as talented and motivated participants consider whether or not to remain with the organization. With the prospect of reputational crises having the power to destroy brand value and even bring a company to its knees, it can be quite revealing to see how internal communications is suddenly given a boost in value by senior managers following a period of crisis.

Organizations that have a mature internal communications plan in place often have contingency plans prepared, too. They are more likely to have a well-rehearsed line management communications plan that can be swung into action at the slightest sign of any trouble brewing on the horizon. Less mature employee communications departments may find it difficult to bring the attention of senior managers to bear on their internal audience, especially when critical stakeholders such as investors or customers appear to be a more pressing problem.

In essence, the real benefits of employee communications come from getting the listening right, rather than telling people what's going on as viewed from the perspective of top management. It's the front-line staff after all who are usually closest to any customer problems, and by listening to what they have to say you will have a better-motivated workforce.

TIP *Feedback from all your people – but especially those at the sharp end – is essential and a non-confrontational feedback system will always give the company information it can use to improve matters.*

Conduits for your messages

Formal channels of internal communications typically fall into one of four broad categories:

1 **electronic** – delivered by Internet, smartphone, television or other devices
2 **print** – such as magazines, newsletters, brochures, posters, and communication packs
3 **face to face** – one-on-one and one-to-many forums where people physically talk to one another, such as team meetings or briefings, conferences and round-table discussions
4 **workspace environment** – including noticeboards and TV screens.

In general terms, 'face-to-face' communications are always the most appropriate where there is a risk of misunderstandings occurring or when emotions are running high.

Informal channels can often turn out to be more effective than official channels, and will often stimulate and create discussion and dialogue between groups. For this reason, if for no other, a company should actually encourage its people to chat at the water-cooler or coffee machine, over the social network, and so on. What used to be considered a time-waster has now been re-evaluated by many leading companies and is actually an excellent way of passing on crucial messages and stimulating ideas within a company.

Long gone are the days of so-called 'line manager cascade' when information was sent down the line to local supervisors, who were expected to deliver it to their subordinates without any corruption, interpretation or deviation. If the company had the foresight, these line managers would also be encouraged to report feedback up the line to the top management. But what a circuitous process! How could anyone have ever expected such a laborious process to generate anything really useful?

Thankfully, in recent years the received wisdom has changed and now concentrates on empowering managers to facilitate discussion rather than simply cascading those management messages to the boredom of all concerned.

SUNDAY

monday

TUESDAY

WEDNESDAY

THURSDAY

FRIDAY

SATURDAY

Promoting internal communications

As with all PR activities, there are numerous channels you can now use to get your chosen messages to your employees. Many companies, for instance, have an intranet system of some sort which should be kept up to date with how the business is getting on, key contracts won, major exhibitions and the like attended, and perhaps even a regular blog from one of the board members.

Each department could also have its own page on this site updating employees on local progress, and how what they are doing ties in with the aspirations of the company as a whole. You could even devolve this system down to project level, if appropriate.

Here are some other ideas for facilitating internal communications:

- As well as, or instead of, an intranet, the main company website is a very important outlet for updating your people, for the majority of staff will visit it from time to time. As well as a weekly or monthly ezine that can be directed at both external and internal audiences, some kind of organizational calendar can give visibility to outside events with which the company is in some way involved.
- The use of email is also extremely important in delivering information to staff, be it in the form of activity reports or direct messages. Aim to communicate something, at the very least, on a weekly basis to your staff.
- Company newsletters can also be delivered as hard copy, rather than as ezines, especially in manufacturing companies where many of the workforce might not have access to a computer for all or parts of the day.
- And, of course, staff meetings, team meetings, coffee meetings, huddles in the coffee area and so on should all be actively encouraged to improve the feeling in all of your employees that they belong to an exclusive club – your company!

Summary

The principles of good internal communication can be encapsulated in that well-worn phrase: 'Do unto others as you would have them do unto you.' In other words, consider how you would like to receive messages rather than how you would impart them; think how you might react to someone else giving you the particular message you want to give out yourself; and then impart your message in the way you know will be received in the best possible way.

For a highly effective internal communications strategy and plan:

- employee-focused communications must be led from the top
- employee communications are not optional extras – they are an essential part of business
- there must be integration between internal and external communications
- communication is a two-way process
- senior managers must always practise what they preach
- consistency of message is vital
- timing of the message is crucial.

SUNDAY
monday
TUESDAY
WEDNESDAY
THURSDAY
FRIDAY
SATURDAY

Questions (answers at the back)

1. Companies should always communicate with their staff...
   a) Because it is a legal requirement in Europe ❏
   (b) Because staff like to feel part of a team ❏
   c) To address employee satisfaction ❏
   d) To encourage their staff to feel motivated for the company ❏

2. Staff should be encouraged to bring up problems that they face, in order to:
   a) Improve customer expectations ❏
   b) Help the overall efforts of the company ❏
   c) Help set the agenda of the company ❏
   d) Prevent them bottling up their feelings ❏

3. Not keeping staff informed about company business can...
   a) Lead to poor morale ❏
   b) Encourage staff to leave the business in search of pastures new ❏
   c) Create a bad public image for the company ❏
   d) All of the above ❏

4. When communicating with staff, the most important thing they want to know is...
   a) What is going on across the company ❏
   b) Why the company is doing what it is doing ❏
   c) That what they are doing has an important role to play in the overall aims of the company ❏
   d) Where they sit in the overall remuneration schemes of the company ❏

5. When undertaking an employee survey, the most important thing to consider is...
   a) Keeping all answers anonymous and confidential ❏
   b) How easily the data from the answers can be collected ❏
   c) How to inform the employees what the survey results reveal ❏
   d) Not making promises that the company cannot keep ❏

6. When surveying your staff, you should always ask them...
   a) Where they work ❏
   b) How old they are ❏
   c) Whether they understand the company's overall goals ❏
   d) All of the above ❏

7. All internal communications need to be made...
a) In close collaboration with the HR department ❏
b) Consistently across the entire workforce ❏
c) Dependent on what communications conduits are available ❏
d) On a face-to-face basis between management and staff ❏

8. An informal gossip network should be encouraged by...
a) Spreading rumours about the company ❏
b) Providing coffee machines where people can congregate ❏
c) Making it easy for employees to give f eedback to management ❏
d) Letting employees know about confidential decisions in the boardroom ❏

9. The main value of employee communication comes from...
a) Listening to staff ❏
b) Letting staff know what is going on at senior management level ❏
c) Telling staff what is expected of them ❏
d) Being able to use staff at times of crisis ❏

10. The best conduit for staff communication...
a) Is through the use of newsletters and noticeboards ❏
b) Via email and ezines ❏
c) Face to face ❏
d) Depends on circumstances ❏

Surviving in tough times

No business is immune from the significant changes in recent years in the economic environment. What we can be sure of is that many sectors will have seen shrinking demand, which is likely to increase the competitive pressures facing businesses. Under these conditions a business must redouble its focus on two key groups – customers and competitors. (Remember that your customers have had a tough time as well!) Here are ten crucial tips you can use to help your business survive and prosper, and boost your future prosperity as an individual too.

1 Have a plan

Have a goal of where you want to be in one week, one month, three months and one year and stick to it as best you can. Think about how many visitors you will need a day, and the conversion rate to customers that you would need to be able to quit your day job (if that is the case with you), be able to break even with your business, be able to take that vacation or buy that car with the proceeds or even just make this month's sales targets. Dream and aim big.

2 Focus on your customers

During difficult times, customers may be changing in terms of their perceived needs, buying habits and attitudes to value.

Marketers must not assume they know what customers are thinking. Use current research to ensure that you have an objective view of the situation. Having up-to-date information on customers will help you identify the right course of action to meet corporate objectives in a changing environment.

3 Listen to your target audiences like never before

Individuals now have a disproportionate level of influence. A blogger in his or her bedroom can achieve a global readership. There are loads of online forums, so this is a really good opportunity for a company to listen to what people have to say about its brand or products. Online PR does not replace traditional forms of PR, but should be used in partnership with the latter to achieve long-term overall success.

4 Focus on your competitors

Businesses will generally adopt three broad approaches during difficult trading conditions. Most commonly, they reduce their prices to stimulate their own customers' demand and to attract competitors' customers. Alternatively, they will increase the benefits they offer while keeping prices steady (e.g. 2-for-1 offers or free trial periods). Firms may also create innovative solutions to customers' perceived needs. The marketer must ensure that information on competitor action is collected and used as part of the strategic decision process. The key is to take the right action at the right time based on sound research.

5 Know your products' benefits

To facilitate an 'exchange', products and services must carry benefits that match the perceived needs of the customer. When economic times are tough, customers are more likely to review their buying decisions and look at alternative ways of meeting their perceived needs. This presents businesses with both a threat (to their current customer base) and an opportunity (where competitors' customers may now be interested in our offerings). Again, we need up-to-date information to ensure that we select the right strategic responses to the current situation.

6 Get promotion right

Communicating with the market is important at any time, but marketers need to be flexible and adaptable when planning their promotional strategies. The marketer has to be ready to change messages and media to respond to customers' needs and competitor actions. Short-term campaigns are required to enable the business to redirect resources as required.

7 Make maximum use of all the social networks

This means Facebook, Twitter, YouTube, et al. You probably use these networks in some way already. So use them for your business as well. Commit to one quick post at the beginning of the day and the end. Post images (do a search on Flickr for a fun/interesting/slightly controversial image) or make one yourself with any of the free image editing software out there. Also, grab related videos from YouTube or sit down in front of your computer and use a free screen capture program or webcam to create one yourself (e.g. http://camstudio.org). Remember: just make it fun and informative. Then post it to your Facebook page and tweet it. When you are on social networks, be social and real. Most of all, make full use of social media by being fun and likable. At the same time, always use a call to action (ask them to like or share your content). Being real and asking for action all the time will naturally make people want to share, both you and your content. To save time in this area, use Hootsuite, a free program that will let you post, tweet and more from one website.

8 Don't get distracted

As you go along you will run across many different ways of doing things or the latest greatest app. Whatever it is, don't just go after it: keep doing what you are doing and then incorporate it if you want. Don't let it distract you from actually doing something on your site. For instance, you can find a webinar for pretty much every day in the week that will give you free tips on Facebook. If all you do is watch webinars though, who will post on your page?

9 Always keep your staff on side

Employees all have needs and aspirations that need to be met if the directors and senior management want to get the best out of them. Good communications throughout and up and down the workforce are therefore an essential part of the management of a company. At times of crisis, they could also mean the difference between survival and going under, since staff need to be fired up and encouraged to behave in a way that supports the long-term ambitions of the organization.

10 PR professionals are worth their weight in gold!

If your organization has compelling news, it may be published whether you like it or not! So it is important to use PR practitioners who understand media operations. If your news is negative, they will know how to mitigate its effects, and if it is positive, they will also be able to advise you on how to get maximum benefit from it. In tough times especially, if you can get *your* company into the news, it means that someone else's company isn't. Use this to your advantage!

Answers

Week 1: Marketing

Sunday: 1a; 2c; 3b; 4b; 5c; 6a; 7b; 8b; 9c; 10d.

Monday: 1b; 2a; 3b; 4a; 5d; 6a; 7d; 8b; 9d; 10d.

Tuesday: 1a; 2b; 3b; 4a; 5b; 6a; 7b; 8b; 9d; 10c.

Wednesday: 1a; 2c; 3b; 4a; 5a; 6b; 7a; 8d; 9a; 10d.

Thursday: 1d; 2c; 3b; 4d; 5a; 6a; 7d; 8c; 9d; 10b.

Friday: 1b; 2c; 3b; 4a; 5c; 6d; 7a; 8c; 9b; 10c.

Saturday: 1a; 2b; 3c; 4a; 5c; 6a; 7a; 8c; 9a; 10a.

Week 2: Digital Marketing

Sunday: 1b; 2b; 3c; 4c; 5d; 6a; 7e; 8a; 9a; 10b

Monday: 1b; 2a; 3c; 4d; 5c; 6b; 7c; 8a; 9d; 10a

Tuesday: 1c; 2d; 3b; 4g; 5b; 6a; 7d; 8c; 9b; 10a

Wednesday: 1c; 2f; 3c; 4a; 5b; 6d; 7e; 8c; 9a; 10a

Thursday: 1a; 2d; 3b; 4d; 5b; 6b; 7d; 8b; 9f; 10e

Friday: 1d; 2a; 3d; 4a; 5c; 6c 7d; 8d; 9b; 10c

Saturday: 1b; 2a; 3b; 4a; 5a; 6d; 7c; 8a; 9d; 10c

Week 3: Social Media Marketing

Sunday: 1d; 2d; 3a; 4b; 5d; 6c; 7d; 8a; 9a; 10c

Monday: 1c; 2d; 3b; 4b; 5a; 6b; 7d; 8d; 9b; 10d

Tuesday: 1b; 2d; 3c; 4d; 5b; 6d; 7a; 8d; 9d; 10c

Wednesday: 1d; 2d; 3b; 4d; 5c; 6a; 7a; 8b; 9d; 10c

Thursday: 1d; 2a; 3a; 4d; 5d; 6b; 7b; 8d; 9d; 10b

Friday: 1b; 2a; 3c; 4d; 5a; 6b; 7c; 8d; 9a; 10b

Saturday: 1d; 2c; 3d; 4d; 5d; 6b; 7d; 8b; 9a; 10d

Week 4: Public Relations

Sunday: 1a; 2d; 3d; 4c; 5b; 6d; 7c; 8c; 9b; 10c

Monday: 1d; 2c; 3c; 4d; 5c; 6c; 7c; 8b; 9d; 10c

Tuesday: 1c; 2d; 3d; 4c; 5c; 6a; 7d; 8c; 9c; 10c

Wednesday: 1a; 2a; 3c; 4b; 5b; 6d; 7d; 8c; 9d; 10b

Thursday: 1d; 2d; 3c; 4b; 5c; 6c; 7a; 8b; 9a; 10d

Friday: 1c; 2d; 3c; 4d; 5d; 6b; 7d; 8c; 9d; 10d

Saturday: 1d; 2c; 3d; 4a; 5d; 6c; 7b; 8c; 9d; 10b

Notes

AVAILABLE IN THE 'IN 4 WEEKS' SERIES

- Accounting & Finance in 4 Weeks
- Job Hunting in 4 Weeks
- Management in 4 Weeks
- Marketing in 4 Weeks
- Selling in 4 Weeks

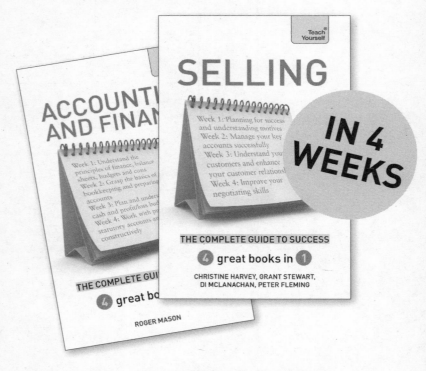
For information about titles in the 'In A Week' series, please visit

www.inaweek.co.uk